AF522384

PRIVATISATION
EVOLUTION OF INDIAN THOUGHT

PRIVATISATION
EVOLUTION OF INDIAN THOUGHT

Edited by
R.K. Mishra • P. Geeta
B. Navin

ANMOL PUBLICATIONS PVT. LTD.
NEW DELHI - 110 002 (INDIA)

ANMOL PUBLICATIONS PVT. LTD.
4374/4B, Ansari Road, Daryaganj
New Delhi - 110 002
Ph.: 3261597, 3278000
Visit us: www.anmolbooks.com

Privatisation: Evolution of Indian Thought

First Edition, 2003

ISBN 81-261-1404-5

PRINTED IN INDIA

Published by J.L. Kumar for Anmol Publications Pvt. Ltd., New Delhi - 110 002 and Printed at Tarun Offset Press, Delhi.

Dedicated

to

T.L. Sankar

A Distinguished Administrator and

Pioneering Researcher

CONTENTS

PREFACE

The privatisation wave has stirred the entire Indian economy. The impact of privatisation is likely to influence the Indian society a great deal. It is very significant at this juncture to trace the evolution of privatisation thought in India to have an assessment of the appropriateness of the progress of the privatisation movement. This book presents a set of papers that were presented in a Workshop on Diversification of Ownership in Public Enterprises, held at the Institute of Public Enterprise, on July 24, 1987. Our research shows that this was possibly the first ever discussion on privatisation held under the auspices of the joint research programme conducted by the London Business School and Institute of Public Enterprise, in collaboration with the Industrial Development Bank of India and the Indian Council of Social Science Research, New Delhi.

The papers presented in the Workshop, delineate the need, extent, form, modalities, machinery, impact and process of privatisation. The British Telecommunications case on British privatisation highlights the modalities that should be adopted in the formulation and implementation of privatisation policies and the outcomes that should accrue to an economy on account of privatisation.

This volume contains basic papers on privatisation based on the Workshop. The papers discuss the role and relevance of state level public enterprises and the scope of privatisation relating thereto, the Indian disinvestment experience in the consequent to the new economic policy and comercialisation and corporatisation of public enterprises. These papers show the development of tentacles providing further scope for acceleration of the privatisation movement in India. The book contains three land mark reports on privatisation viz., Report of the Committee to Review Policy for Public Enterprises (Arjun Sengupta Committee Report), Report of the Committee on Disinvestment of Shares in Public Sector Enterprises (Rangarajan Committee) and the Report of the Comptroller and Auditor General of India.

We are dedicating this book to Shri. T.L. Sankar who was Former Director, Institute of Public Enterprise, and Principal, Administrative Staff College of India and currently Member, Disinvestment Commission, Government of India, during whose period, the studies on diversification of public ownership commenced. He was instrumental in flagging the research collaboration between London School of Business and Institute of Public Enterprise in 1983 which lasted a full term of ten years continuing upto 1993. Mr. Sankar, initiated the tradition of dispassionate and holistic research on privatisation to benefit the economic system and judge the performance of industry not from ownership angle but from the angle of financial and economic performance. This work was a precursor to a number oft cited forceful analytical studies taken up at the Institute later. We have been encouraged in this work by eminent public policy makers, scholars, social scientists and public sector managers. We express our gratitude unto them.

R K Mishra
P Geeta
B Navin

LIST OF CONTRIBUTORS

Dr. Geeta Gouri, Director, Andhra Pradesh State Electricity Regulatory Commission, Hyderabad, and Former Professor and Chairperson, Economic & Development Policy Division, Institute of Public Enterprise, Hyderabad.

Dr. Y. V. Reddy, Executive Director, International Monetary Fund and Former Deputy Governor, Reserve Bank of India and Principal Secretary and Ex-Officio Commissioner, Department of Public Enterprise, Government of Andhra Pradesh.

Dr. Nitish K Sengupta, Member of Parliament and Director, International Management Institute, New Delhi and Former Member Secretary, Planning Commission, New Delhi.

Prof. David Chambers, Dean, London School of Business, Sussex Place, London.

Prof. R. K. Mishra, Senior Professor and Dean (Research), Institute of Public Enterprise, Hyderabad.

Dr. R. Nandagopal, Director, School of Management, PSG Institute of Technology, Coimbatore and Former Programme Director, MBA-PE Programme, Institute of Public Enterprise, Hyderabad.

T. L. Sankar, Member, Disinvestment Commission, Governmenmt of India, New Delhi and Former Director, Institute of Public Enterprise, Hyderabad and Principal, Administrative Staff College of India, Hyderabad.

A. Lateef Syed Mohammed, Professor of Finance, Chicago Business School, Former ICSSR Teacher Fellow, Institute of Public Enterprise, Hyderabad.

K Balaramamoorthy, Former Director, Institute of Public Enterprise, Hyderabad and Chairman and Managing Director, Nuclear Fuel Complex, Hyderabad.

Dr. P. Geeta, Research Division, Institute of Public Enterprise, Hyderabad.

Dr. B. Navin, Research Division, Institute of Public Enterprise, Hyderabad.

1

PUBLIC ENTERPRISES IN THE PHASE OF ECONOMIC LIBERALISATION

— Geeta Gouri

In the Indian context, economic liberalisation has more often implied relaxation or removal of controls prevalent in the economy. These controls, primarily have been exercised in significant areas such as industrial licensing, import-policy, foreign collaboration, and technology transfer. Broadly they epitomise the entire gamut of quantitative restrictions evolved for achieving (i) rapid industrial growth with minimum foreign dependence; (ii) balanced dispersal of industries; (iii) prevention of concentration of economic power. The rationale for controls was inherent in the strategy of import-substituting industrialisation of growth with equity inaugurated during the early fifties.

The strategy of industrialisation conceives of a specific role of the state and its intervention in economic activities public sector enterprises (PEs) form an integral part of the same. In the Import-substituting industrial strategy, PEs were conceived as catalyst to achieve 'growth with equity'. The current phase of liberalisation may inevitably affect the role and functioning of PEs. In this paper we shall examine some of the possible effects of economic liberalisation in PEs. The relationship between economic liberalisation and PE can be placed in proper perspective with a brief reference to significant developments in the Indian Industrial scene.

Industrial development in India has been slow especially after the mid sixties. Deceleration in growth rates has been most pronounced in the capital goods sector.[1] At the same time, a diversified industrial base developed, which, however, suffered from three inadequacies: (i) high cost; (ii) relatively obsolete technology in some areas; and (iii) poor quality products. Lack of competition, internally and externally, has been identified by many[2] as responsible for the above mentioned inadequacies. Regulations and controls of import - substituting industrial strategy were basically time consuming with approval adherences bogged down in bureaucratic red tapism. In the process, internal competition was dampened. Absence of internal competition encouraged uneconomic scales of production units to exist and protected the prevalent high cost industrial structures. Insulation of foreign competition through tariff barriers and quantitative restrictions isolated Indian industry from the mainstream technological developments. A situation characterised by lethargy, with Indian industry slow to respond to changing developments emerged. PEs were part of the general trend and suffered from the same inadequacies.

Liberalisation is an attempt to correct the prevalent situation through the introduction of competitive market conditions by dismantling quantitative restrictions. In their place, economic activities will be regulated by indirect signals given by monetary and fiscal policy. The present phase of economic liberalisation is therefore, a half-way house between total control and complete freedom. The strategy of industrialisation is still 'growth with equity', only the instruments to achieve this goal have changed. The slogan of liberalisation can be stated as efficiency and competitiveness.

A halfway house may land itself to contradictory situations without hope of dreaming of liberalisation schemes. In this paragraph we shall examine some of the measures of liberalisation—can it contradict the very objectives they were set up for or the earlier gains of regulation. On both counts the main aim of liberalisation is lost. The present liberalisation phase is very current (1985) hence empirical evidence to support our arguments will be scanty. We can only hypothesise on probable tendencies. The canvas of investigation as mentioned earlier will be PEs. The new role for PEs in the phase of economic liberalisation is summed up in the Seventh Plan Document. To quote:

> "The public sector has sustained and initiated the industrial transformation of India. It shall continue to play its pivotal role in modernising industry and in reducing the concentration of economic power. To perform its historic task, the public sector has to undergo basic structural changes to confirm to the plan priorities of efficiency and productivity. Only in the measure that public sector generates investable surplus can it play its indispensable social role of providing an adequate infrastructural base for the economy, being a vehicle for the introduction and absorption of new technology in critical sections of the economy".[3]

What is efficiency and productivity in the context of PEs? How can efficiency be introduced? What are the basic structural changes required to make PEs efficient? Does competition ensure efficiency? These are some of the questions which would require special attention in the current phase of economic liberalisation.

The present phase of liberalisation can be dated to the policy changes of 1985. Elements of this can however, be traced to the Industrial Licensing Policy (ILP) of 1973. The ILP of 1973 in turn represented a deviation from the Industrial Policy Resolution (IPR) of 1956 on the following counts. First, the concept of exempted sector was introduced in under which investment upto a limit of Rs. 1 crore required no license. Second, industries were classified into five schedules. In this reclassification of schedules, special areas were reserved for small-scale sector. Third, Monopoly Houses were defined in terms of the lower limit of Rs. 20 crores. Fourth, to the Monopoly Restrictive Trade Practices Act a list of core industries open to large houses were added as Appendix 1.

Subsequent to the Industrial Policy statement of 1973 further steps were taken to liberalise licensing requirements. Between 1975 and 1985 many of the present liberalisation measures were introduced such as broad banding, re-endorsement of capacity etc. only the scope was limited in 1973. The secretariat for Industrial Approvals (SIA) was set up to handle delicensed industries. The Secretariat is only a registration body and not a licensing authority.

The liberalisation efforts of 1973 were examined by the study groups on Industrial Regulations (1978) headed by G.V. Ramakrishna and the group was of the view that "regulation and licensing of industry is relevant in the Indian context...." The study group is however, of the view that licensing policies can be made considerably more selective and procedures streamlined.[4] The Dagli Committee on Controls and Subsidies (1979) was critical of the existing system of controls and subsidies. The Committee provided insights into the working of the control system. It was, the Narasimhan Committee on the Possible Shift from physical to Financial Controls (1986) which was categorical and forthcoming on the need for sustained liberalisation.

This brief historical narration of liberalisation prior to 1985 points to one major fact: liberalisation in India is an outcome of disillusionment with the regulatory mechanism to achieve the desired objectives of 'growth with equity'.

The main features of the current liberalisation phase are:

1. **Delicensing**: In March 1985, 25 broad categories of industries were delicensed. In December 1985, delicensing was extended to 22 out of the 27 MRTP industries exempt under section 21 and 22 of the MRTP Act. In July 1986, roller flour mills industries was delicensed. In September 1986, delicensing was also extended to certain chemical industries. Delicensing is over and above the exemption limit of Rs. 5 crores which formed the small-scale sector. Delicensed industries required only SIA approval,

provided (i) such undertakings do not come within the purview of MRTP Act or FERA unless located in backward areas; (ii) the article is not reserved for small-scale sector; (iii) the concerned undertaking is not located within the specified urban limits; (iv) import requirements are not more than Rs. 75 lakhs.

2. Broad-banding in selected industries to secure better capacity utilisation. In January 1986, 28 industry group were covered under this facility. During 1986 this facility was extended to cover glass, steel pipes and tubes, metallurgical machinery, earth-moving machinery, synthetic fibres and synthetic filament yarn, electrical cables and wires, ball and roller bearings, specified categories of agricultural machinery, soya products, textile machinery, chemical industries, cranes railway wagons, steel fabrication, auto ancillaries. The same set of caveats applicable to delicensing are valid here.

3. Re-endorsement of capacity was introduced to encourage maximisation of capacity utilisation which had achieved 80 per cent capacity utilisation. The re-endorsed capacity is calculated by taking the highest production achieved during any of the five years plus one-third thereof. The undertakings which are able to achieve capacity utilisation equal to the re-endorsed level would get further re-endorsement. Re-endorsement is not available for (i) small scale sector; (ii) 21 industries listed as suffering from acute raw material shortage or involve high pollution; (iii) industries in urban limits.

4. Licensing of capacity upto minimum economic scales would be automatic. The minimum economic scale will not apply to (i) small scale sector; (ii) 21 identified industries in which there is acute shortage of raw material or likely to result in high pollution; (iii) industrial undertakings located in urban areas; (iv) MRTP and FERA companies of Non-Appendix-

1; (v) restrictions of the scheme to drugs and pharmaceutical units. The earlier list involved 65 industries now extended to 73 industries. These industries fall into 9 categories.

5. Industries off the MRTP Ambit -- A list of 27 industries was selected to which section 21 and 22 of MRTP Act would not apply. Such exemption is besides those in force already for 100 per cent exports units and industries of high rational importance as notified from time to time. These industries would require a license but are exempt the purview of MRTP Act. Some of the industries are Electrical motors with starters, alternate energy devices and systems, transmission line towers, electronic components, automotive components and spares, chemical process plants etc.

6. MRTP Companies are permitted to set up industries in areas of high technology which are referred to as Appendix 1 industries.

7. New Technology Policy linked to foreign collaboration - No clearance is required for foreign collaboration in investments upto Rs. 10 crores. Further, a policy for encouraging foreign collaboration upto 40 per cent equity is part of the package. This encouragement is in view of the foreign exchange crunch.

8. Trade Policy - Gradual shift from quantitative restrictions to tariffs. This was matched with a shift of many crucial components, project equipment and raw material to Open General License (OGL). The changes in Trade Policy were guided by the Abid Hussain Committee on Trade Policies.

The domestic liberalisation schemes are aimed towards (1) minimum economic scale; (2) better capacity utilisation; (3) encouragement towards more industrial investments liberalisation on the trade front is aimed towards (i) upgradation of technology and (ii) cost and quality consciousness for modernisation.

In the above list we have not included the New Textile Policy, New Electronic Policy. Further, Liberalisation also involves changes in Administered Pricing. Rationalisation of administered prices is necessary to provide the correct signals for (i) investment decisions and (ii) to evolve cost consciousness.

In this section we shall assess the possible repercussion of two liberlisation schemes on PEs. They are (i) capital goods imports; (ii) investment expansion schemes such as delicensing and broad banding.

Liberalisation of capital goods imports was motivated by two considerations. First, cheaper imports of components and spare parts for modernisation in order to facilitate Indian manufacturers to be competitive internationally. Second, exposure to international competitive conditions is an attempt to inject dynamism into the industry. The underlying presumption behind both the considerations is that the capital goods sector in India is inefficient and technologically obsolete. Towards rectifying this situation in 1985 capital goods imports were placed on the Open General License. At the same time, import duties were reduced. Capital goods imports are divided into project and non-project imports. Project imports involved a duty of 65 per cent and non-project imports of 100 per cent. In the 1985 Budget project import duties were reduced to 45 per cent. Within capital goods power equipment attracted a duty of 25 per cent and fertilizer project equipment of zero per cent. The duty on non-project imports remained at 100 per cent. In the 1985 Budget project import duties were reduced to 45 per cent. Within capital goods power equipment attracted a duty of 25 per cent and fertilizer project equipment of zero per cent. The duty on non-project imports remained at 100 per cent. An immediate repercussion of these measures was a doubling of capital goods imports from Rs. 2,000 crores to Rs. 4,000 crores, mainly under the heading of project imports.

The capital goods industry is the pride of import-substituting industrial strategy. This sector with a large public sector investment helped PE's to reach the goal of 'commanding heights' of the economy. Tariff Barriers nurtured the industry by protecting it from international competition. Protection paid rich dividends in terms of (i) developing a diversified industrial base and (ii) in achieving a breakthrough on the export front with exports of equipment and technology and to compete successfully for turnkey projects abroad. Despite these achievements the capital goods industry experienced slowdown in its growth rate contributing to the general deceleration in Indian industrial growth rate. Low capacity utilisation with high capital-output ratios reflected the deceleration. It is pertinent to enquire how far high capital - output ratios are an outcome of inefficiencies in the capital goods industry, or, whether low capacity utilisation is due to diversion of demand towards imports. Advocates of liberalisation would support the first argument. Efficiency can be evaluated by comparing price differentials between domestic prices and international prices of capital goods. Studies by individual scholars[5] and the World Bank[6] have revealed that capital goods industry in India is by and large efficient comparable to international firms. To quote from one of the studies, "this differential (between domestic prices and international prices) varies depending on the commodity being considered, with domestic prices exceeding international prices by anywhere between 15.38 per cent and 248.22 per cent. This range is particular large in the case of HEC Ranchi, which is known to be a sick public sector unit, but is much smaller in the case of HMT (86.23 - 137.6) and BHEL (56.2 - 99.06)". [7] Higher raw material costs of steel, non-ferrous metals, alloys and infrastructural costs of power explain the price differentials. Heavy import duties paid by domestic producers contributed to the high raw material and components costs. Paradoxically, high tariffs which nurtured Indian capital goods industry resulted in negative effective rate of protection.[8] Administered price of infrastructure added to the high costs.

Liberalisation of capital imports instead contributed to low capacity expansion by diverting demand towards imports. This has resulted in low profitability and poor performance with serious implications for profitable public sector enterprises like BHEL. Let us examine the case of BHEL in more detail. By all indicators of efficiency BHEL has performed well. First, BHEL as compared to many PEs has maintained a financial credibility. In 1985-86 it generated internal resources to the extent of Rs. 153 crores.[9] Second, BHEL has the technological capability to produce power generating equipment upto 250 MW. Third, BHEL has been successful in exporting technology and turn key projects. In recent times BHEL has witnessed a steady decline in capacity utilisation in the manufacture of thermal and hydro-sets and other related equipment. According to projections made by BHEL on the basis of the current rate of receipt of orders for the power projects, capacity utilisation in the last two years of the Seventh Plan and a year beyond (1988-89, 1989-90, 1990-91) will be as low as 52 per cent, 50 per cent and 16 per cent for thermal sets and 32 per cent, 39 per cent and 22 per cent for hydro sets.[10] Diversion of demand to imports has been largely responsible for this situation.

This was hardly the opportune moment to open the economy for international producers in the capital goods industry. A world-wide recession is on in the power equipment industry. Against annual average world demand of 22,500 MW installed capacity is of the order of 1,25,000 MW.[12]

To overcome recessionary conditions international producers are involved in cut throat competition willing to sell at prices lower than marginal cost. Their efforts have been backed by provision of 'soft loans' or 'tied aid' from their respective countries. Receptive to the adverse repercussion the 1987 Budget has attempted to rectify the situation by levying uniform import duties of 85 per cent on both project and non-project imports. Budget has only tried to rationalise the tariff structure.

The capital goods example provides certain insights to PE performance and liberalisation. First, efficiency in PE is not always related to competition. PE are often inefficient because of higher conversion costs. This calls for structural changes within the economy. Often the profitability of PE is determined by factors outside their control for example location of industrial units or the control on prices. Second, indiscriminate liberalisation can negate the gains of import substitution. In this particular case a profitable PE is made sick contradicting the very aims of liberalisation.

Indiscriminate delicensing and capacity expansion can also have perverse impact on the efficiency of PE and in turn on industrial growth rate. To understand this outcome, we have to be sensitive to investment decision-making psyche of the Indian entrepreneur. The Indian industrialist with his trader mentality, is guided by quick profits. In an unregulated market expansion of investment in non-priority (in terms of the Seventh Plan) areas can be anticipated. Consumer goods with large quick profits are high on the list. Further the possibility of foreign collaboration without regulation is an added attraction. Group behaviour is also strong among Indian Industrialists with the result investments tend to get concentrated in certain 'green fields'. Such behaviourial patterns may be observed from a glance at SIA approvals. In the last one year SIA approvals have been in roller flour grinding (27.5 %), electronic components (16.7 %), special alloys - sponge iron (6.4 %) and auto -ancillaries (6.3 %). Without planned investment and assessment of market potentiality, there is every possibility for such investments patterns to stagnate and then fall sick. Without a policy of death this signifies an additional burden to PE's in terms of take over of sick industries. In a half-way house the Government may not be willing to emulate the harsh process of selection adopted by the market. Sick industries are not allowed to die. Instead, financial institutions pump in more money. Eventually they are nationalised.

The two examples of the possible outcomes of liberalisation and PEs suggests that further rethinking is required. Both the examples of liberlisation proved inimical to the efficient functioning of PEs, efficiency defined in terms of financial performance. On such limited evidence it is not possible to state that liberalisation is ill-advised. The evidence only points to two facts. First, liberalisation measures have to be discriminatory. It cannot be a blanket step. In some areas such as the capital goods efficiency may require further protection rather than liberalisation. Second, the market structure in India has to develop further for liberalisation to succeed. To put it crudely it has to become more capitalist.

Our analysis also suggests that PEs cannot be treated as homogenous entity judged purely by financial indicators. PEs are a mixed lot. Those with economic objectives may be judged by financial ratios while those with social objective require different criteria. Further, PEs with economic objectives can again be divided into those functioning in competitive environment and those functioning in non-competitive environment. The theory of contestable markets has reduced the boundaries between the two categories.[11] Nevertheless, where PEs by virtue of large investments are natural monopolies or limited market size forces them to operate in monopolistic market conditions, Introduction of competition is self-defeating. This Institute has examined some of the aspects in their report to the Economic Advisory Committee.

Liberalisation and PEs will invariably require a policy for defining new areas of investment for PEs. Such a policy has to be complimented with an alternate scheme for weaning PEs from unprofitable activities. Undue emphasis on efficiency in financial terms may result in PEs becoming eventually redundant. In the ultimate analysis the role of PEs is a political question.

NOTES

1. For example see., I.J. Ahuwalia, *Industrial Growth in India, Stagnation since the Mid-Sixties,* Oxford University Press., New Delhi, 1985. K.N. Raj, *The New Economic Policy,* V.T. Krishnamachari Memorial Lecture, Institute of Economic Growth, New Delhi, 1985.

2. The first to raise these inadequacies were J. Bhagawati and P. Desai, *Planning for Industrialisation: Industrialisation and Trade Policies since 1951,* Oxford University Press, New Delhi, 1975. S.S. Marathe, *Regulation and Development, India's Policy of Experience of controls over Industry,* Sage Publications, New Delhi, 1986.

3. *Seventh Plan Document 1985-90,* Vol. I, Government of India,

Planning Commission, New Delhi, pp. 6.

4. Report of the Study Group on Industrial Regulation and Procedures (Chairman G.V. Ramakrishna), 1978.

5. C.P. Chandrasekhar, "Investment Behaviour, Economies of Scale and Efficiency in an Import Substitute Regime", Paper presented at the seminar on Indian Industrialisation, Centre for Development Studies, Trivandrum, 1987.

6. World Bank, *Industry Development India: Non-Electrical Machinery Manufacturing*, A sub-sector study, report No. 5095 - In May 18, 1984. Quoted in ibid.

7. *Optcit.*

8. Y.K. Alagh, "Industrial Policy in India: Theory Measurement and Practice", paper presented at the Seminar on Indian Industrialisation, Centre for Development Studies, Trivandrum, 1987. He estimated ERP to be ranging between .99 to -0.78.

9. Economic Advisory Council, *Public Enterprises in India: Some Current Issues*, May 20, 1987.

10. *Ibid.*

11. See W.J. Baumol, "Theory of Contestable Markets" Chapter I in his book *Micro Theory*, Wheatsheaf Books, Sussex, 1986.

2

PRIVATISATION: A CONCEPTUAL AND CONTEXTUAL FRAMEWORK

— Y Venugopal Reddy

In the Indian situation there are two distinct positions on Privatisation namely, "private is pariah" or "market is moksha". The advocates of both these extreme approaches have three things in common: First, intellectual inspiration from realities outside the country; second, tendency to be prisoners of the precept and practice of the past; and third, varying perceptions of what Privatisation means. Therefore, for a meaningful understanding of the issue in a policy-context, it is necessary to understand the concepts and practices in other countries and relate them to the conditions in India. The objectives of this chapter are to:

1. Clarify the concept of privatisation in the light of: the historical growth of the role of the State, the recent questioning of the expanding role of the State and consequently the parameters of strengthening the market;
2. Analyse the policy effects of the above process in international context;
3. Explain the pressures towards privatisation in the Indian context;

4. Indicate the unique features of the privatisation debate in the Indian context; and
5. Identify the major areas requiring clarification, research and study, with a view to firm up a well-understood policy-frame.

Concept of Privatisation

Broadly speaking, there has been a large expansion in the role of the State all over the world – both developed and developing – from the time of the Second World War until the 70's. The role of the State has expanded in four broad areas, namely:

(a) Increased regulation of economic activity to ensure resources – conservation, ecological balance, competition itself, etc.

(b) Expansion in the provision of social welfare measures through health care schemes, pensions, unemployment benefits, etc.

(c) Increased public investments to provide physical capital (such as highways) and knowledge capital (through educational facilities, research and development, etc.)

(d) Nationalisation of existing industries or commercial enterprises and also starting such enterprises in the public sector usually subsumed under the title of public enterprise.

In short, therefore, the State has expanded its role as, regulator, welfare provider, facilitator or promoter of development and entrepreneur.

Such an expanding role for the State was questioned (particularly since 60s and late 70s, respectively) on a number of counts – theoretical and pragmatic. Firstly, in liberal democracies it was felt that the freedom and liberty of the individual is being threatened by the expanding role of the Government (for instance, by Milton Friedman). Secondly, it is argued that the nature of politics and bureaucracy as such that public institutions are not conducive either for 'efficiency' or 'welfare' (for instance, Public choice theory, the Property Rights Theory and the Capture Theory of Regulation).

At a more pragmatic level there have been a number of factors responsible for a review of the role of the State with a marked preference towards privatisation.

(i) The macro economic environment resulting in recession or slow recovery was partly attributed to the expanding role of the State and the limits imposed on free flow of trade and capital.

(ii) The pressures on the budgets with increasing tendency towards deficits and consequent inflationary pressures forced the Governments to look at ways of pruning the budget burdens, and one of the relatively easier ways of reducing the budget pressures was perceived to be a reduction in the role of the State in general.

(iii) It was felt that the unions in the public sector have developed as a powerful lobby cornering the benefits in the economy disproportionate to their contribution. The Government felt that the only way of reducing this burden without serious political repercussions was to privatize enterprises and where possible functions performed in the Government.

(iv) Certain technological developments that have taken place, particularly in areas like telecommunications, have opened up possibilities for competition (hence private ownership also) and consequent efficiency that did not exist before.

(v) The evolution of organisational structure and information revolution has brought about greater opportunities for regulating the functioning of the market system by the State and promoting the private sector to provide services in a socially acceptable and more efficient way compared to the past.

Policy Effects – International Context

Without going into the merits or demerits of these factors, for the present purpose it is proposed to indicate the policy package that logically follows from accepting the thrust towards privatisation indicated earlier, followed by an enumeration of the actual policy packages adopted along with the effects that can be observed.

As a policy package, privatisation starts with the premise that strengthening the market forces in the form of introducing competition would result in a greater level of operational and allocative – efficiency and involves the following elements.

(i) This would imply regulation to the extent of removing the barriers to entry and the barriers to exit. At the same time, it might imply regulation to ensure a continued atmosphere of competitiveness (i.e., at least contestability).

(ii) The prices have to be right, reflecting the relative scarcities. The prices should reflect the relevant scarcities not only in the domestic market but with reference to the international situation also.

(iii) The State element has to be replaced by a private element in production and / or funding of the economic activities. Privatisation need not be restricted to the commercial or potentially commercial areas only but could extend even to other areas where, if necessary voluntary and non-governmental agencies could replace government. Such a process of privatisation can take place with reference to establishment and / or operation of such a production / funding facility. Private ownership and control is, in the final analysis a necessary but not sufficient condition though private control or operation can surrogate for ownership to some extent.

Differing weights of the above elements can be observed in the actual expression of the policy in different countries –

reflecting the country-specific socio-political and economic conditions. Results, where they can be assessed, have been mixed. A quick review of broad patterns which helps a better focus on the Indian context, follows:

(i) Privatisation is often equated with supply-side management of the economy which includes a review of the role of the Government in regard to budget, employment, Government provision of welfare and regulatory atmosphere. Two prime examples would be USA and UK. The privatisation elements in terms of reduction of the size of the federal Government and deregulation was emphasised more in USA. However, the actual results of the first six years in USA do not indicate reduction in the outlays of public expenditure, employment in Government, budgetary deficits, etc., though to some extent elements of welfare state have been marginally substituted by elements of warfare state.

(ii) The privatisation of public enterprises has been taken to wean transferring the public assets to the private sector and thus enhancing efficiency as well as competitiveness. Prime examples would be UK, Japan, and to some extent, Canada, Italy, Germany etc. In these cases also, some of the objectives of introduction of ownership-democracy do not seem to have been achieved. However, profitability has increased, but what amount of it can be attributed to the fact of privatisation, is a moot point. "Window dressing" of the enterprise undervaluation of shares, special privileges being given, are some of the criticisms. The medium term impact on the fiscal situation of the sale is still a matter of serious debate and the accusation of "selling the silver" or "pawnshop" approaches continue to be raised. In regard to developing countries as a whole, the thrust has been in terms of re-privatisation of those which were nationalised and in select sectors like food, textiles, hotels and banking.

Other areas being actively considered are telecommunications, airlines and transport. Overall, however, it is estimated that the actual privatisation compared to the intentions would be in the range of 10-15%. Apart from political / union pressures, thin domestic capital markets and financial institutions hampering progress. Some analysts see an intended gap between pronouncements and real intentions.

(iii) There has been an intensive review of the functioning of public enterprises with a view to making them simulate the working of the private sector through a variety of instruments, including distancing them from the Government in terms of financing and operations. The instrument of Memorandum of Understanding practised by France is being advocated on a large scale in many developing countries also. Some of the holding companies in developing countries, including Canada and Italy, are also keen to introduce some elements of private sector approach in their units. It is expected that there will be a medium and short-term impact in terms of financial gains but the extent to which this will harm the "public purpose" of these enterprises, including their creativity and technological advances, is a moot point. In any case, a review of the public enterprises has almost universally resulted in a process of deceleration or a virtual halt of further expansion of public enterprise in most economies and allowing private enterprise to enter areas which were hitherto reserved for the public sector.

(iv) Deregulation and introduction of competitive forces within the economy seem to be an important area, particularly in developing countries practising a comprehensive planning approach. It is too early to make an assessment of the impact of such deregulation, though by and large, there has been a greater thrust towards removal of barriers to entry rather than removal of barriers to exit.

(v) The liberalisation in terms of promoting international trade through more realistic foreign exchange regime, as well as relaxation of restrictions on imports and exports has been advocated. While in some countries like UK, this has resulted in opening up participation in their equity by other countries like USA, in most developing countries it has resulted in a greater role for multinationals. The impact on the domestic economies, both in Latin America and Africa, as a result of liberalisation in the short term appears to be somewhat unsettling.

(iv) Contracting out and giving franchises to Private sector has been attempted in USA, UK and Western Europe with some success. Some developing countries, particularly in East Asia have started these measures in transportation and urban sector.

(vii) The donor agencies, in particular the International Monetary Fund and the World Bank are advocating a whole package of measures towards privatisation, and the flow of resources from these institutions is overtly related to appropriate policy response from the recipients. The major donor countries in the world are acting in close union with the multilateral agencies in regard to the policy thrust. There is as yet little evaluatory study made by these institutions on the results of the thrust towards privatisation, but the fragmentary evidence that is available in the reviews made in the recent past does not conclusively establish the superiority of 'Market' though failures of 'State' are well-established.

If one were to make very broad generalisations on the basis of experience, four lessons will emerge. First, the scope for privatisation in developing countries in terms of selling the assets of public enterprises is limited; second, the market environment for introducing competition in many developing countries is not very conducive; third, there are costs in the medium term of a policy of liberalisation as a concomitant of privatisation which can be borne only in the given political environment; fourth, any policy will, therefore, have to be selective country and sector specific and within the socio-political context and political will.

Pressure in the Indian Context

Thus, it is very clear that any analysis of scope and limits to privatisation in India should be based on a clear understanding of the Indian socio-political and economic context. The pressures towards the privatisation in India can be attributed to a number of factors, the most important no doubt being the fact that India is a subsystem of the world capitalist system. More specifically, the disenchantment with the working of the large public enterprise sector in basic and heavy industry operating from commanding heights is a prime mover. The disenchantment relates to the high cost economy produced by these enterprises, the financial burden on the difficult financial situation of the Government, the quality of service rendered, the wage levels and the level of productivity, etc. There is no doubt an intensive debate as to whether the blame should be more on the Governmental interference or on the inherent levels of operational efficiency of the public enterprises. Further, there has also been concern at the way the regulatory framework has been used to achieve results totally in opposition to the stated objectives of reducing concentration of economic power and ensuring allocation of resources of investment towards socially desirable goals. In fact the inefficiency of private enterprise (as in the case of public enterprise) is attributed to governmental interference / regulation. There is almost universal condemnation of the regulatory role of the State in the area of industry leading to a plea for removal of the regulations (with an implied assumption that the Government is not capable of regulating for public purposes). The persistent trade-deficit and the increasing dependence on foreign savings to finance current account deficit makes the plea for review of the role of the State in the context of the international economy even more pressing and urgent. At a socio-political level, there has been a greater assertion of the pluralistic nature of the Indian policy and pressures towards decentralisation of decision-making. This is reflected in the changing character of the parties that are elected to different levels of Government, a plea for review of the Union/State relations and the variety of measures suggested or implemented towards decentralisation of the Government to local bodies, autonomous agencies and voluntary organisation.

There has been opposition to these pressures mainly on grounds of effect it will have on the policy due to increased presence of Big Business and Multinationals. Equity issues are also flagged. Further, the disappointing performance of private sector is also cited.

Unique Features of the Indian Debate

1. In this background, it would be useful to identify the unique features of the debate on privatisation in India and how it differs from the policy environment in which other societies in the world are approaching the issue of privatisation.

    (a) contrary to the pressures in USA and UK, there is no public articulation in India to impose cuts on welfare provision by the Government. The funding of such welfare activities by the Government is supported universally though there may be at the margin some advocates for encouraging private provision. If at all, the public pressure in India is towards greater funding and provision of welfare, partly due to political compulsion and partly due to the argument for removing demand constraints. Of late, there have been questions raised on the level of outlay on defence, but the provisions for welfare at large are seldom seriously questioned. In brief, supply-side economics in regard to management of public finance in India is not applicable to the expenditure side though in a limited way, similar strategy has been adopted in regard to raising of revenues.

(b) There has been emphasis on increasing the public investment rather than rolling back public investment. The demand for public investment far outstrips the availability of resources and the privatisation debate is to be viewed in the context of providing greater resources for public investment (and perhaps public consumer expenditure also in terms of welfare provision).

(c) The issue of subsidies is coming to the fore and has been dealt with in the Seventh Five-Year Plan also in a candid fashion. The major areas where subsidy is provided by the Union Government relate to food, fertilizers, exports and interest payments. In the State budget it relates to irrigation and indirectly to power and transport. While concern is expressed in a general way, and a plea is made to charge the beneficiaries for the services rendered, the roll back by the State in terms of its participation is an issue which is more or less restricted to the Road Transport Corporation sector.

(d) Of greater relevance to the Indian situation is the issue of concealed subsidies in the operations of public enterprises and the pricing mechanisms. Subsidies to favoured clientele, not open to Parliamentary control or public debate, through political patronage via public enterprises, are being flagged by academicians for attention.

(e) The largest area that is commanding the attention of the Government relates to the review of the area of operations of public enterprises, the role of public enterprises and their functioning. The areas of control and autonomy are put at the fore but the actual roll back in terms of area of operations of the existing enterprises is a non-starter. However, a number of areas hitherto the monopoly of public enterprise are now being opened up for the private sector.

(f) In terms of regulatory atmosphere, maximum attention is paid to this aspect and there appears to be almost universal support to the idea of removing physical controls and replacing them with non-discriminatory controls. One area of serious disagreement relates to the large houses and the accommodation that is being shown in the process of liberalisation to these large houses. This is a matter closely related to issues of political economy.

(g) In its international dimensions, the privatisation debate relates to the liberalisation and here the controversy is somewhat intense. Areas of concern relate to the possible harmful role of multinationals in the Indian economy and more important, Indian politics; the harmful effects of such liberlisation on the consumption and demand patterns; the effect of import of capital and intermediate goods on the capital goods industry; the implications on the economy and question of relaxing foreign exchange regulations and promoting collaborations; and, in the limited context of public enterprises, the concerns expressed at the threat to the markets of public enterprises, and in particular to BHEL.

2. Most of the privatisation debate, it may be noted, relates to industry and marginally to infrastructure. More important, the thrust is towards a review of the role of public enterprises and functioning of the Government vis-à-vis public enterprises and regulating the private sector. There is nothing in the debate to indicate a positive orientation towards private sector as a more effective,

efficient or a viable option to the public sector. Indeed, the thrust towards privatisation is meant to enable greater public investment rather than reduce the role of the Government in investment and in welfare. Finally, there is a growing feeling that in the Indian context, the privatisation debate has helped only to divert the attention of the nation away from the more pressing and urgent issues of poverty, unemployment, land distribution and regional development that affect the most vulnerable and largest segment of India's population.

Area for Further Studies in India

The above analysis of the conceptual frame, the international experience and the Indian context can help identify the major areas requiring further study to provide an appropriate package of measures relevant to the conditions of the Indian policy and Indian economy situation.

The Macro Economic Issues

Five broad areas covering macro economic framework will have to be considered in detail. First relates to the linkage between allocative and operational efficiencies and the extent to which they can be separated in the context of the structure of the Indian economy today as a precondition to defining the roles of the public and private sectors. In other words, the areas that could be left to market forces in terms of operations and the pricing mechanism that can be used to improve the market will have to be derived from this analysis. Further the role of budgetary subsidies (in terms of who pays and who benefits) on welfare and productivity will become an integral part of study of role of prices. Second, the scope for utilising non-discriminatory controls and means by which these can be exercised should be related to role of prices and distinction between owned-monopoly and private regulated monopoly. Third would require a distinction between the economic consumer and the welfare consumer of any goods of service. To the extent the welfare consumer predominates, the public element will have to take a leading role. Fourth concerns with the possible role of large houses and foreign multinational issues have to be linked to the more fundamental equity issues relevant to the country. Finally, the greatest perceived problem of the Indian economy is the level of productivity and the technological change. Arrangements by which this can be ensured should provide the lead in a dynamic sense and the relevant roles of public and private sector will have to be developed from this angle.

The Public Enterprise Issues

The first step towards analysing the area of operations of public enterprises should be to identify the nature of social obligations inherent in the establishment and continuing to be valid in its operations today. The second step would be to identify the linkage between the extent of subsidisation and the social obligations defining more clearly social groups that benefit from such subsidies. Third, the functioning of the public enterprises has to be reviewed with reference to the market environment in which they operate, namely, whether the source of supplies and the market are private or public and the input and output prices are controlled, administered or free competitive. Fourth, a disaggregated analysis of the public interest element in the public enterprise and the nature of economic environment will lead to a greater refinement in determining the nature of control and the role of Government vis-à-vis the public enterprises. The autonomy and the control issues are related to the extent of public interest that subsist in its operations. An analysis of the above factors would be possible only on the basis of a totally disaggregated enterprise-specific analysis of the factors which may ultimately lead to determining the patterns.

Private Sector

Any debate on privatisation will be incomplete unless the capacity, existing performance and the potential of the private sector is fully analysed. This has to encompass the small, medium and large scale sectors, cooperative and non-cooperative sectors, joint sector and areas such as contracting and trading which interface with public sector and operate in what is generally perceived to be a large segment of the black economy. Naturally the state of capital markets and equity-participation by public at large would be important elements. In brief, what is the potential (financial and non-financial) of private-corporate sector in India for taking over greater responsibility.

Cooperative Sector

India had begun with emphasis on the cooperative sector but due to a variety of reasons, including perhaps a tendency towards centralised political regime, this sector has tended to be ignored in the debate. The scope and potential for viewing the cooperative sector as an alternative to the public and private sector will have to be examined afresh before dispensing with this option.

Issues of Public Administration

These extend to the broader area of non-enterprise sector also, particularly those covering services and in particular education and health. A review will have to cover these elements. While this may not be actively on the debate now, there are indications that his is coming to the fore. This would involve an examination of the procedures as well as the scope for decentalisation to lower formations in the Government with necessary decentralisation of political elements.

Politics of Privatisation

In the final analysis, privatisation is not a technical issue though the identification of scope and more important the implementation of policies would be intensely technical. The issues are very closely related to matters of political philosophy. Hence, the current debate on privatisation in India will have to take into account the broad spectrum of the political implications to the national unity (for instance by freeing private enterprise and freezing sub-national governments there can be a threat to the nation). The emphasis on availability to all of a service, even if it is substandard or costly, rather than making it available to a few people / regions, and more important issues of equilibrium among the various sections of society (in particular big business, multinationals), and specially those outside the organised industrial sector, will have to be analysed to fully appreciate the limits that have to be set towards any attempt at privatisation.

3

NOT PRIVATISATION, BUT PUBLIC SHARE-HOLDING

— Nitish K Sengupta

The outright sale by the British Government of the British Airways through an open offer of sale to the public (oversubscribed to the extent of 6 billion pounds), and several examples of denationalisation in France have added new dimensions to the raging controversy over so called 'privatisation' in many countries. They have certainly much relevance for India where many thousands of crores of rupees are lying invested in 100 p.c. government-owned enterprises yielding only very marginal returns and needing handsome budgetary support from the Government every year adding to tax burden. The word privatisation has in recent years been extensively, but somewhat poorly used to describe a move for government disinvesting from government owned enterprises and transferring partial or entire ownership to private hands. Unfortunately the issue has acquired ideological overtones, and what can be a sound pragmatic policy irrespective of a socialist or free enterprise economy is being unnecessarily regarded as the touchstone of a country's socialism.

Traditionally a public sector enterprise has been viewed as one in which government has 100 p.c. ownership. But there can also be enterprise where government holds the majority share-holding of the controlling block of share-holding allowing the general public to subscribe to the balance share-holding. Such an enterprise need not be called an example of privatisation , but just a modern joint stock corporation with a mixture of both government and public share-holding. In fact even in the Indian scene there are leading examples of such enterprises with mixed ownership for example, Indo-Burma-Petroleum, Balmer-Lawrie, Andrew Yule, Hyderabad Allwyn, Gujarat State Fertilizers Corporation, Gujarat Narmada Fertilizer Corporation. These are all quoted on the Stock Exchanges. Even State Bank of India has a small percentage of public share-holding. The issue is whether as a measure of resource gathering from the capital market through public subscription, or as a measure of making these enterprises more flexible and result-oriented less of bureaucratically run departmental undertakings we should not encourage this mixed form of enterprise as a pervasive feature in our mixed economy. In other words more and more wholly owned government enterprises can be converted through partial public subscription into joint sector corporations. This cannot be called privatisation or denationalisation, but simply a case of limited public share-holding in an otherwise government-owned corporation. Today there are so many public enterprises which have established a steady record of profitability. As the general public will be interested in subscribing to the share capital of only profitable concerns, a start could be made selectively among some of them. Government could sell upto 49% shares to the public or the equity base of an undertaking could be expanded and 49% of the enlarged capital, or at least 24% could be thrown open to public subscription at a fair price of these shares to be calculated by the Controller of Capital Issues of the Central Government according to his standard formulas. Public response is likely to be overwhelming to such offers from companies such as H.M.T., BHEL, ITC, MMTC, Indian Oil Corporation, Bharat Petroleum, Air India, Indian Airlines, ITDC. Such companies will no longer need to depend on government's budgetary support on a regular basis.

Fixing a proper selling price for the shares of an enterprise may pose some problems. The net assets value and profit earning value as calculated according to the standard guidelines should apply *mutatis mutandis* in such cases. Special factors such as monopolistic position will also be given due credit. Initially, selling some shares in small lots so as to establish a trading price before they are offered in bulk for sale may be a workable starting point. In some cases there will have to be an agreed price on a willing buyer willing seller basis. Interestingly, the J.R.D. Tata Planning Group on Civil Aviation in the year 2000 has made recommendation for permitting partial public share-holding in both Air India and Indian Airlines. In this way, according to the Group not only can the two enterprises raise substantial funds, but also they become less dependent on the government for future growth, more self-reliant and can raise resources from the market on commercial terms, as the Singapore Airlines or Thai Airlines are doing. This will boost up the capital market by increasing the floating stock. It will also give the public at large a sense of participation and partnership in the nation's public sector. Stock market quotations will also provide an independent criterion for a company's future, and is a true indicator of a company's health. The substantial rise in the market value of shares such as Andrew Yule, Hyderabad Allwyn and Balmer Lawrie in recent years indicates that these companies by recording vastly improved working results have regained investors' confidence. Balmer-Lawrie shares with a face value of Rs. 100 are being quoted at Rs. 800. This corporate restructuring will not in any way dilute government's overall control while at the same time making the company management responsive to share-holding from the public some of whom are bound to ask difficult questions at the annual general meetings. The present pattern of wholly owned government companies makes management bureaucratic, non-responsive and rigid. They are almost extensions of the administrative ministry. Public share-holding upto 49 percent or 24 percent will bring in much needed relish in corporate management.

It will bring some key non-political, non-establishment criteria for evaluating and improving corporate efficiency, e.g. raising finances from the capital market, scrutiny by public share-holders, market quotation of share prices, and better preparedness for the annual general meetings. This will make for all round improvements in corporate discipline. Also, this will bring about a true partnership between the public and private sectors based on commonality of approach to issues and economic problems. As for the government, the budgetary benefits will be multiple directly through release of funds consequent on the sale of large blocks of shares, which could be reinvested in other priority areas and indirectly through better profitability and performance of the enterprises and better tax receipts and lesser dependence on subsidies from the government. Eventually, the proposed restructuring, so called privatisation will have to be reflected in economic efficiency of the enterprises. That is the end. Partial privaitisation is only the means to an end just as public sector is not an end in itself but only the means to an end viz. economic growth with social justice. Corporations jointly held by the government and the public are envisaged by the Companies Act, 1956 and the Industrial Policy Resolution, 1956. They need not be found ideologically objectionable by orthodox Marxism. Widely dispersed share-holding is a phenomenon of the 20th century.

It did not exist when Marx and Engels formulated their theories of private capitalism. Few of the 17 million share-holders of General Motors can be described as capitalists. They are, by and large, small investors. Similarly ownership was the only conceivable means of control when Marx and Engels conceptualised Communism. Hence the insistence on State ownership of the means of production and distribution. Today's State is qualitatively different from the State of these days. It is socialist. It is also powerful enough to impose its policies on private sector without owning it. In such a situation direct ownership by the government does not have any practical significance as long as ownership is widely diffused in the public, and the government in any case subjects the non-government sectors to very tight discipline in larger public interest.

An interesting straw in the wind is the recent report that Poland will soon offer shares in several State Companies to private citizens and might even open a State Exchange in order to rejuvenate her socialist economy (Lecture at the Swedish Foreign Policy Institute by Jerzy Urban, a Polish official - See Statesman of 8th April, 1987.) Simultaneously State subsidies to industry is to be cut by 15% so as to force outdated and unprofitable parts of industry into bankruptcy and to move out of the system of centrally subsidised industry. According to Mr. Urban this is not an ideological set-back, and "there were no doctrinaire barriers standing in the way of working out new motors of economic change". Further, the role of socialism is to distribute prosperity, not poverty". With such strong winds of change flowing in some of the citadels of Marxist orthodoxy we need not be overzealous on ideological counts. We, therefore conclude with a plea for allowing partial public share-holding over as much of the economy as possible thereby releasing huge government funds for redeployment and bringing about a meaningful partnership between government and the public with over riding emphasis on professional management running these mixed enterprises which will no doubt improve our economic performance.

4

PRIVATISATION IN THE UK: PROCEDURES AND OUTCOMES

— David Chambers

There are several reasons why Britain's current re-moulding of its nationalised industries may be viewed as a useful laboratory experiment by public enterprise managers in other countries. At the centre of the experiment, of course, is the Conservative Administration's programme of floating a series of important public enterprises (PEs) on the stock markets (see Exhibit 1) but the effects and the debate have extended far beyond those industries directly in line for privatisation.

Opponents of privatisation have been just as eager as its advocates to look at the fundamental rationale for keeping particular enterprises in the public sector. At the same time, PE managers have found themselves working in unfamiliar territory. What has been learned can be summarised in the answers to two questions:

> What were the classical arguments for setting up PE's in the UK and to what extent do they still hold good?
>
> What lessons of permanent value have been provided in the UK during the 1980's About reforming and rehabilitating PE's?

The Classical Arguments

The arguments which were used when PE's were being established in the UK are listed in this section with an accompanying commentary on how these would be reformulated today.

Promoting Economic Growth: One group of arguments for public ownership based the case on evidence of the systematic under-investment in certain sectors by private owners. This was for two distinct sets of reasons:

a) The absentee landlord syndrome. This applies to sectors such as coal where many private owners had undoubtedly squeezed dividends out of their companies rather than reinvest in up to date equipment.

b) "Missed opportunities". There were frequent examples, for example in the steel industry, where specific innovations were not taken up because the firms were individually too small, because no firm wanted to risk taking the lead or because they thought in terms of domestic rather than world markets.

Again, industries like Electricity Supply failed to achieve operating economies prior to nationalisation because no one company was able to exert the force and leadership necessary for full exploitation of a national grid. Breaking deadlocks can be a reason for nationalisation. In such cases, external intervention may prove necessary to owners' achievement of their own best interests (though in this example, intervention could be through other methods than complete nationalisation). This route to better achievement of their own interests is referred to (in a deceptively simple phrase) as "realising natural monopolies".

Both sets of reasons recur, with appropriate changes, in current discussion. The absentee landlord reappears in the shape of a City financial institution more interested in immediate dividends than in the long-term prosperity of an industry. "Short termism" is the phrase currently used to refer to this tendency. Again, divergence of interests between owners and employees is a key issue in the context of capital outflows from the country. The owner (perhaps in the shape of a pension fund or life assurance society) may prefer that incremental investments should be in other economies offering better returns, to the detriment of domestic employment and perhaps the longer-term development. It becomes a fine judgement to decide whether the long-term social interest is better served by open capital markets or active encouragement of domestic capital investment.

The argument from missed opportunities has been used to justify state intervention in fields like microchip manufacture (e.g. Inmos) and in current advocacy of a national fibre-optics grid. An investment which offers an acceptable combination of risk and return from the national point of view (e.g. from the point of view of future wage-earners and taxpayers) may be unacceptable to any single company. In the UK the story of Thorn-EMI's steady retreat from information technology and back to the safe ground of high-street retailing of electrical goods is a case in point.

Eliminating Wasteful Competition: Here the histories refer to sectors like banking, bus transport, insurance where there is a social interest in having standards of safety and prudence scrupulously observed and where the forces of competition can easily push some operators into unacceptable practices. Other cases illustrate suicidal competition. The survivor may turn out to be not the company with the most efficient operation but rather the one with the deepest pocket. In the UK, newspapers and beer offer relevant case-histories.

None of these cases provides a cast-iron argument for public ownership. Instead, the important arguments relate to the form of public intervention and to its duration. Safety standards in the beer industry are fairly easy to monitor and the social interest will not be seriously affected by leaving the companies to battle it out. The regulatory regime is much harder to specify and implement in the fragmented bus industry or in banking or insurance. At a particular point of time, and perhaps for a limited period of time, public ownership may appear as the most practicable solution.

Exploitative Employers: Historically, important arguments for public ownership were based on (a) the poor working conditions of workers in the industry and (b) poor service to consumers. Neither of these arguments would be advanced with much conviction in the UK today. In fact the wheel has turned full circle. A major argument for privatisation has been that some public-sector Trade Unions had increased their power to the point that they in turn had become the exploiters, with consumers and taxpayers as the exploited. Needless to say, the particular form of privatisation used in the UK (with public monopolies becoming private monopolies) is not best adapted to correcting these tendencies.

Preferential Purchasing: The argument that public enterprises can be directed to purchase from named (and presumably domestic) suppliers has again lost its force as the flaws of the command economies have become more evident. For practical and transitional reasons the argument survives in the form e.g. of a constraint on the Central Electricity Generating Board that it must buy nearly all its coal from the UK National Coal Board.

Instruments of Macro-economic Policy: The use of public enterprises as an instrument for implementing price-control policies, credit-control policies, wage-level policies, balance-of-payment policies, credit-control policies, wage-level policies, has been a very important feature of government practice. The opportunities for using the industries in these ways were mentioned at the time when they were being nationalised, but these arguments played only a small part in the justifications for nationalisation. There is now a much wider realisation that the industrial base has been damaged by these interventions, and the arguments from tighter control of the macro-economy would not be use today in justification of any extension in public ownership.

Rehabilitation: Intervening to help sick industries has been a major reason for taking companies into the public sector, in the UK as in other countries, and numerous studies have been published on individual cases. These interventions have often been in response to specific emergencies or to local political pressures. Any such intervention today would probably have to be justified in generalisable terms which would mean spelling out the rules and understandings under which public support would be provided. Thus the exemplary case may be one where government intervenes to help a company through a temporary crisis. From the start, government's aim is then to put the company back on its feet and after that to withdraw. The rules and understandings determine how long a period to allow before there is sufficient evidence to show whether or not the enterprise can be restored to health. If the evidence indicates that it cannot, then the objective of support switches: further support will be used to arrange the decline and demise of the enterprise in a socially responsible way. This way of managing rehabilitation also gives a role to privatisation. Because interventions are time-limited, a company can be returned to private ownership once it has been restored to health, and the proceeds from sale can be cycled back to provide the means for the next interventions. This amounts to a politically neutral use of the privatisation device.

Reforms in the Management of PEs

By forcing each British PE to think about whether and why it should or should not be privatised, the current debate has provoked reactions and had elicited evidence which may be of interest beyond the UK.

First, the question of the "success" of a PE now figures in public discussion in a new way. There is now a large body of individuals, belonging to several different groupings or constituencies, and external to the PE sector, with a direct interest in "talking up" the success of particular PE's. In the past the tenor of public discussions has been just the reverse.

Second, there is a new awareness of the PE as a going concern which has, potentially, a valuation. What would it be worth if it were floated on the stock market? Moreover, and significantly, how is this constraint on the PE's operation? In the past, the somewhat metaphysical concept of the potential market valuation of a PE has not figured prominently in public debate or governmental policy. Specific investments have been assessed for their incremental effects on the corporation's Net Present Value, (and hence on its value to its owners, the taxpayer) but examples are not easy to find where a directive on pricing or on preferential purchasing has been assessed in quite this way. As commentators come to think of a PE as an entity with a valuation to its owners which changes form day to day (or, like a quoted company, from minute to minute) as the markets assess the significance of the flows of current news, then the full consequences of different interventions become much harder to fudge.

A third aspect of the British Experiment is also noteworthy. Just as there is a new interest in "success", so there is a more discriminating appreciation that there are differences in kind between certain ways of making something called "success" come about. It is common ground that for a PE to be privatised, first it must be seen to be a "success" at least in the sense that it is capable of yielding an income flow to the purchasers of its stock. Some PE's in the UK achieved this by what would be generally accepted as good management. The tiny Amersham International and the giant British Gas Corporation belong to this category.

But for other PE's (British Aerospace, British Airways, even British Telecom) some of the most interesting footwork has been in the various restructuring prior to flotation, to make this Corporation an entity that reasonable investors would wish to buy. Exhibit 2 is an extract from a Report by the National Audit Office, illustrating some of these arrangements in the case of

BT. Starting with the year 1983-84, BT changed its accounting bases. Had the revised bases been in force in the previous year, a reported profit of pounds 365 m would have been revised upward to pounds 1,031 m. The fascinating question, not lost on those PE's which are going to remain in the public sector, is this: if such efforts are to be put into re-moulding Bae, BA etc., into a shape the stock market will associate with success, might not similar efforts be used to improve the coherence, focus and identity of the PE's that remain?

A fourth reason why current British experience may offer wider lessons is that everyone engaged in any way in the business of UK PE's has been forced to think again about the social objectives towards whose achievement the PE was to have been a means, about who had actually gained from the adoption of this organisational form (consumers? Employees? Low-income groups? Government ministers?), and about judging PE's as against other possible means for achieving the same social objectives.

What in summary can now be seen as the important and generalisable lessons of UK experience? Not the rather obvious lesson that privatisation is possible and not the sometimes questionable means of carrying it out. You can sell anything at a price: most of the UK privatisation issues have been priced at levels at which they were heavily oversubscribed, and the costs of floating British Gas, which amounted to pounds 40 m. in advertising and underwriting, were condemned by critics ranging from the Trades Union Congress to the National Audit Office.

What has been most significant in the British experience is to be found in the period leading up to privatisation. Here the UK demonstrates a concerted and serious effort to reshape public enterprises and to make them "viable" in terms the private sector would understand. What happened in the UK in this period offers models to those working for the reform of PE's in other countries. Mr. Gorbachev's struggle to introduce a form of internal free market within the public sector is the most dramatic example. Privatisation happens to have been the rallying-cry in the UK but the significant reforms have taken place before privatisation, while the enterprises still occupied the public sector. For many other countries it is the UK reforms, and not the UK privatisations which are worth watching.

Changed Perspectives

Looking beyond Britain, a future historian will observe the almost simultaneous flowering in the early 1980's in many different countries, of new ideas about the management of public sector industry. In these years, the idea that at least some PE's should be run to earn real profits won widespread support. Such profits began to be seen as part of the potential input to a social and economic infrastructure. A particular PE's best contribution to social goals (such as regional policy or income redistribution) might be to earn funds which could be channeled to agencies specifically targeted on these goals, rather than itself aiming for the full range of goals.

Manpower reductions in a PE were no longer taboo subject. This was a special case of the previous argument. The cause of employment creation might be better served by running an efficient PE whose profits were channeled to other job-creators, than by accepting over manning as the natural condition for a PE. The PE's goal would then become "aiming profit subject to operating in an exemplary fashion" rather than aiming simultaneously at employment-creation and profit.

Competition between PE's within PE's and between PE's and private enterprises began to be seen as a basis for dynamism and growth. The dismissive phrase wasteful competition was used much less freely.

Privatisation was seen as a topic that had arrived to stay. Enterprises and parts of enterprises could enter or leave the public sector in the future for pragmatic and opportunistic rather than from strictly ideological reasons. PE's boundaries had been shown to be moveable, and judgements over whether and when to move them constituted a whole new field of enterprise policy.

Finally, many PE managers gained a new confidence in this period that organisational structures were not immutable and that constraints could be challenged. It was possible for able managers to negotiate the elbowroom for effective action. Paradoxically, this was a very good time to be a Public Enterprise Chairman.

EXHIBIT I

Main UK Privatisations and Sales of Shareholdings

	Year or years Of privatisation	*Sales proceeds (net of costs, pounds m)*
Amersham International	1982	64
Associated British Ports	1983	94
British Aerospace	1981, 1985	349
British Airways	1987	415
British Gas	1986	1796
British Gas Debt	1986	750
British Petroleum Shares	1979, 1983	827
British Telecom	1985	2598
BT Loan Stock	1985	105
Britoil	1982, 1985	1052
Cable and Wireless	1981, 1983, 1985	1045
Enterprise oil	1984	1045
Jaguar	1984	297
National Freight Consortium	1982	5

EXHIBIT 2

Restructuring of British Telecommunications (BT) Prior to Privatisation

(Extract from National Audit Office, Report by the Comptroller and Auditor General, Session 1984-85, HC 495

Restructuring in Preparation For Sale Revision of Accounting Policies

9. Under the 1981 Act it was the duty of the Corporation to prepare an annual statement of accounts giving a true and fair view of its state of affairs and of its profit or loss. This statement had to comply with any requirement notified by the Secretary of State, after consultation with the Corporation and with the consent of the Treasury, relating to the information to be contained in the statement, the manner in which that information was to be presented and the methods and principles according to which the statement was to be prepared. It was to be audited by auditors appointed by the Secretary of State after consultation with the Corporation.

10. In accordance with these provisions, the Corporation's main accounts up to 31 March 1983 were prepared under the historic cost accounting convention modified by the charging of additional depreciation to reflect the estimated replacement value of fixed assets. In accordance with accepted accounting practice, the supplementary depreciation charges were not included in accumulated depreciation but were credited directly to reserves. In the Report of the auditors, which referred to the modification of the accounting convention, they stated their opinion that the historic cost accounts for the year to 31 March 1983 gave a true and fair view of BT's state of affairs and profit in accordance with the modified convention. The Report of the auditors also drew attention to the

fact that the 1982-83 accounts did not anticipate any effects on the Corporation's financial operations which might result from the Telecommunications Bill (which was enacted as the 1984 Act) then before Parliament. The auditors also confirmed that, subject to stated limitations, supplementary statements prepared on current cost accounting principles complied with the relevant Statement of Standard Accounting Practice (SSAP).

11. To reflect changes in the business environment brought about by the 1984 Act, in particular the abolition of its exclusive privilege and the introduction of competition in the provision and operation of telecommunications systems, together with the need to take account of developments in technology, the Corporation, revised its bases of accounting with effect from 1 April 1983. First, in the main historic cost, accounts it ceased to charge supplementary depreciation which in 1982-83 had amounted to pounds 626 million. Secondly it shortened the estimated useful lives of a number of fixed assets and changed the accounting policy concerning expenditure on certain other assets so that previously capitalised was charged against revenue as incurred. In consequence of the latter changes the opening value of fixed assets stated in the 1983-84 accounts was reduced by pounds 933 million with a corresponding reduction in reserves. The amount comprised pounds 584 million in respect of depreciation arising from changes in asset lives and pounds 349 million which would have been charged to revenue had the revised policy regarding capitalisation of fixed asset expenditure been followed from the outset. The Corporation considered that the circumstances leading to the shortening of the estimated asset lives were exceptional and the adherence to the provisions of the relevant SSAP under which the pounds 584 million of depreciation would be charged against future profits

would have caused the accounts to give a misleading view. Therefore in accordance with the Explanatory foreword to SSAPs they departed from the provisions of the relevant SSAP and included a note to the accounts to that effect. The historic cost accounts for 1983-84, which restated the results for 1982-83 in accordance with the revised policies, gave, in the opinion of the auditors a true and fair view of the Corporation's state of affairs and of its profit. Reflecting the responsibilities of the Secretary of State in connection with the Corporation's annual statement of accounts, (paragraph 9), the proposed changes in the bases of accounting were considered in discussions between the Department, the Corporation and its auditors. The auditors informed the Department that they agreed that the changes and in particular those relating to asset lives were necessary to reflect fairly the state of affairs of the business and its results.

12. The Corporation's accounts for 1983-84 stated that, had the revised accounting bases been effective in 1982-83, the reported profits for the year would have been pounds 1,031 million compared with the stated amount of pounds 365 million. The increase of pounds 666 million comprised pounds 626 million from cessation of charges in respect of supplementary depreciation and pounds 40 million arising from the revised policies concerning asset lives and capitalisation of fixed asset expenditure. The reported profits for 1983-84 on the revised basis were pounds 990 million.

5

PROBLEMS OF INTERFACE BETWEEN PRIMARY AND SECONDARY MARKETS

— Nitish K Sengupta

The chaotic conditions prevailing in the stock market in recent months, with unprecedented fluctuations of the prices of certain pivotals and the near total stoppage of activities following the income-tax raids on the offices of some brokers, should set everyone thinking on the need for certain overdue long-term reforms in the stock exchange system. Cassandras are back in their game of creating an impression that all is lost, and that unless, the Government retreats from the policy of 'raids', the future of the capital market is doomed.

What is not realised is that the so-called market price of most of the pivotals was grossly overvalued, thanks to reckless speculation, that in actual fact there are only few transactions in these pivotals at the quoted price, that genuine investors have no cause for apprehension even in TISCO or Reliance shares tumble by around hundred rupees, and that only those who indulge in pure gambling as distinct from speculations stand to loose.

The truth is that while the primary capital market has since 1979 expanded by 15 times or so, the structure and the method of working of the secondary market has by and large remained unchanged. A structural reform of the stock market is, therefore, the prime need of the hour and does not brook any delay whatsoever. We have to provide a healthy secondary market where genuine investors can freely buy and sell and there is enough room for healthy speculation, but not reckless gambling indulged in by a handful of brokers without any regard for either the health of the market or the health of the economy.

Phenomenal Upsurge

Few events in India's economic development after independence are comparable to the phenomenal upsurge in the capital market between 1980 and 1985 in terms of the magnitude of the changes within a short time span. While the annual average raising by companies from the market between 1947 and 1979 was only Rs. 58 crores, the annual figures jumped to about Rs. 1,000 crores by 1984 starting with Rs. 120 crores in 1980 and are now almost touching Rs. 3,000 crores a year.

There has been both deepening and widening of the shareholding structure. The capital market from having been confined to only the cities of Bombay, Calcutta, Delhi, Madras and Ahmedabad has now extended to many newer areas and reached non-traditional sections, such as agriculturists, the middle class and the non-resident Indians.

As against only about five or six stock exchanges which operated a few years ago, today they are 13 of them. In the olden days, an issue of Rs. 2 or 3 crores was considered a big issue, but in recent years there have been numerous cases of companies raising staggering sums between Rs. 100 and Rs. 300 crores in a single issue, the most notable case being of a company recently raising Rs. 370 crores through an issue of non-convertible debentures.

At the same time, many more companies have become broad-based. While until 1981 the company with the largest number of shareholders had only about 80,000 today there are any number of companies with lakhs of shareholders. In a way, these Indian companies, widely held and professionally managed, are becoming similar to the modern public corporations of the west. This has happened largely because of a well thought-out Government policy, relentlessly pursued, from 1980 onwards of compelling MRTP companies whenever they sought permission for expansion to raise substantial portion of the cost of the project from the market through shares or debentures rather than relying almost wholly on long-term institutional finance as they had been doing till then.

The demonstration effect of several such cases of successful public issues during 1980 and 1981 was phenomenal. Convertible debentures became the main instrument of these issues. It gave the investors both a good return from the beginning and the certainty of conversion into risk capital by the time the company will have reached the stage of profitability. Convertible debentures, therefore, became a highly popular instrument and mainly did the trick. Many more companies, aware of the newly - found strength of the capital market, and the fact that public response was expected to be overwhelming if they had a business reputation and if the project in question was sound, now went to the public.

A number of industrial houses, which throughout the 70s had been sitting on the sidelines and not gone in for any expansion for fear of the convertibility clause, also followed suite with new projects and concomitant public issues. Indeed, a new horizon had been created for the corporate sector. At the same time, pressure on the financial institutions substantially eased as companies were no longer dependent on them for raising their requirement of long-term capital.

Secondary Market

But this growth of the primary market has created serious problems of interfacing with the secondary market, viz. The stock exchanges which still, by and large, continue to retain the same old infrastructure and way of working suited to the narrow base of the capital market in the yester years. Unless the secondary market is reoriented so as to discharge the new responsibilities cast on it by the vastly enlarged primary market, this will act as a drag on the future growth of the primary market itself. Investors who are anxious to buy new securities are bound to get disenchanted if they face serious problems while trying to buy or sell scripts.

The existing stock exchange regulations were essentially meant for times when buyers and sellers as also the stock brokers were small in number and mostly located in the same city or at most in the few stock exchange centres. They have little relevance in today's context when the number of shareholders has gone up to around 15 million and they are dispersed over the length and width of the whole country. Restrictions on shares transfer under Section 108 (1) (a) and (1) (b) requiring transfer forms to be stamped by a prescribed Government official, and the validity of such transfer deeds lasting only for about two months have outlived their utility.

A shareholder located, say, at Jabalpur is first required to obtain the transfer deed from stock exchange centre and thereafter send it to the stock broker, say, at Delhi or Kanpur for arranging the sale. More often than not, by the time the transfer deed is presented to the company, its validity period would have expired. Normally all correspondence between the company and the shareholders, including the despatch of share certificates is required to be done by registered post. This, coupled with an inefficient postal system, lead to delays and often loss of the share scripts in transit. The dilatory and inefficient working of the banking system under which cheques take longer to be encashed makes it difficult to make necessary payment in reply to calls or in connections with the subscription for issues. This also affects the system. Also FERA restrictions on inflow and outgo of foreign exchange mitigate against the efficient functioning of the secondary market at a time when a large number of non-resident Indians have shares in Indian companies. The situation is very much like the problems that will be faced by a small airstrip which is accustomed to handling only Vayudoot Donniers if it is suddenly called upon to handle jumbo jets without broadening the runway or making necessary changes in the infrastructure.

Majority of the stock exchange members are old fashioned, lacking in both modern education and spirit of service to the clients. Many of them need to graduate from their role as pure stock brokers into a newer role as investment counsels or investment brokers. They are reluctant to permit new members and want to retain all control. There needs to be a substantial enlargement of the number of brokers in major stock exchanges, such as Bombay, Calcutta and Delhi. Further, some of the existing brokers are engaged in reckless speculation. For over a decade, forward trading was not recognised by law and yet permitted in the major exchanges through extra-legal means over which laws and regulations had no control.

Reform of Exchanges

In the last few years, the Bombay Stock Exchange passed through several severe payment crisis largely because of speculation and over-trading when deals were entered into without even a minimum volume of scripts. Since 1983, a limited volume of forward trading upto three months has been permitted and this should partially solve the problems caused by the absence of *de jure* forward trading. But the basic question remains one of giving a hard look at the existing rules and regulations, whether under Company Law or Stock Exchange Regulations or FERA, to find out how many of them have outlived their utility and, are, anachronistic in the context of the sea changes that have taken place in the capital market. Thus, for instance the restrictions imposed under Section 108(1)(a) and (1)(b) could be done away with. Also, it is necessary to take stock of the available infrastructure. Time has come when stock exchange boards need not be viewed as mere private clubs of the brokers. Essentially, the stock exchange is a public institution in which the Government, the industry and the public are vitally interested.

Thus, there should be representatives from all these interests on the board of exchanges. Indeed, such representatives should constitute the majority. At present, the majority consists of the elected representatives of the stock brokers who very often find it difficult to distinguish between their own private interests and the larger public interest. There should be uniformity of working hours amongst the exchanges. They should be linked to one another with computer terminals. In fact, there is a strong case for greater computerisation in stock exchanges.

Another consideration is that the secondary market still has a very narrow base where two or three Government institutions, viz. UTI, LIC or GIC have a cramping influence. When they start selling, prices automatically go down. A market can be said to exist only when there are hundreds and thousands of independent decision-makers. In spite of the vast changes, the stock market is still handicapped by the fact that decision-makers are few. Trusts and provident funds should be permitted to buy and sell stocks into a small percentage of their funds - say one or two per cent.

New Mechanisms

Also, the commercial banks which have been, by and large, absent from the market since 1969 should be allowed to utilise a small percentage of their funds to buy and sell shares. Considering the tremendous difficulty faced by investors in buying or selling their shares on time, it is necessary that we should think in terms of a separate body - say Stock Holders' Corporation - which can assume the responsibility of arranging transfer of shares on behalf of the buyers or sellers who may agree to become account-holders in that corporation. Organisations, like UTI or ICICI could take the lead in setting up subsidiary bodies to discharge such functions.

Also, brokers should be encouraged to do part of their business amongst themselves form their respective offices without necessarily going to the stock exchange floor. It is understood that in the New York Stock Exchange, a very substantial part of the business is carried on amongst members from their own business premises. A related area where attention needs to be given is the steep rise in the cost of public issues. A look is needed at the Company Law propositions and Stock Exchange Regulations covering areas, such as brokers' commission and the requirement of the number of prospectus etc. to be printed, with a view to reducing the cost of issues. In fact, the high cost of a public issue has been driving many companies to resort to rights issues rather than public issues in recent years.

Finally, having regard to the enormous increase in the size of the capital market, and the difficulties being experienced in successful running of the stock exchanges, it is high time that consideration is given to the idea of having a Security and Exchange Commission to coordinate and effectively supervise the activities of the exchanges.

6

FINANCIAL IMPLICATIONS OF PRIVATISATION OF PUBLIC ENTERPRISES IN INDIA

— R. K. Mishra & R. Nandagopal

The purpose of this chapter is to examine the status of Public Enterprises (PEs) amenable to privatisation, evolve the methods and procedures to implement such a programme and present estimates of its financial implications. The scope of the chapter is limited to PEs owned and managed by the Central Government. The chapter does not make an attempt to build up a case for or against the privatisation. It presupposes that the policy makers are already seized with this issue on account of numerous reasons and are in search of appropriate decision criteria to initiate the privatisation programme. The term 'privatisation' in the present context connotes diffusion of the public ownership and management in varying degrees in PEs giving due regard to their nature and specific characteristics.

I

Status of PEs Amenable for Privatisation

The PEs which are amenable to privatisation can be identified with reference to two criteria: (I) They fulfil the statutory requirements, and (ii) They have a suitable capital structure.

Statutory Requirements

The statutory provisions, among other things, mandate that no decision about change in management and financial structure of an undertaking could be taken in contravention of the provisions contained in the Acts under which such public corporations have been incorporated. Thus, privatisation of PEs by the Executive wing of Government belonging to the statutory corporation form of organisation could be ruled out at the very outset. Similarly, some of the Central PEs have been incorporated as Government companies under Section 25 of the Indian Companies Act, 1956. These companies have been mainly entrusted with the task of organising certain promotional activities on "no-profit, no loss" consideration on the limited liability basis. These companies fall outside the purview of any scheme of privatisation. In other words, PEs incorporated as Government companies alone emerge as suitable candidates for privatisation.

It is appropriate to recapitulate here the essence of arguments advanced in favour of this form. It has been said that the Government company form of organisation provides maximum commercial flexibility and freedom to PEs as compared to the departmental and public corporation forms. It is also the form that is most convenient and expeditious to separate existing departmental undertakings into self regulating autonomous agencies. It is also the easiest form of organisation to lend new government owned ventures to execute government policies and programmes. A study of the evolutionary process of the form of organisation in PEs shows that over the last fifty years, governments world over shifted from the departmental undertakings to the statutory corporation forms initially and have later adopted the company for the State owned undertakings.

The Central Government has invested monies in some enterprises, predominantly by way of debt and does not have, therefore, direct responsibility for their management. The enterprises under this category do not instantaneously qualify for privatisation as long as their debt capital is not converted into equity and the ownership of such enterprises is passed on to the Government consequently.

The Public Enterprises Survey published by the Bureau of Public Enterprises for the year 1985-86 lists the names of PEs under different ministries. A study of this list reveals that out of the 236 PEs mentioned, nine are public corporations, four are Section 25 companies, nine are undertakings with Central Government investment but without direct responsibility for management and one does not have any equity investment. Thus, only 213 companies could be considered for privatisation. The detailed breakup of these enterprises has been provided in Annexure-I.

Capital Structure

The term lending institutions have prescribed the broad norm of 2:1 debt-equity ratio for the financing of industrial units. This 2:1 norm has been liberalised for certain industries. The financial institutions vary this norm in view of the capital intensity and postulated rate of return for particular industry. The 2:1 norm is considered a sound financial measure with regard to the optimisation of the earning per share and valuation of the firm. We have confined the scope of the present study to the PEs having a debt-equity ratio of 2:1 or more. Annexure-2 provides the list of PEs which have a debt-equity ratio of 2:1 or more. The number of such enterprises as on March 31, 1986 was 79. Of these 78 units, 39 had incurred losses and 40 units had earned profits in 1985-86. These units had been operating under three conditions of price control, viz., no price control (NPC), non-administered price control (PCNA) and administered price control (PCA). A study of the nature of the 79 enterprises under reference in terms of profit earning, success, and price control status, competition brings out the following eight-fold pattern of PEs:

(i) **Competitive, Successful, No-Price Control PEs:** These are the PEs making profit faced with no-price controls. They are in competition with their counterparts in the private sector. These units are engaged in construction, light and medium engineering, and textile sectors. Some of these units were set up to achieve an improved production planning and control and mitigate supply shortages. Twenty such units have an equity investment of Rs. 686.25 crores and a total investment of Rs. 3704.83 crores. The textile units numbering eight under this category are taken over sick units.

(ii) **Competitive, successful, price control non-administered PEs:** These enterprises are similar in nature to the enterprises in the earlier category excepting the difference that they operate under price control orders promulgated from time to time by the administrative ministries controlling them. Such orders are applicable to their counterparts too, in the private sector. Only two drugs and pharmaceuticals units figure in this category of PEs. The equity and the investment in such units are Rs. 1.39 crores and 3.52 crores respectively.

(iii) **Competitive, non-successful, no price control PEs:** These enterprises are losing units despite the price control and a large number of their counterparts in the private sector are earning profits. Twenty-seven in number, these units have an equity investment of Rs. 333.19 crores and a total investment of Rs. 1589.31 crores. These units include the taken over sick textile units, medium and light engineering units, tea companies, chemical and pharmaceutical firms and jute units.

(iv) **Competitive, non-successful, non-administered price control PEs:** These enterprises, unlike the private sector units governed by the similar price control orders, and incurring losses positively because of operational and managerial inefficiencies, commercial imprudence, rigid financial framework and inconducive interface with the Government. The drugs and pharmaceutical firms prominently figure in this category. Three units in this category have an equity investment of Rs. 4.35 crores and a total investment of Rs. 14.31 crores.

(v) **Non-competitive, Successful, Administered Price Control PEs:** The entrepreneurial role of PEs in the economic development of the country needs no elaboration. Many PEs have been set up in such sectors of the economy which are vital for growth but have continued to be unattractive to the private sector. The policy frame evolved by the administrators and planners has allocated the commanding heights of the economy to the public sector. PEs engaged in the fulfillment of these tasks do not have to compete with the private sector units and obtain the 'non-competitive' status.

Some of the non-competitive PEs operating under the administered price formula have not only been able to break even, but even yield huge surpluses. Eight such units, belonging to the petroleum industry, have an equity investment of Rs. 64.96 crores. The total investment in these units is of the order of Rs. 4790.20 crores.

(vi) **Non-competitive, Non-successful, Price-Control Administered PEs:** These units function in the core sector of the economy. In our case three such units have an equity investment of Rs. 1,072.66 crores and a total investment of Rs. 1,159.74 crores. The units under reference belong to the coal industry. The coal prices are controlled by the administered pricing formula. The woe of the coal industry is unprofitable pricing. The industry has been complaining time and again about the increase in administered prices are not commensurate with the increase in the cost of its inputs.

(vii) **Non-competitive, Successful, Non-administered Price Control PEs:** These enterprises enjoy the non-competitive status presently on account of the deregulation policy of the government. Initially, they enjoyed this status on account of importance attached to their operations in the public sector without any conceivable competition being offered to them by the private sector. The shyness of private entrepreneurship in making a march to such areas and explore the unexplored has helped these enterprises to continue to enjoy this status. Ten enterprises with a total investment of Rs. 3,885.28 crores make up this category. The equity investment in these enterprises is Rs. 486.66 crores. The telecommunication and air transport units are the principal companies of this category.

(viii) **Non-competitive, Non-successful, Non-administered Price Control PEs:** Despite the non-competitive status, these enterprises have not been able to turn the corner because either they have been setup to regulate the economic activity without much levy to manouvre charges for their services or they cannot price their products appropriately since their real decision making power in this area rests with some other enterprises who have been responsible for their creation. Six enterprises have a total investment of Rs. 830.76 crores and an equity investment of Rs. 235.17 crores in this category. The ship building and inland water transport units are the principle components of this category.

Decision Model for Privatisation of PEs in India

Having identified PEs amenable for privatisation, we propose to specify a decision model for privatisation of PEs in India. The decision model is explained in the 2 x 2 matrix. The four quadrants of this matrix specify the privatisation criteria based on two factors viz., success and competition.

Cell I: This has reference to the competitive units which are successful and are operating under no price control or price control non-administered. The enterprises which are competitive can be straightaway privatised. The equity investment in these enterprises is of the order of Rs. 686.25 crores. As these enterprises are profitable there should not be any difficulty in selling their shares. Only the stock markets have to be approached to achieve this objectives. The shares can be unloaded in one shot or in a few installments. The outcomes of the privatisation of PEs in U.K. indicate that the one shot off-loading in most of the cases did not enable the government to realise the best value. On the other hand the enterprises going in for off-loading in stages realised better value of their shares. Similarly, the fixed price method has been found superior to the tender method in U.K. In other words, Decision Model for Privatisation of PEs in India trade-offs have to be decided by Government keeping in view the conditions prevailing in the stock markets, the preparedness of the investing public and the control it proposes to exercise on enterprises singled out for privatisation. In our view the Government can think of privatisation of the shareholding in these enterprises in any range it deems suitable. The most ideal proposition would be to off-load the entire shareholding.

Another kind of PEs in this Cell are those which are operating under non-administered price controls. Two such enterprises are Karnataka Antibiotics & Pharmaceuticals Ltd. And Orissa Drugs & Pharmaceuticals Ltd. They are producing bulk formulations and mass drugs. And the price of these products are controlled under the price control order by the Government to the disadvantage of these units. To achieve the objective of complete privatisation, we suggest the removal of price controls on such enterprises. This will improve their competitive status and consequently the privatisation potential. An action on these lines would push them up in this quadrant. The privatisation strategy applicable to the non-price control units in this category will then hold good for these units, too. To sum up, the Government can get back an investment of Rs. 700 crores from the units pertaining to Cell I, if it decides to opt for their privatisation.

SUCCESSFUL

Cell I	*No. of Enter-prises*	*Equity (Rs. in Lakhs)*	*Cell II*	*No. of Enter-prises*	*Equity (Rs. in Lakhs)*
i) Competitive, Successful, Non-price Control (NPC) - Privatise - De-control Management	20	68625	i) Competitive, non-successful, Non-price Control (NPC) - Privatise/ Liquidate/ - Close/ Managerial change	27	33319
ii) Competitive, Successful, price Control Non-administered (PCNA) - Remove Price Controls - Privatise	2	139	ii) Competitive, non-successful, price Control Non-administered (PCNA) - Financial liberalisation/ - Remove Price Controls/ - Managerial changes/ selling out/ - Liquidation	3	435
Total	22	68764	Total	30	33754

COMPETITIVE

Cell III			*Cell IV*		
i) Non-competitive, Successful, Price Control Administered (PCA) - Remove Price Controls, - Set up a board for regulation/ - Financial liberalisation	8	69146	i) Non-competitive, non-Successful, Price Control Administered (PCA) - De-regulate price controls	3	107260

ii) Non-competitive, successful price control, non-administered (PCNA) - Remove price controls - Financial liberalization	10	48666	ii) Non-competitive, non-successful price control, non-administered (PCNA) - Joint sector management - Deregulate prices - Price liberalization	6	23517
Total	18	117812	Total	9	130777

Cell II: In this cell are discussed the privatisation strategies regarding the competitive units which are unsuccessful both with and without price controls. We suggest that the competitive, non-successful, non-price control PEs should also be privatised. In case their privatisation is not possible, liquidation or closure of such enterprises can be resorted to. However, an honest effort should be made to introduce managerial changes in such organisations in case there is a need to do so. The managerial changes would include, among other things merger of units and a greater freedom in the operational matters. The desired operational freedom can be guaranteed to these enterprises through MOUs (Memorandum of Understandings). 26 enterprises of this type have the equity investment of Rs. 333.19 crores. The managerial change in these enterprises may help them turn the corner and thereby make their shares attractive to the general investor in the country.

The other kind of enterprise under this category are competitive, non-successful and non-administered price control PEs. We suggest removal of price controls to make their scrips attractive. These enterprises should be benefited by financial liberalisation by way of incorporating suitable changes in their debt-equity ratio. They should also be covered by the measures related to managerial changes outlined in para. This will improve the financial working of such enterprises and make them amenable for privatisation failing which selling out their assets or liquidation might be the only alternatives left with the government. Three enterprises in this category have an equity investment of Rs. 4.35 crores and it is possible to privatise their shareholdings by introducing requisite financial and managerial changes to a large extent.

Cell III: The non-competitive successful enterprises with the administered price control and non-administered price control have been included in this Cell. The privatisation strategy for the enterprises with administered price control is the removal of price controls in the present form and setting up a board for regulating the pricing patterns of these enterprises. The model suggested in this regard is a board of the type set up for the British Telecom. As these enterprises are working in the core sectors of the economy and the private sector being not keen enough to set up units in such fields of economic activity it may not be able to transfer their ownership to the entrepreneurs in the private sector. We, therefore, suggest that such units may be allowed to benefit by the financial liberalisation. This may entail the floatation of bonds in the capital market and mobilising money from foreign capital markets through appropriate securities. Further, it will be worthwhile to off-load shares to the tune of 49 per cent in the case of non-competitive units which are characterised by high profit earning. In this quadrant there are eight enterprises in the oil sector with an equity investment of Rs. 691.46 crores These enterprises are controller by the pricing formula administered by the Oil Pricing Committee. The non-competitive enterprises earning profits under non-administered price control system numbering ten have equity investment of Rs. 486.66 crores. As suggested the enterprises of both kinds could be privatised to the tune of 49 per cent yielding resources to the tune of about 580 crores.

Cell IV: This cell deals with the privatisation strategy for non-competitive enterprises which have not been making profits are operating under either administered price control or non-administered prices. In view of the unprofitable operations we do not suggest off-loading of their shares in the capital markets. We suggest measures to improve the status of these enterprises in terms of operational efficiency and profitability so as to evaluate them to shift from Cell IV to Cell III. In the case of non-competitive, non-successful enterprises covered by administered price control, we suggest that their prices should be deregulated and a board should be set up to keep an eye on their price patterns as suggested in the case of enterprises falling in quadrant III.

In the case of non-competitive, non-successful enterprises operating under non-administered price control, we suggest that management can be given to workers. Alternatively, new concept of joint sector management may be given a fair trial. It is further suggested that pricing liberalisation will be in order in the case of these enterprises. The Government may consider giving greater autonomy to the management of these enterprises.

In fine, the strategic decision model for the privatisation of PEs indicates that competitive PEs are at the top in the list of privatisation. The techniques of privatisation will range from 100 per cent off loading of public share holdings to selling of assets and any number of permutations and combinations favouring the implementation of the programme.

Financial Implications of Privatisation

We quantify in this section the resources expected to accrue to the Government by the privatisation of PEs under reference and explore the possibility of their mobilisation through capital markets. Finally, we consider the implications of such a drive on the units not included in the scope of this paper.

Nature of PEs	*Resource Expected (Rs. in lakhs)*
Competitive, Successful	68764
Competitive, Non-successful	33754
Non-competitive, successful	61400
Total	Rs. 1639918

Resource Generation: According to the strategic model outlined in the previous section, the Government may expect to receive resources to the tune of Rs. 1639.18 crores as explained above.

Privatistion of PEs in the U.K. has been an enormously rewarding proposition. During the period 1982-86 it has yielded resources to the tune of pounds m. 9818 or Rs. 19638 crores. In the U.K. the privatisation strategies have comprised even transfer of ownership to workers in PEs. Approximately 10,300 workers used savings and/or loans to raise pounds 6,187,500 (12.38 crores) to bring their own company, the National Freight Consortium. The amount of shareholdings brought by workers was 82.5 per cent. This is worth trying in our context also.

Approaching the Capital Markets: The capital markets in India have come of age. Between 1947 and 1975 , Indian companies annually raised only Rs. 58 crores on an average from the capital markets. But starting with Rs. 120 crores in 1980, this figure jumped to almost Rs. 1000 crores by 1983 and is expected to touch a mark of Rs. 5000 crores in the current financial year. The resources mobilised are expected to be around 2.5 per cent of the G.D.P. in 1987-88. In the developed countries, mobilisation of resources through capital markets has been around 8-9 per cent of the G.D.P. This shows the shape of things our economy should strive to achieve in the times ahead. The number of stock exchanges has gone upto 14 against three in the USA. Some of the stock exchanges are modernising their operations in a big way and making effort to open up. The Indian Capital Markets are aiming to securitise the financial assets. However, the space of these sweeping reforms have been throttled by the fiscal policy of the Government and the setback caused by the dubious companies which mobilised resources from the capital markets during the last three years. The shares of such companies are selling at discount in the stock markets. The Government and the financial institutions are taking concerted steps to instill confidence in capital markets. But the removal is not seen round the corner.

The issues by PEs at this juncture are expected to lead to the revival of capital markets in more than one way. The investors will have not only the investing opportunities in the financially sound companies which are active on the economic scene for quite some period. There is no reason to believe that the offer of PE shares to certain reasonable level would siphon-off private enterprises resources from the capital markets as the potential of the capital market is quite high compared to the level of shares offered for public sector.

PEs need to prepare themselves fully to meet the challenges arising out of the decision to approach the capital markets. Taking a cue from the U.K. French, Italian, Japanese and the Malaysian experience, the Government may set up a "Public Enterprise Financial Bank" to manage PE issues and minimise the costs involved in the fluctuations and portfolio management. Further, all efforts should be made to create and enlarge a secondary market to ensure the liquidity of such issues. It will be worthwhile to encourage the non-Resident Indians (NRIs) and the international capital markets to subscribe to these issues. Further, the methods of selling out the securities should be very carefully worked out to discourage speculations and prevent any possible loss of inflow of money to the Government. Two years back, the employees stock ownership schemes were initiated by the Government. Steps should be taken to popularise them. Care need to be taken to enlarge the distribution of shareholdings or sale of assets to a maximum number of people. Unlike the U.K., USA, Canada, Japan and France, the capital and financial markets in India in conjunction with the Government need to make an attempt to diversify the ownership base to the widest possible extent. The mutual funds may be attracted to contribute to the success in this regard. The capital markets should work for integrations with the international capital markets. A part of the off-loading should be effected through the international capital markets, Indian funds set up abroad and other possible methods.

Implications to PEs in General: The privatisation of PEs in general, and resorting to the capital markets in particular, are expected to make PEs business-like and improve their interface with the Government. For expansion and financing the working capital needs, PEs may like to approach the capital markets more frequently than the Government and banks. The cost of funding through capital markets may work out cheaper than banks. In course of time, PEs with a debt-equity ratio of below 2:1 can also obtain the privatisation benefits. The past experience shows that PEs have done very well in raising the public deposits. The bond issues by the Indian Telephone Industries Ltd., National Thermal Power Corporation Ltd., Rural Electrification Corporation of India Ltd., Mahanagar Telephone Nigam etc., have proved a great success. It has been said that the commercial banks have subscribed heavily to these bonds and therefore, they have not clicked with the general investing public. But this has been the case with the other securities also.

To conclude, the privatisation of PEs in India is financially a viable proposition

Annexure-1

LIST OF CENTRAL GOVERNMENT ENTERPRISES AS ON 31.3.1986

I. **Statutory Corporations**

1. Air India
2. Indian Airlines
3. International Airports Authority of India
4. Delhi Transport Corporation
5. Central Warehousing Corporation
6. Food Corporation of India
7. Oil and Natural Gas Commission
8. Industrial Development Bank of India
9. Industrial Finance Corporation of India

II. **Section 25 Companies**

10. Artificial Limbs Manufacturing Corporation of India
11. Indian Dairy Corporation
12. National Research Development Corporation of India
13. Trade Fair Authority of India

III. **Undertakings with Central Government Investment But Without Direct Responsibility for Management**

14. Damodar Valley Corporation Ltd.
15. Hindustan Diamond Company Ltd.
16. Indian Explosives Ltd.
17. Machinery Manufacturers Corporation Ltd.
18. Sikkim Mining Corporation Ltd.

19. Singareni Collieries Ltd.
20. Sindhu Resettlement Corporation Ltd.
21. Visvesvaraya Iron and Steel Company Ltd.
22. Wagon India Ltd.

IV. Enterprise With Total Debt Investment

Delhi Transport Corporation (mentioned in Category I at the Serial No. 4).

V. Government Companies Amenable to Privatisation

23. National Seeds Corporation Ltd.
24. State Farms Corporation of India Ltd.
25. The Fertiliser Corporation of India Ltd.
26. The Fertilizers & Chemicals (Travancore Ltd.)
27. Hindustan Fettilizer Corporation Ltd.
28. Madras Fertilizers Ltd.
29. National Fertilizers Ltd.
30. Pradeep Phosphates Ltd.
31. Project and Development India Ltd.
32. Pyrites, Phosphates & Chemicals Ltd.
33. Rashtriya Chemicals & Fetilizers Ltd.
34. Cardamom Trading Corporation Ltd.
35. The Cashew Corporation of India Ltd.
36. Export Credit Guarantee Corporation of India Ltd.
37. The Mica Trading Corporation of India Ltd.
38. The Minerals & Metals Trading Corporation of India Ltd.
39. The Projects & Equipment Corporation Ltd.
40. The State Trading Corporation of India Ltd.

41. Tea Trading Corporation of India Ltd.
42. Hindustan Teleprinters Ltd.
43. Indian Telephone Industries Ltd.
44. Telecommunications Consultants (India) Ltd.
45. Bharat Dynamics Ltd.
46. Bharat Earth Movers Ltd.
47. Bharat Electronics Ltd.
48. Garden Reach Shipbuilders & Engineers Ltd.
49. Goa Shipyard Ltd.
50. Hindustan Aeronautics Ltd.
51. Mazagon Dock Ltd.
52. Mishra Dhatu Nigam Ltd.
53. Praga Tools Ltd.
54. Bharat Coking Coal Ltd.
55. Central Coalfields Ltd.
56. Central Mine Planning & Design Institute Ltd.
57. Coal India Ltd.
58. Eastern Coalfields Ltd.
59. Neyveli Lignite Corporation Ltd.
60. Western Coalfields Ltd.
61. National Hydroelectric Power Corporation Ltd.
52. National Projects Construction Corporation Ltd.
63. National Thermal Power Corporation Ltd.
64. North Eastern Electric Power Corporation Ltd.
65. Rural Electrification Corporation Ltd.
66. Andaman & Nicobar Islands Forest & Plantation Development Corporation Ltd.

67. General Insurance Corporation of India
68. Life Insurance Corporation of India
69. National Insurance Company Ltd.
70. The New India Assurance Company Ltd.
71. The Oriental Insurance Company Ltd.
72. United India Insurance Company Ltd.
73. Hindustan Vegetable Oils Corporation Ltd.
74. Modern Food Industries (India) Ltd.
75. North Eastern Regional Agricultural Marketing Corporation Ltd.
76. Hindustan Latex Ltd.
77. Hospital Services Consultancy Corporation (India) Ltd.
78. Indian Medicines Pharmaceutical Corporation Ltd.
79. Rehabilitation Industries Corporation Ltd.
80. Educational Consultants India Ltd.
81. Bengal Chemicals & Pharmaceuticals Ltd.
82. Bengal Immunity Ltd.
83. Goa Antibiotics & Pharmaceuticals Ltd.
84. Hindustan Antibiotics Ltd.
85. Hindustan Fluorocarbons Ltd.
86. Hindustan Insecticides Ltd.
87. Hindustan Organic Chemicals Ltd.
88. Indian Drug & Pharmaceuticals Ltd.
89. Indian Petrochemicals Corporation Ltd.
90. Karnataka Antibiotics & Pharmaceuticals Ltd.
91. Maharashtra Antibiotics & Pharmaceuticals Ltd.

92. Orissa Drugs & Chemicals Ltd.
93. Punjab Maize Products Ltd.
94. Rajasthan Drugs & Chemicals Ltd.
95. Smith Stanistreet Pharmaceuticals Ltd.
96. The Southern Pesticides Corpn. Ltd.
97. Uttar Pradesh Drugs & Pharmaceuticals Company Ltd.
98. National Small Industries Corporation Ltd.
99. Andrew Yule & Company Ltd.
100. Banarhat Tea Company Ltd.
101. Basmatia Tea Company Ltd.
102. Bharat Brakes & Valves Ltd.
103. Bharat Heavy Electricals Ltd.
104. Bharat Heavy Plate & Vessels Ltd.
105. Bharat Leather Corporation Ltd.
106. Bharat Opthalmic Glass Ltd.
107. Bharat Process & Mechanical Engineers Ltd.
108. Bharat Pumps & Compressors Ltd.
109. Bharat Wagon & Engineering Company Ltd.
110. Braithwaite & Company Ltd.
111. Burn Standard Company Ltd.
112. Cement Corporation of India Ltd.
113. Cycle Corporation of India Ltd.
114. Damodar Cement and Slgg Ltd.
115. Engineering Projects (India) Ltd.
116. Heavy Engineering Corporation Ltd.
117. Hindustan Cables Ltd.

118. HMT Bearing Ltd.
119. HMT Ltd.
120. HMT (International) Ltd.
121. Hindustan Newsprint Ltd.
122. Hindustan Paper Corporation Ltd.
123. Hindustan Photo Films Manufacturing Company Ltd.
124. Hindustan Salts Ltd.
125. Hooghly Dock & Port Engineers Ltd.
126. Hooghly Printing Company Ltd.
127. Hoolungooree Tea Company Ltd.
128. Instrumentation Ltd.
129. Jessop & Company Ltd.
130. The Legan Jute Machinery Company Ltd.
131. The Mandya National Paper Mills Ltd.
132. Maruti Udyog Ltd.
133. The Mim Tea Company Ltd.
134. Mining & Allied Machinery Corporation Ltd.
135. The Murphulani (Assam) Tea Company Ltd.
136. Nagaland Pulp & Paper Company Ltd.
137. National Bicycle Corporation of India Ltd.
138. The National Industrial Development Corporation Ltd.
139. National Instruments Ltd.
140. National Newsprint & Paper Mills Ltd.
141. Rajgarh Tea Company Ltd.
142. Rajasthan Electronics & Instruments Ltd.
143. Richardson Cruddas (1972) Ltd.

144. Sambhar Salts Ltd.
145. Scooters India Ltd.
146. Tannery & Footwear Corporation India Ltd.
147. Triveni Structurals Ltd.
148. Tungabhadra Steel Products Ltd.
149. Tyre Corporation of India Ltd.
150. Weighbird (India) Ltd.
151. National Film Development Corporation Ltd.
152. India Tourism Development Corporation Ltd.
153. Balmer Lawrie & Company Ltd.
154. Bharat Petroleum Corporation Ltd.
155. Biecco Lawrie Ltd.
156. Bridge & Roof Company Ltd.
157. Bongaigaon Refinery & Petrochemicals Ltd.
158. Cochin Refineries Ltd.
159. Engineers India Ltd.
160. Gas Authority of India Ltd.
161. Hindustan Petroleum Corporation Ltd.
162. Hydro Carbons India Ltd.
163. Indian Oil Blending Ltd.
164. Indian Oil Corporation Ltd.
165. I.B.P. Company Ltd.
166. Lubrizol India Ltd.
167. Madras Refineries Ltd.
168. Oil India Ltd.
169. Central Electronics Ltd.
170. Bharat Aluminium Company Ltd.

171. Bharat Gold Mines Ltd.
172. Hindustan Copper Ltd.
173. Hindustan Zinc Ltd.
174. Mineral Exploration Corporation Ltd.
175. National Aluminium Company Ltd.
176. Bharat Refractories Ltd.
177. Ferro Scrap Nigam Ltd.
178. Hindustan Steelworks Construction Ltd.
179. IISCO Ujjain Pipe & Foundry Company Ltd.
180. India Firebricks & Insulation Company Ltd.
181. The Indian Iron & Steel Company Ltd.
182. Kudremukh Iron Ore Company Ltd.
183. Manganese Ore (India) Ltd.
184. Metallurgical & Engineering Consultation (India) Ltd.
185. National Mineral Development Corporation Ltd.
186. Metal Scrap Trade Corporation Ltd.
187. Neelachala Ispat Nigam Ltd.
188. Rashtriya Ispat Nigam Ltd.
189. Sponge Iron India Ltd.
190. Steel Authority of India Ltd.
191. Vijayanagar Steel Ltd,
192. The British India Corporation Ltd.
193. Brushware Limited
194. Cawnpore Textile Corporation Ltd.
195. Central Cottage Industries Corpn. of India Ltd.
196. The Cotton Corporation of India Ltd.
197. The Elgin Mills Ltd.

198. The Handicrafts & Handlooms Exports Corpn. of India Ltd.
199. The Jute Corporation of India Ltd.
200. National Handlooms Development Corporation Ltd.
201. National Jute Manufacturers Corporation Ltd.
202. National Textile Corporation Ltd.
203. National Textile Corporation (Andhra Pradesh, Karnataka, Kerala & Mahe) Ltd.
204. National Textile Corporation (Delhi, Punjab and Rajasthan) Ltd.
205. National Textile Corporation (Gujarat) Ltd.
206. National Textile Corporation (Madhya Pradesh) Ltd.
207. National Textile Corporation (Maharashtra North) Ltd.
208. National Textile Corporation (South Maharashtra) Ltd.
209. National Textile Corporation (Tamil Nadu & Pondicherry) Ltd.
210. National Textile Corporation (Uttar Pradesh) Ltd.
211. National Textile Corporation (West Bengal, Assam, Bihar & Orissa) Ltd.
212. North Eastern Handicrafts & Handlooms Development Corporation Ltd.
213. Air India Charters Ltd.
214. Helicopter Corporation of India Ltd.
215. Hotel Corporation of India Ltd.
216. Vayudoot
217. Airline Allied Services Ltd.
218. Indian Railway Construction Company Ltd.

219. Rail India Technical & Economic Services Ltd.
220. Central Inland Water Transport Corporation Ltd.
221. Cochin Shipyard Ltd.
222. Dredging Corporation of India Ltd.
223. Hindustan Shipyard Ltd.
224. Indian Road Construction Corporation Ltd.
225. The Mogul Line Ltd.
226. The Shipping Corporation of India Ltd.
227. Hindustan Prefab Ltd.
228. Housing & Urban Development Corporation Ltd.
229. National Building Construction Corporation Ltd.
230. Water & Power Consultancy Services (India) Ltd.
231. Electronics Corporation of India Ltd.
232. Indian Rare Earths Ltd.
233. Uranium Corporation of India Ltd.
234. C.M.C. Ltd.
235. Electronics Trade & Technology Development Corpn. Ltd.
236. Semi Conductor Complex Ltd.

Annexure-2

S.No.	Name of the Enterprises	Year of Incorporation	Paid up Capital	Loans	Total	Competitive Status	Price Control Status	Net Profit/ Net Loss 1985-86
1.	The Projects and Equipment Corporation Ltd.	1971	150	820	970	C	NPC	76
2.	Indian Telephone Industries	1950	8800	18401	27201	NC	PCNA	1266
3.	Telecommunications Consultants India Ltd.	1978	30	289	319	NC	PCNA	558
4.	Nbharat Earth Movers Ltd.	1964	3000	11422	14422	NC	PCNA	2317
5.	Garden Reach Shipbuilders & Engineers Ltd.	1967	4090	8541	12631	NC	PCNA	-789
6.	Hindustan Aeronautics Ltd.	1964	7200	59978	67178	NC	PCNA	4344
7.	Mazagon Dock Ltd.	1934	8185	20222	29007	NC	PCNA	-3898
8.	Bharat Coking Coal Ltd	1972	45000	105716	150716	NC	PCA	-13994
9.	Eastern Coalfields Ltd.	1975	37369	125334	160703	NC	PCA	-6997
10.	Western Coalfields Ltd.	1975	24891	79664	104555	NC	PCA	-9905
11.	National Projects Construction Corpn. Ltd.	1957	1609	4099	5708	C	NPC	120
12.	Rural Electrification Corporation Ltd.	1969	16100	166901	183001	NC	PCNA	1624

S.No.	*Name of the Enterprises*	*Year of Incorpo-ration*	*Paid up Capital*	*Loans*	*Total*	*Competitive Status*	*Price Control Status*	*Net Profit/ Net Loss 1985-86*
13.	Rehabilitation Industries Ltd.	1959	411	2809	3220	NC	PCNA	-735
14.	Maharashtra Antibiotics and Pharmaceuticals Ltd.	1979	100	225	325	C	PCNA	-50
15.	Goa Antifibiotics & Pharmaceuticals Ltd.	1981	85	167	252	C	PCNA	-35
16.	Karnataka Antibiotics & Pharmaceuticals Ltd.	1981	85	237	344	C	PCNA	16
17.	Orissa Drugs & Pharmaceuticals Ltd.	1979	54	119	173	C	PCNA	1
18.	Punjab Maize Products Ltd.	1975	250	604	854	C	PCNA	-201
19.	Bengal Chemicals & Pharmaceuticals Ltd.	1981	855	2032	2887	CT	PCNA	-590
20.	Hindustan Flurocarbons Ltd.	1983	491	1400	1891	NC	PCNA	221
21	The National Small Industries Ltd.	1955	2149	4266	6415	C	NPC	78
22.	Braithwalle & Co. Ltd.	1976	1318	5129	6447	CT	NPC	-1214
23.	Burn Standard Co.. Ltd.	1976	2783	8668	11451	CT	NPC	-46
24.	Jessop & Co. Ltd.	1958	3004	7643	10647	CT	NPC	-169

S.No.	Name of the Enterprises	Year of Incorporation	Paid up Capital	Loans	Total	Competitive Status	Price Control Status	Net Profit/ Net Loss 1985-86
25.	Mining and Allied Machinery Corporation	1965	4847	11475	16322	NC	PCNA	-1230
26.	Bharat Brake & Valves Ltd.	1977	254	615	869	CT	NPC	-252
27.	HM.T. Ltd.	1953	3732	14350	18082	C	NPC	762
28.	Instrumentation Ltd.	1964	878	1786	2664	C	NPC	247
29.	National Instruments Ltd.	1957	373	2047	2420	C	NPC	-234
30.	Richardson & Cruddas Ltd.	1972	880	2416	3296	CT	NPC	-698
31.	Scooters India Ltd.	1972	756	4669	5425	C	NPC	-46442
32.	Bharat Opthalmic Glass Ltd.	1976	556	1747	2303	C	NPC	-505
33.	Tannery & Footwear Corporatrion of India Ltd.	1969	1296	3141	4437	C	NPC	-929
34.	Engineering Projects (India) Ltd.	1970	800	8459	9259	C	NPC	-3443
35.	The Min Tea Company Ltd.	1979	5	34	39	CT	NPC	-2
36.	Bharat Process & Technical Engineer Ltd.	1980	362	1110	1472	CT	NPC	-312
37.	Weighbird (India) Ltd.	1980	25	111	136	CT	NPC	-85

S.No.	Name of the Enterprises	Year of Incorpo-ration	Paid up Capital	Loans	Total	Competitive Status	Price Control Status	Net Profit/ Net Loss 1985-86
38.	National Bicycle Corporation of India Ltd.	1980	528	1110	1638	CT	NPC	-496
39.	HMT Bearing Ltd.	1981	295	601	896	C	NPC	13
40.	Bharat Petroleum Corporation Ltd.	1976	2785	22180	24965	NC	PCA	6132
41.	Cochi Refineries Ltd.	1965	700	23837	24537	NC	PCA	25
42.	Hindustan Petroleum Corpn. Ltd.	1976	6384	45834	52218	NC	PCA	233
43.	Indian Oil Blending Ltd.	1963	40	115	155	NC	PCA	35
44.	India Oil Corporation Ltd.	1964	12327	37708	50035	NC	PCA	12897
45.	Madras Refineries Ltd.	1965	9825	22013	31838	NC	PCA	2615
46.	Oil and Natural Gas Commission	1965	34285	251678	285963	NC	PCA	132847
47.	Balmer Lawrie & Co. Ltd.	1929	285	648	933	CT	NPC	306
48.	Engineers India Ltd.	1965	50	200	250	C	NPC	1034
49.	Oil India Ltd.	1981	2800	6517	9317	NC	PCA	6832
50.	Indian Firebricks & Insulation Co. Ltd.	1960	217	1005	1222	CT	NPC	-279
51.	'Manganese Ore (India) Ltd.	1977	323	688	1011	C	NPC	-10
52.	Metal Scrap Trade Corporation Ltd.	1964	110	224	334	NC	PCNA	872

S.No.	Name of the Enterprises	Year of Incorporation	Paid up Capital	Loans	Total	Competitive Status	Price Control Status	Net Profit/ Net Loss 1985-86
53.	Hindustan Steel Works Construction. Corporation. Ltd.	1964	2000	7983	9483	C	NPC	215
54.	Ferro Scrap Nigam Ltd.	1979	200	471	671	C	NPC	239
55.	The Cotton Corporation of India Ltd.	1976	1700	8953	10653	NC	PCNA	-1069
56.	The Jute Corporation of India Ltd.	1971	500	3693	4193	C	NPC	-2402
57.	North Eastern Handicrafts & Handloom Development Corporation	1977	100	206	306	C	NPC	-31
58.	National Textile Corporation Ltd.	1968	30553	74614	105167	CT	NPC	53
59.	NTC (Andhra Pradesh, Karnataka, Kerala & Mahe) Ltd.	1974	3196	8817	12013	CT	NPC	-1117
60.	NTC (Delhi, Punjab & Rajasthan)	1974	2651	5539	8190	CT	NPC	-893
61.	NTC (Gujarat) Ltd.	1974	1735	6430	8165	CT	NPC	-1751
62.	NTC (Madhya Pradesh) Ltd.	1974	2567	10584	13151	CT	NPC	-1452
63.	NTC (Maharashtra North) Ltd.	1974	4584	9975	14559	CT	NPC	837
64.	NTC (South Maharashtra) Ltd.	1974	3415	12780	16195	CT	NPC	1
65.	NTC (Tamilnadu & Pondicherry) Ltd.	1974	1648	4528	6176	CT		
66.	NTC (Uttar Pradesh) Ltd.	1974	1629	8025	9654	CT	NPC	-1271

S.No.	Name of the Enterprises	Year of Incorpo-ration	Paid up Capital	Loans	Total	Competitive Status	Price Control Status	Net Profit/ Net Loss 1985-86
67.	NTC (West Bengal), Bihar, Assam & Orissa) Ltd.	1974	4064	16085	20149	CT	NPC	-2634
68.	National Jute Manufacturers Corpn. Ltd.	1980	641	13781	14422	CT	NPC	-2377
69.	The British India Corporaiton Ltd.	1981	507	1244	1751	CT	NPC	10
70.	The Elgin Mills Co. Ltd.	1981	110	3040	3150	CT	NPC	181
71.	Cawnpore Textiles Ltd.	1983	60	229	289	CT	NPC	123
72	Air India	1953	7436	43628	51064	NC	PCNA	6600
73.	Indian Airlines	1953	5004	31566	36570	NC	PCNA	6322
74.	Indian Railway Constn. Corpn. Ltd.	1976	495	6053	6548	NC	PCNA	1877
75.	Central Inland Water Transport Corporaiton Ltd.	1967	3684	7559	11243	NCP	PCNA	-2166
76.	The Mogul Line Ltd.	1938	1901	11638	13539	C	NPC	-2073
77.	The Shipping Corpn. of India Ltd.	1961	7000	96498	103498	C	NPC	506227
78.	National Building Constn. Corpn. Ltd.	1960	1300	9373	10673	C	NPC	122545
79.	Housing & Urban Dev. Corpn. Ltd.	1970	8100	54853	62953	C		1413

NPC = Non Price Control. PCNA = Price Control Non-Administered PCA = Price Control Administered
C = Competitive CT = Competitive Takeover NC = Non-competitive

7

DIVESTMENTS IN PUBLIC ENTERPRISES: THE INDIAN ENTERPRISES

— T. L. Sankar, R. K. Mishra &
A. Lateef Syed Mohammed

Historical Background

PEs have been a part of the socio-economic and political philosophy of the Indian nation for a long time. In ancient India, PEs functioned in the areas of manufacturing, trading, public utilities, services and social welfare sectors. The Kautilya's *Arthasastra* (278 BC) presents a glorious picture of how PEs were conducting themselves successfully by striking a judicious balance between the "Public" and "enterprise" components governing the personality of these enterprises. The motto of PEs in ancient India was the achievement of business goals with excellence which comprised consumer satisfaction, accountability, public good and business ethics. PEs continued to flourish in medieval India (AD 1000-AD 1600). It was during this period that Karkhanas were set up and run by the Mogul kings in phenomenon. However, the sovereign parts of the Indian State and the princely to spur the economic development of their subjects, promoted PEs vigorously. This led to the setting up of PEs in crucial areas of the economy such as agriculture, industry, trade, transport, mining and defence production by the princely states origin to the resolutions passed by the all-India National Congress at its Karachi and Lahore annual sessions in 1931 and 1932 respectively and the blueprint evolved by Sir M. Visveswaraiah in 1934[1].

The First Industrial Policy Resolution (IPR) of the Government of India, announced in 1948, laid down a four-fold division of industries. The first category included industries which were solely reserved for the public sector. In the second category were included industries which had to be progressively nationalised though they were marked with the presence of both the public and private sectors. The third category constituted industries where the private sector dominated but the entry of public sector was not ruled out. It was only the fourth category of industries which was left solely to the private sector. The planned era in India commenced in 1951. From then to the present, all the Five-Year Plans except the present one, i.e. the Eighth Five-Year Plan has scaled down the allocation to the public sector substantially to about 49 per cent of the total plan outlay. The size of the public sector has been fixed at Rs. 3,92,000 crores within the overall plan size of Rs. 8,10,000 (Rs. 30 is equal to US$ 1 and Rs. 100 000 (Rs. One lakh) was equivalent to US$ 3,000 or 2,000 sterling, approximately, as on 15 August 1992). The Eighth-Year Plan came close on the heels of the Third Industrial Policy Resolution announced in 1991. The foundations of the directions contained in these two documents were laid down in the Second Industrial Policy Resolution announced in 1956 which reduced the division of the industries from four to three categories. While it provided for the retention of the monopoly of the public sector on the first category of industries included in the First IPR, 1948, it merged the second and third categories to create a single category in which both the sectors were free to set up units and compete. This was the first measure of liberalisation in which the private sector was assigned a greater role, in that the threat of nationalisation which loomed large on the third category of industries included in the First IPR, 1948, was ruled out. The Third IPR of 1991 has further enlarged the scope for the private sector as the number of industries reserved for public sector have been reduced to a bare minimum of eight. The Eighth Five-Year Plan, drawing its linkages from the IPR, 1991, besides reducing the plan size for the public sector, calls upon PEs to generate resources to support their operations as well as the future growth. PEs are expected to contribute to the exchequer too. As a corollary, both the Eighth Five-Year Plan and the IPR, 1991, plead for larger business autonomy through performance contracts between PEs and the government.

The Economic Administration Reforms Commission, in its various reports on public sector undertakings, provided forceful support to the present move of economic liberalisation and privatisation of PEs.

Current Scenario

PEs operate three levels of administration in India: Central, State and Municipal. The Central PEs are owned and managed by the central government. The State Level Enterprises (SLPEs) are owned and managed by the 25 state governments forming the Indian Union. The Municipal PEs are owned and managed by the local self-governments. The central PEs are mainly engaged in the manufacturing and production of goods such as steel, minerals and metals, coal, lignite, power, petroleum, fertilizers, chemicals and pharmaceuticals, heavy, medium and light engineering, transport equipment, consumer goods, agro-based industries and textiles. The enterprises providing the services operate in sectors such as trading, marketing, transport services, contract and construction services, industrial development and technical consultancy services, tourist services and financial services. The SLPEs operate mainly in the fields of manufacturing, trading, financial, promotional and welfare activities. The municipal enterprises have confined their activities to providing city transport, power supply and generation, and milk supply. PEs organised in different forms numbered about 1,400 as of 31 March 1991. The investment in these enterprises amounted to Rs. 3,000,000 crore as of that date. PEs contribute about 15 per cent to the net domestic product of the country while the public sector as a whole contributes 25 per cent. The investment and revenue in the PEs is about 60 per cent of the total investment by the public sector as a whole comes to about 55 per cent.

TABLE I

Ranking of Top Ten Central PEs in Terms of Investment

S.No.	*Name of the PE)*	*Amount of investment (Rs. in crores)*
1.	National Thermal Power Corp. Ltd.	12,848.92
2.	Coal India Ltd.	10,248.65
3.	Steel Authority of India Ltd.	7,648.11
4.	Rashtriya Ispat Nigam Ltd.	7,122.75
5.	Oil and Natural Gas Commission	7,019.25
6.	Rural Electrification corp. Ltd.	4,065.88
7.	Indian Railway Finance Corp. Ltd.	3,988.94
8.	Nation Hydro Electric Corp. Ltd.	3,886.71
9.	Mahanagar Telephone Nigam Ltd.	3,257.80
10.	National Aluminium Company	3,683.23
	(a) Total	63,214.29
	(b) Total in 244 Central PEs	113,233.68
	(c) (a) as percentage of (b)	55.15 per cent

Source: Department of Public Enterprises, Government of India, New Delhi, Public Enterprises Survey 1990-91, Vol. 1, March 1992

The central PEs form the backbone of the PE system in India. As of 31 March 1951, five central PEs had an investment of Rs. 29 crores. The number of operating enterprises on 31 March 1992 was 246. During the 1980s the rate of growth of investment in central PEs turned out to be 15 per cent per annum on compounded basis. The rate of growth of the country as a whole was 3.5 per cent per annum during the 1980s. the turnover of these enterprises, their capital employed, the dividends paid by them and the net profits earned during 1990-91 amounted to Rs. 1,18,355 crores, Rs. 1,01,703 crores, Rs. 2,368 crores respectively. These enterprises contributed Rs. 19,466 crores to the central exchequer by way of dividends, corporate tax, excise duty, customs duty, and other duties in 1990-91 and their export earnings amounted to Rs. 7,096 crores during the same year. The ranking of central PEs as per investment, turnover, profits and losses are given in Tables I-IV.

TABLE II

Ranking of Top Ten Central PEs in Terms of Turnover

S.No.	*Name of the PE)*	*Amount of investment (Rs. in crores)*
1.	Indian Oil Corporation	19,553.94
2.	Oil and Natural Gas Commission	9,594.38
3.	Steel Authority of India Ltd	8,359.19
4.	Food Corp. of India	8,330.21
5.	Hindustan Petroleum Corp.	6,283.25
6.	Minerals and Metals Trading Corp	5,622.98
7.	Bharat Petroleum Corp	5,283.06
8.	Bharat Heavy Electricals Ltd.	3,237.16
9.	National Thermal Power Corp. Ltd.	2,400.59
10.	State Trading Corp.	1,819.97
	(d) Total	70,484.73
	(b) Total in 244 Central PEs	118,355.21
	(c) (a) as percentage of (b)	59.55 per cent

Source: Department of Public Enterprises, Government of India, New Delhi, Public Enterprises Survey 1990-91, Vol. 1, March 1992

TABLE III

Ranking of Top Ten Central PEs in Terms of Profits

S.No.	*Name of the PE)*	*Amount of investment (Rs. in crores)*
1.	Oil and Natural Gas Commission	12,848.92
2.	National Thermal Power Corp. Ltd.	10,248.65
3.	Coal India Ltd	7,648.11
4.	Steel Authority of India Ltd	7,122.75
5.	Rashtriya Ispat Nigam Ltd	7,019.25
6.	Oil and Natural Gas Commission	4,065.88
7.	Rural Electrification corp. Ltd	3,988.94
8.	Indian Railway Finance Corp. Ltd	3,886.71
9.	Nation Hydro Electric Corp. Ltd	3,257.80
10.	Mahanagar Telephone Nigam Ltd	3,683.23
11.	National Aluminium Company	63,214.29
	(g) Total	113,233.68
	(h) Total in 244 Central PEs	55.15 per cent
	(i) (a) as percentage of (b)	

Source: Department of Public Enterprises, Government of India, New Delhi, Public Enterprises Survey 1990-91, Vol. 1, March 1992

TABLE IV

Ranking of Top Ten Central PEs in Terms of Loses

S.No.	*Name of the PE)*	*Amount of investment* (Rs. in crores)
1.	National Thermal Power Corp. Ltd.	12,848.92
2.	Coal India Ltd	10,248.65
3.	Steel Authority of India Ltd	7,648.11

4.	Rashtriya Ispat Nigam Ltd	7,122.75
5.	Oil and Natural Gas Commission	7,019.25
6.	Rural Electrification corp. Ltd	4,065.88
7.	Indian Railway Finance Corp. Ltd	3,988.94
8.	Nation Hydro Electric Corp. Ltd	3,886.71
9.	Mahanagar Telephone Nigam Ltd	3,257.80
10.	National Aluminium Company	3,683.23
	(j) Total	63,214.29
	(k) Total in 244 Central PEs	113,233.68
	(l) (a) as percentage of (b)	55.15 per cent

Source: Department of Public Enterprises, Government of India, New Delhi, Public Enterprises Survey 1990-91, Vol. 1, March 1992

Performance

Table V presents the profitability profile of the central PEs. Its is clear from the Table that the central PEs generate less than 3 per cent of net profits on the capital employed. Further, their profitability does not bear any consistent pattern. This should be seen against the backdrop that the bank rate is 12 per cent.

Forty-seven central PEs utilized less than 50 per cent of installed capacity in 1990-91, whereas 59 units utilised their installed capacity between 50 to 75 per cent during the same period. The percentage of turnover to capital employed was 116.37 in 1990-91. In other words, the capital input-output ratio was 1.16:1 which was low by all standards. The cost of production exceeded 93 per cent of the turnover of these enterprises which left very little margin to exceed interest charges.

The profitability status of the private corporate sector enterprises is superior to that of PEs. The cost of production amounted to 85 per cent of their turnover in 1990-91. Their net profits to capital employed was 10 per cent during the same period and their capital input-output ratio exceeded 3:1.

Problems

The environment of PEs poses the most complex problem responsible for their poor performance. Under the present disposition of procedures and rules they are not in a position to make autonomous investment, financing and dividend decisions. Their style of operation is a replica of the Government's style. The recruitment, promotion, marketing mix, production planning, and project management decisions are often substantially influenced by the Government's inaction and excessive involvement. Public Accountability has become a great paradox for these enterprises. While strangling management and workers in these enterprises, it empowers the Parliament Secretariat, bureaucracy and Comptroller and Auditor General of India to interfere fully in their policy-making, and substantially in their day-to-day working. Despite the introduction of the Memorandum of Understanding (MoU) which describes the responsibilities of the Government to the PEs, on the one hand, and the obligations of PEs to the Government on the other, the transgression of the latter's autonomy has not come to a halt. PEs have still to depend on the Government for seeking access to capital markets, enlisting the support of foreign firms for technological collaboration, revising wage agreements and incentive structures for their workers, fixation of prices monopoly markets and evolving appropriate capital structures. They are subject to excessive bureaucratic controls and professionalism, as such, is lacking in their executive management.

An excessive governance of PEs puts them to a considerable disadvantage. The provisions with regard to the government companies contained in the Companies Act mar the initiative to be competitive. The articles of association of these enterprises compel them to inform the Government, seek its permission, and take its directions on a large number of matters. As PEs are more or less 100 per cent Government owned and managed enterprises, the commercial banks and suppliers ask for the Government guarantee which is both an expensive and arduous proposition. The general rules of the game which make a business create rhythm for its continued survival and growth are not to be found operating in PEs, as they are plagued by the safety first principle and avoid the risk-taking phenomenon.

The Indian economy is passing through an unprecedented financial crisis. Whereas the internal resources have dried up, the foreign exchange reserves have been depleted, so much so that the country's ability to pay the interest as well as the principle in respect of foreign borrowings was adjusted as doubtful in 1991. This forced the country to approach the International Monetary Fund for a massive borrowing which was conceded subject to the condition that the Indian Government would embark on the structural adjustments programme to reduce PE losses drastically, and provide budgetary support to these enterprises, food and fertilizer subsidies and spendings on government departments. It is thus clear that PEs have to bear the brunt of the burden of the restructuring programme. Having had lukewarm success in its previous attempt to improve PE performance, the Government has no choice but to launch the programme of divestment of shareholdings in these enterprises. While there is no doubt that this is the only sensible remedy left in the hands of the Government, it must be ensured that the programme is designed, implemented and monitored in a foolproof way lest it should become another failure.

Philosophy of Divestment

The philosophy of divestment in PEs is based on strong logical foundations. First, divestment ushers PEs into the domain of acquiring and developing their own corporate identity. Although PEs are clothed with the Morrisonian concept of "enterprise" which provided for their independence from the Government, it could be said without any prejudice that in India they have been treated very differently. A caged tiger can never be healthy unless it is set free. Drawing an analogy from this, we could say that PEs also need to enjoy a reasonably high degree of independence. The divestment liberates PEs from the superfluous controls of their principals. With this change in the agent-principal relationship there is so much for both the parties to gain. The Government can attend to some other investment propositions and save itself from the criticism of making imprudent business decisions on account of lack of technical and procedural rigidities with which it has burdened itself. On the other hand, PEs could keep pace with the market dynamism flowing from quick business reflexes resulting from their being distanced from the Government.

The divestment of shareholdings enables a PE to develop its own financing plans, thereby reducing its dependence on the Government. The concept of cost of capital guides the decision-making with regard to approaching the capital market, deciding about the period and sources of finance and several other financial issues which introduce the element of optimisation in the various aspects of PE management.

The internal systems, procedures and practices undergo a total restructuring as the assumption of this concept forces the enterprises to divested to come closer to the customer and accept the market signals, which may even lead to an attitudinal change on the part of both the management and workers. They may fashion their behaviour on the style of an entrepreneur or owner instead of acting as agent as they do at present.

The divestment makes available the scarce capital invested by the Government in PEs for alternative uses in projects of greater importance, pruning budgetary deficits or repaying the public debt. In the days of rising prices, the divestment could act as a forceful check on containing inflation.

Divestment Process

The divestment process comprises two major elements, namely the formulation of a decision model for selecting the portfolio of PEs for divestment, an also setting up a committee to select appropriate techniques of share valuation for enterprise proposed to be divested. Such a committee should also be overseeing the divestment process and advising the Government on its various facets.

Developing a pragmatic model for deciding the portfolio of PEs whose shareholdings have to be divested is the most critical component of the divestment process. The literature on PEs neither shows how such a model could be formulated nor offers any guiding principles. The model could, therefore, take into account a host of factors, namely financial success, marketing structure, social obligations, classification of PEs into certain cognate groups, etc. Venugopal et al. [2] have suggested a 2 X 2 matrix for divestment on PEs which takes into consideration factors such as the financial success and marketing structure. According to their model, which is depicted in Table VI, financially successful PEs operating in the competitive market are the most appropriate candidates for divestment. The 2 X 2 matrix gave a four-quadrant classification of PEs as shown in Table VI.

The 2 X 2 matrix suggests that financially successful PEs in the Competitive enterprises need to be hived-off from the PE portfolio. The financially unsuccessful PEs in the competitive sector need to undergo financial reforms to be brought in line with the working of the financially successful competitive PEs. Once this is achieved they can also be unloaded from the PE portfolio. Coming to the financially successful non-competitive PEs, the matrix introduces the idea of breaking them into smaller units to introduce competition, thereby making them eligible for finally off-loading to the private sector. The financially non-successful, non-competitive enterprises will first have to be transformed into financially viable units. They may subsequently given up to the private sector. In the event of their continuous dismal financial performance, they will have to face closure or sell out. The application of a 2 X 2 matrix will introduce selectively in the retention of PEs in the public sector.

Sankar, Mishra and Nandagopal [3] have presented another model outlining the approaches for divestment of the shareholdings in the SLPEs which is known as 3 X 2 matrix for a divestment decision. The same can be made applicable to central PEs as well. PEs are considered as high and low on three factors, namely social purpose, profitability and resource mobilisation. According to the model, Table VII, PEs operating in competitive markets having low social purpose and also low resource mobilisation are most suitable candidates for divestment. The three-dimensional matrix could be used to segregate core PEs from non-core ones.

TABLE VI

Classification of Central PEs in Terms of Market-Financial Performance

Market structure	*Financial success*	
	Good	*Bad*
Single Source	A	B
	Non-competitive	Non-competitive
	successful PEs	unsuccessful PEs
	No. 54	No. 23
	Net profit Rs. 2429	Net loss Rs. 969
crores		crores Paid-up
capital	Paid-up capital	
	Rs. 11,771 crores	Rs. 2,589 crores
Multiple	C	D
Source	Competitive	Competitive
	successful PEs	unsuccessful PEs
	No. 68	No. 66
	Net profit Rs. 444	Net loss Rs. 887
crores		crores Paid-up
capital	Paid-up capital	
	Rs. 6,138 crores	Rs. 3,898 crores

Source: [3]

The three-dimensional matrix, for the purpose of arriving at the portfolio for retention, could be presented as showed in Table VII.

It is obvious that if a PE has a "High" score on all the three dimensions (H1, H2, H3), it is a fit candidate for being in the state sector while a PE which has a "Low" score on all three dimensions (L1, L2, L3) would qualify for drastic action such as closure or privatisation. But all the PEs do not fall into such convenient categories.

TABLE VII

The three-dimensional Matrix

Factors		*High*	*Low*
1.	Public purpose	H1	L1
2.	Mobilization of resources of financial institutions	H2	L2
3.	Profitability	H3	L3

TABLE VIII

Classification of Central PEs in terms of Efficiency, Social Obligation and Externalities

Sl. No.	*Market Structure*	*Efficiency*	*Social Obligations externalities*	*Portfolio of privatization options*
1	Competitive	High	Low	Create further competition by allowing private sector units or by divestiture
2	Competitive	High	High	Non-divestiture options (a) Management transfers (b) Marketization
3	Competitive	Low	Low	Divest
4	Competitive	Low	High	Non-divestiture options (a) Sub-contracting, etc. (b) Joint-ventures marketization
5	Monopoly	High	Low	Create competition by allowing private sector entry and through exposure to

				international competition thus increasing scope for marketization
6	Monopoly	Low	Low	Divest
7	Monopoly	Low	High	Create competition by splitting the enterprise into different units
8	Monopoly	High	High	Regulate with divestiture options or encourage dilution of equity

Suresh Kumar[4] has evolved a 3 X 2 X 4 , matrix which categorizes PEs in terms of their being high or low with reference to market structure, efficiency and social obligations. This model makes the performance improvement in PEs a precondition for their divestment. The model suggests sale of equity to the public in the case of efficient and competitive enterprises having low obligations and externalities. As shown in Table VIII, this model suggests divestment, through sale to workers or private sectors, of such of those PEs which are inefficient and characterised by low social obligations.

The Government of India, as a part of its new economic policy, has decided to divest the shareholdings of PEs. It selected 31 enterprises for divestment in 1991-92. The financial profile of these enterprises is shown in Table IX.

Table IX shows that the selection of enterprises for divestment is not consistent operating at the cutting-edge of industrial such as the Computer Maintenance Corporation of India Ltd, have been picked up for divestment. A group of enterprises having very low profitability, including the Fertilizers Corporation of India and National Fertilizers Corporation, have been chosen for divestment. Further, some selected enterprises comprise units that have been earning extremely low net profits and their asset base is disproportionate to their earning power. This category of enterprises includes the Steel Authority of India Ltd, Bharat

Heavy Electricals Ltd. Andrew Yule and Company, Bharat Earth Movers Ltd. etc. Also, the dividend record of many units has not been encouraging. For instance, the Computer Maintenance Corporation of India Ltd., Dredging Corporation Ltd. Fertilizers and Chemicals of Tryancore Ltd, National Aluminium Company, Neyveli Lignite Corporation and Steel Authority of India Ltd. did not pay dividends during the period 1988-89 to 1990-91. Though it was proposed to divest 20 percent of the equity of the 31 undertakings in 1991-92, the equity divestment turned out to be less than 9 per cent of the paid-up capital. The percentage of equity divested in 31 enterprises shows wide fluctuations. Whereas Bharat Earthmovers Ltd., Bharat Electronics Ltd, Bharat Heavy Electrical Corporation and Bharat Petroleum Corporation, etc. are at the top of the table with 20 per cent divestment of equity, the Dredging Corporation of India Ltd, Fertilizers and Chemicals (Travancor) Ltd, Hindustan Machine Tools Ltd and Minerals and Metals Trading Corporations, etc. are at the bottom of the table with divestment of their equity at the rate of 1.5 per cent.

Organization

It goes without saying that any major programme of divestment should be supported by a suitable mechanism capable of getting the best value for the state and ensuring the fulfillment of its dominant objectives. The Government's divestment efforts are marked by a number of gaps. The Government did not think it proper to appoint a standing committee of experts who could look into the multifaceted aspects of divestment and advise it about the modus operandi for launching this long-term programme. Having admitted more than once that divestment of shareholdings is an ongoing process, it is difficult to understand what prevented the Government from creating a permanent mechanism. This has given rise to the suspicion that the programme has been launched to benefit not the "State" but certain groups of people who thrive on the cost to the public exchequer. This criticism does not appear to be totally unfounded as a number of questions continue to remain unanswered. It would be relevant to know:

1. Why did the Department of Public Enterprise and the Ministry of Finance unnecessarily hasten the decision to sell the shares of PEs through mutual funds?
2. Why did the Government sell the shares to the mutual funds, whereas one of the objectives of the divestment programme is building up an access for PEs to the capital markets?
3. What was the basis for determining the upset price for selling the shares to the mutual funds?
4. Was the upset price so settled a sound economic proposition for the Government?

It appears that the administration did not bother much to learn from the recent experience of the divestment programme in the United Kingdom, France and several other countries. There was no need to have a one-shot deal with the mutual funds, as the pulse of the market could easily have been known by divestment of shareholdings in two to three small releases. Also, it was unethical on the part of the Government to have compelled the mutual funds to buy PE shareholdings compulsorily, as they manage the money of small investors who are risk-shy. The fixation of a uniform upset price is also open to strong criticism. One wonders how a uniform upset price was fixed when PEs selected for divestment differed on the grounds of their product profile, investment base, market-structure and profitability.

There are indications that the price, initially pegged at Rs. 15 to 20 per share was readjusted to Rs. 30 in the second round. It could, therefore, be argued that the upset price hardly sensed the mood of the capital market. Consultations with the management of PEs were not held. On top of this, launch was not discussed with the stock market authorities or experts on capital markets.

S. No.	Name of the PE	Earning per share 1989-90 Rs.	Earning per share 1990-91 Rs.	Dividend per share 1989-90 Rs.	Dividend per share 1990-91 Rs.	Paid up value 1990-91	Book value per share 1989-90 Rs.	Book value per share 1990-91 Rs	Equity divested (Rs. in crores) 1990-91	Equity divested (%) 1991-90
1.	Adrew Yule & Co.	3.33	4.92	1.50	1.50	10.00	38.11	41.37	1.50	13.57
2.	Bharat Earth Movers	1533.67	1538.00	120.00	120.00	1000.00	10230.67	11668.67	6.00	20.00
3.	Bharat Electronics	276.37	428.12	120.00	120.00	1000.00	2911.62	3282.50	16.00	20.00
4.	Bharat Heavy Electricals	491.62	150.92	100.00	100.00	1000.00	3367.97	3418.86	48.95	20.00
5.	Bharat Petroleum Corp	2451.40	2556.20	200.00	200.00	1000.00	10924.00	13280.20	10.00	20.00
6.	Bongaigaon Ref.& Petrochemicals	145.03	242.77	40.00	50.00	1000.00	1490.16	1682.88	39.96	20.00
7.	Computer Maintenance Corp	56.67	451.33	0.00	0.00	1000.00	1600.00	1172.00	2.53	16.69
8.	Cochin Refineries	99.80	88.29	21.00	21.00	100.00	298.11	366.59	6.90	10.01
9.	Dredging Corp of India	333.93	527.50	0.00	0.00	1000.00	3363.57	3851.07	0.40	1.44
10.	Fertilizers and Chemicals (T)	0.09	0.69	0.00	0.00	10.00	10.72	11.41	5.28	1.54
11.	Hindustan Machine tools	73.55	180.11	0.00	30.00	1000.00	3334.13	3211.38	4.27	5.43
12.	Hindustan Cables	144.21	50.61	60.00	0.00	1000.00	2681.55	2735.87	1.67	3.64
13.	Hindustan Petroleum Corp	3136.90	1881.89	200.00	200.00	1000.00	10704.57	12386.43	12.77	20.00

S. No.	Name of the PE	Earning per share 1989-90 Rs.	Earning per share 1990-91 Rs.	Dividend per share 1989-90 Rs.	Dividend per share 1990-91 Rs.	Paid up value 1990-91	Book value per share 1989-90 Rs.	Book value per share 1990-91 Rs	Equity divested (Rs. in crores) 1990-91	Equity divested (%) 1991-90
14.	Hindustan Photofilm Mfg. Co.	71.65	18.76	5.00	0.00	1000.00	1372.96	1345.68	19.18	16.05
15.	Hindustan Organic Chemicals	598.56	648.13	60.00	65.00	1000.00	2874.66	3458.12	9.87	20.00
16.	Hindustan Zinc	265.76	225.39	0.00	0.00	1000.00	1483.33	1569.06	80.75	20.00
17.	Indian Petrochemicals Corp	436.77	481.50	100.00	100.00	1000.00	3497.47	3745.27	37.20	20.00
18.	Indian Railways Construction Corp	3614.87	1,812.49	210.00	100.00	1000.00	3554.25	3740.50	0.10	0.27
19.	Indian Telephone Industries	33.50	40.99	6.00	6.00	100.00	308.56	345.89	17.60	20.00
20.	Madras Refineries	440.11	442.91	210.00	210.00	1000.00	2095.48	2328.38	22.83	20.00
21.	Mahanagar Telephone Nigam	320.48	159.67	0.00	0.00	1000.00	1767.03	1766.10	120.00	20.00
22.	Maruti Udyog Ltd	38.09	43.84	7.00	8.00	100.00	181.28	217.18	9.92	9.00
23.	Minerals and Metals Trd Corp	1193.83	220.80	20.00	20.00	100.00	807.14	1000.20	0.34	0.67

S. No.	Name of the PE	Earning per share 1989-90 Rs.	Earning per share 1990-91 Rs.	Dividend per share 1989-90 Rs.	Dividend per share 1990-91 Rs.	Paid up value 1990-91	Book value per share 1989-90 Rs.	Book value per share 1990-91 Rs	Equity divested (Rs. in crores) 1990-91	Equity divested (%) 1991-90
24.	National Aluminium Company	121.73	55.83	0.00	0.00	1000.00	1094.42	1150.25	35.05	2.72
25.	National Fertilizers	23.65	60.62	20.00	0.00	1000.00	1389.74	1455.00	11.19	2.18
26.	Neyveli Lignite Corp	703.81	663.31	0.00	0.00	100.00	14358.27	14733.25	71.79	5.00
27.	Rashtriya Chemicals and Fertilizers	88.47	73.88	20.00	20.00	1000.00	1538.71	1592.53	31.12	5.64
28.	Shipping Corpn of India	38.70	36.46	4.34	0.00	100.00	181.44	217.90	52.25	20.00
29.	State Trading Corp	105.70	77.10	20.00	20.00	100.00	1039.03	1096.13	2.38	7.93
30.	Steel Authority of India	47.94	61.46	0.00	0.00	1000.00	1130.71	1190.19	199.29	5.00
31.	Videsh Sanchar Nigam	948.00	1309.67	300.00	300.00	1000.00	4741.50	5753.00	12.00	20.00

Source: Centre for Monitoring Indian Economy, A Statistical Review of Central Government Enterprises: 1990-91, April 1992, Mumbai

Techniques

In the literature on valuation of shares for divestment decisions, reference is made tc the following five distinct methods:

(1) Net Tangible Asset Method:

(2) Market Value Method:

(3) Earning Capacity Value Method:

(4) Fair Value Method:

(5) Face Value Plus Interest Method:

These methods are explained as follows.

Net Tangible Asset Method (NTAV)

The net tangible assets value is computed with the help of the latest audited balance sheet. First, the figure of total assets is worked out. As a second step, the balances in respect of current liabilities, long-term debt, intangibles, including goodwill and assets to be written-off, are then deducted from the total assets. In the third stage, the assets are revalued and any increase or decrease on account of this has to be effected. The ultimate figure arrived at gives the value of the net tangible asset. The net tangible asset per share is arrived at by dividing net tangible assets by the number of shares with the company. While computing the net asset value certain points have to be given due credit. The new bonus issue and the fresh issue of equity should be taken into account while computing the net tangible asset per share. Any reserves which have not been created out of genuine profits should not be taken into account. Provisions for any other terminal benefits to the employees should be deducted as liabilities. In other words, this method equates the value of the firm to the net worth of the business. The contingent liabilities which impair the net worth of the company are deducted from the assets of the company.

One of the limitations of the net-tangible assets method is that it does not show the true book value of the assets if they have not been revalued in the in the recent past. Similarly, if any firm does not follow a sound depreciation policy, the net tangible asset method would not provide a fair valuation.

Market Value Method (MV)

The market value method can be used only in such cases where the companies are listed on one or more stock exchanges. There have been some cases of both central and state enterprises being listed on the stock exchanges. These enterprises earlier belonged to the private sector. The stock exchange method is very easy to understand and operate. By this method, the market value acts as the guiding factor for valuation of shares. The underlying principle is that the market presents a genuine assessment of the managerial and economic strengths of the enterprises through pricing of its scrips on a day-to-day basis. However, it is argued that the market price of the scrips can always be manipulated, especially with the help of information that insiders have about the probable course that is likely to take place in respect of the ownership transfer of a company. This problem is quite serious in an imperfect capital market such as India. Further, the recent security scam has also created doubts about the validity of the market value as a real measure of the true value of the shares. This can, however, be overcome by averaging out the prices of the scrips of a company for a period ranging from three months to three years. This method was widely used while nationalising private undertakings in the United Kingdom and India. Another way to overcome this problem is to take high and low values of the shares over a period of time and then average them out.

Profit Earning Capacity Value Method (PECV)

This method suggests the valuation of the company by capitalizing the average of profits after tax. According to the guidelines[5] issued by the Controller of Capital Issues of India, the capitalisation of profits for industries in various lines of operation could be done on the following basis:

(1) 15 per cent on capital employed in the case of manufacturing concerns;

(2) 20 per cent in the case of trading companies;

(3) 17.5 per cent in the case of intermediate companies (an intermediate company is one wherein the turnover from trading activity is more than 40 per cent but less than 60 per cent of its total turnover).

The case of manufacturing enterprises exceptions may have to be made to the capitalization rate of 15 per cent. If there is a staggering difference between the market price and the price arrived at of 15 per cent of capitalization rate, it would be advisable to have a higher rate of capitalization for negotiating a price at which the enterprise can be transferred to the private sector. In the case of well-diversified and multi-product enterprises, it is advisable to charge something over and above 15 per cent of capitalisation rate. It must be ensured that the profits shown in audited accounts of the company are true profits, completely shorn of window-dressing. Normally, a period of three years is taken to average out the profits. If the profits of the last three years are stable, they may be averaged out on the basis of the simple arithmetic mean. However, if the profits are rising year after year steadily, it is useful to take the help of weighted average method. It is very easy to apply this method. However, the only difficulty with the profit-earning capacity value method is selecting an appropriate capitalisation rate.

Fair Value Method (FV)

This method is not an independent method of share valuation. The average of the NTAV and the PECV (with 15 per cent capitalization rate) is called "fair value" or value based on best reasonable judgement. Although market value will not be taken as a direct input in calculating fair value, it will be used as a guiding factor for reworking the capitalization rate for readjusting PECV. The CCI guidelines provide for such readjustment if the fair value is less than market value by over 20 per cent. However, it is clear that the capitalization rate should not be reduced below 8 per cent. Where the PECV is negligible or nil, the fair value should be limited to half of the net asset value. If, however, the net assets comprise mostly liquid assets, the fair value may be fixed up to two thirds of the net asset value or up to the actual cash.

Fair value does not provide the maximum value of shares as it is based on the principle of averages. PEs with low profiles or having the net asset value below the face value of shares may be valued with the help of the fair value method.

Face Value Plus Interest Method (FI)

According to this method the valuation of a firm is done by taking into consideration its total investment at the time of acquisition and adding an equivalent of 15 per cent interest every year. From the total sum so computed, the total amount of dividends paid to shareholders from the date of acquisition up to the date of valuation has to be deducted. The remainder is divided by the total number of shares to compute the value per share of the company. This method is suitable for the valuation of companies which have non-volatile assured income stream. The method turns out to be very useful even for those companies that make capital additions only occasionally. It is of no use for those enterprises having a negative net worth.

Which method is most suited for share valuation for PEs? The special features of the various techniques point out that no one method could meet the requirements of the situation. A basket of techniques needs to be used to arrive at a fairly value method would be the right choice. For companies with staggering investments but low profit making, the net worth method would be appropriate, although it would need to be modified to provide for the inflation factor. For medium/high profit making companies or dividend paying companies, the profit earning capacity value method would be an ideal choice. For companies with stable operations and moderate growth, the face value plus interest method could provide genuine estimates.

The share valuation of divested units is shown in Table X.

Expectations and Outcomes

The Government of India, in its annual budget for 1991-92, laid down a target of Rs. 2,500 crores from divesting 8 per cent shareholdings. It realized about Rs. 3,038 crores by divesting 8 per cent of equity in 31 PEs in two rounds. The 31 companies were divided into seven or eight companies per package. Each package contained a mix of highly profitable companies and a pair of marginally profitable ones. A total of 47 packages were prepared containing different amounts of shares of each constituent company. These were further subdivided into 825 sub packages each requiring an investment of Rs 3-4 crores. The Government proposes to raise Rs. 2,500 crores each year up to 1994-95 beginning with 1992-93. In the current year, i.e. in 1992-93, Rs. 2,500 crores would be raised through divestment, of which Rs. 1,500 crores would be mopped up to reduce the budgetary deficit and the remaining Rs. 1,000 crores are proposed to be invested in the National Renewal Fund, which has been set up to retrain and redeploy the labour force declared surplus by the industry on account of the restructuring undertaken as part of the structural adjustment programme. Taking the cue from the Government's intentions, it could be said that divestment of shareholdings is a long-term programme. As observed earlier this divestment effort should result in the best value to the Government. However, the outcomes of the divestment efforts have been different. Table XI shows the best alternative value of the divestment of shareholding effected by the Government for the 31 companies in 1991-92. An analysis of Table XI shows that the Government could have mopped up Rs. 6,356.20 crores by selling 8 per cent of its equity in 31 PEs against the proceeds of Rs. 3,038.00 crores accruing on the basis of the jumble sale method. This clearly indicates that the shares were understood as a result of a hasty decision. This view is also supported by many who have blamed the Government for underselling the PEs' shares. Nevertheless a member of the Planning Commission who was heading the Committee for Divestment said[6]:

The Government obviously did not have enough time and found the safest method of disinvestment. The first tranche of disinvestment was to meet the budgetary deficit so it was done in a bit of a hurry.

Conclusions

The divestment of PE shareholdings is an economic necessity. At a time when the country was on the brink of economic disaster and facing the threat of being declared insolvent by the external economic community, the Government rightly swung into action to initiate the divestment of shareholdings of PEs. While this move needs approbation, our analysis points out that the Government failed to realizes not only the best value but also the other objectives of the divestment programme.

The Government launched the programme without creating the required conditions for its takeoff. It did not get PEs listed on the stock markets. Adequate efforts were not make to build up the much needed PE-capital market linkages. Opportunities were frittered away to sell PE shares when favourable conditions existed in the Capital markets.

Suitable methods t oversee the divestment of PE shareholdings were not adopted. The Department of Public Enterprise and the Finance Ministry adopted techniques and methods which resulted in far lower realizations than were justified. It would be appropriate to suggest that a permanent committee of divestment be set up in the Cabinet Secretariat of the Government of India to remove these distortions. The Committee should advise about both the portfolio of PEs for divestments and the timings for the task. Learning from the pitfalls of the earlier exercises, it could be said that there is no need to follow a uniform method for divesting the shareholding of PEs. PEs selected for divestment should be classified into various categories based on their special features and the best price should then be arrived at by choosing one or a blend of share valuation methods. The study of expected outcomes and the results attained shows that the Government realized assets for lower amounts than were justified from the disinvestment of shareholdings in PEs.

TABLE X

Valuation of Shares by Different Methods

S.No.	Name of the PE	No. of Shares	Paid up Shares Rs.	Value method Rs.	NA method	PECV Interest	Face value + Interest method	Best Value method
32.	Adrew Yule & Co	10570000.00	10.00	41.38	22.33	25.12	35.50	41.38 NA
33.	Bharat Earth Movers	300000.00	1000.00	11668.67	8849.62	8720.38	5050.00	11668.67 NA
34.	Bharat Electronics	800000.00	1000.00	3285.50	2240.83	2378.89	6550.00	6550.00 FI
35.	Bharat Heavy Electricals	2447600.00	1000.00	3418.86	1006.43	430.58	16005.00	16005.00 FI
36.	Bharat Petroleum Corp	500000.00	1000.00	13280.20	1716.44	17780.44	5500.00	17780.44 PECVWA
37.	Bongaigaon Ref.& Petrochemicals	1998200.00	1000.00	1682.86	1120.79	1264.03	3550.00	3550.00 FI
38.	Computer Maintenance Corp	1551500.00	1000.00	1160.40	-795.03	-1328.18	3400.00	3400.00 FI
39.	Cochin Refineries	6893000.00	100.00	366.47	533.42	566.73	520.00	566.73 PECVWA
40.	Dredging Corp of India	280000.00	1000.00	3851.07	1993.64	2292.07	3250.00	3851.07 NA

S.No.	*Name of the PE*	*No. of Shares*	*Paid up Shares Rs.*	*Value method Rs.*	*NA method*	*PECV Interest*	*Face value + Interest method*	*Best Value method*
41.	Fertilizers and Chemicals (T)	342770000.00	10.00	11.41	1.81	2.01	53.50	53.50 FI
42.	Hindustan Machine tools	785600.00	1000.00	3210.29	400.82	511.01	6700.00	6700.00 FI
43.	Hindustan Cables	458400.00	1000.00	2735.60	1822.28	1183.83	6850.00	6850.00 FI
44.	Hindustan Petroleum Corp	638400.00	1000.00	12386.43	16720.62	15938.81	3550.00	16720.00 PECVWA
45.	Hindustan Photofilm Mfg. Co.	1055300.00	1000.00	1345.68	-80.65	-287.12	5650.00	5650.00 FI
46.	Hindustan Organic Chemicals	493500.00	1000.00	3457.55	3574.02	3944.17	5650.00	5650.00 FI
47.	Hindustan Zinc	3729100.00	1000.00	1569.06	1258.27	1379.54	4750.00	1569.00 NA
48.	Indian Petrochemicals Corp	1860000.00	1000.00	3745.27	2876.82	2637.22	4350.00	4350.00 FI
49.	Indian Railways Construction Corp	49500.00	1000.00	37393.94	12076.36	11124.58	3250.00	37393.94 NA
50.	Indian Telephone Industries	8,800,00	100.00	345.89	251.97	254.29	745.00	745.00 FI
51.	Madras Refineries	1141300.00	1000.00	2328.40	2966.02	2964.65	4900.00	4900.00 FI

S.No.	Name of the PE	No. of Shares	Paid up Shares Rs.	Value method Rs.	NA method	PECV Interest	Face value + Interest method	Best Value method
52.	Mahanagar Telephone Nigam	6000000.00	1000.00	1766.10	2001.00	1711.41	16500.00	16500.00 FI
53.	Maruti Udyog Ltd	11024000.00	100.00	217.19	208.41	223.27	250.00	250.00 FI
54.	Minerals and Metals Trd Corp	5000000.00	100.00	700.14	636.93	241.31	520.00	700.14 NA
55.	National Aluminium Company	1288600.00	1000.00	1150.25	456.91	514.64	2500.00	2500.00 FI
56.	National Fertilizers	4905800.00	1000.00	1455.50	209.46	265.72	355.00	355.00 FI
57.	Neyveli Lignite Corp	143582000.00	100.00	147.33	41.04	42.43	625.00	625.00 FI
58.	Rashtriya Chemicals and Fertilizers	5516900.00	1000.00	1592.52	648.11	578.22	295.00	1592.52 NA
59.	Shipping Corpn of India	26123000.00	100.00	217.91	197.54	222.80	650.00	650.00 FI
60.	State Trading Corp	3000000.00	100.00	1096.13	836.22	859.74	625.00	1096.14 NA
61.	Steel Authority of India	39815100.00	1000.00	1039.49	371.63	351.15	4750.00	4750.00 FI
62.	Videsh Sanchar Nigam	600000.00	1000.00	5753.00	7232.97	7407.97	7600.00	7600.00 FI

TABLE XI.

Actual and Realizable Value from Sale of Shares Divested

S.No.	Name of the PE	No. of Shares	No. of Shares divested	Shares divested (%)	Paid up value of divested	Paid up value per share shares (Rs. in crores)	Best Value per share (Rs.)	Amount realisable under best value method (Rs. in crores)
1.	Adrew Yule & Co	10570000.00	1434349.00	13.57	1.50	10.00	41.38	5.94
2.	Bharat Earch Movers	300000.00	60000.00	20.00	6.00	1000.00	11668.67	70.01
3.	Bharat Electronics	800000.00	160000.00	20.00	16.00	1000.00	6550.00	104.80
4.	Bharat Heavy Electricals	2447600.00	489520.00	20.00	48.95	1000.00	16005.00	783.48
5.	Bharat Petroleum Corp	500000.00	100000.00	20.00	10.00	1000.00	17788.44	177.80
6.	Bongaigaon Ref.& Petrochemicals	1998200.00	399640.00	20.00	39.96	1000.00	3550.00	141.87
7.	Computer Maintenance Corp	1551500.00	258945.00	16.69	2.53	1000.00	3400.00	88.04
8.	Cochin Refineries	6893000.00	689989.00	10.01	6.90	100.00	566.73	39.10
9.	Dredging Corp of India	280000.00	4832.00	1.44	0.40	1000.00	3851.07	1.55
10.	Fertilizers and Chemicals (T)	342770000.00	5278658.00	1.54	5.28	10.00	53.50	28.24

S.No.	*Name of the PE*	*No. of Shares*	*No. of Shares divested*	*Shares divested (%)*	*Paid up value of divested*	*Paid up value per share shares (Rs. in crores)*	*Best Value per share (Rs.)*	*Amount realisable under best value method (Rs. in crores)*
11.	Hindustan Machine tools	785600.00	42658.00	5.43	4.27	1000.00	6700.00	28.58
12.	Hindustan Cables	458400.00	16686.00	3.64	1.67	1000.00	6850.00	11.43
13.	Hindustan Petroleum Corp	638400.00	127680.00	20.00	12.77	1000.00	16720.00	213.48
14.	Hindustan Photofilm Mfg. Co.	1055300.00	169376.00	16.05	19.18	1000.00	5650.00	95.70
15.	Hindustan Organic Chemicals	493500.00	98700.00	20.00	9.87	1000.00	5650.00	55.77
16.	Hindustan Zinc	3729100.00	745820.00	20.00	80.75	1000.00	1569.00	117.02
17.	Indian Petrochemicals Corp	1860000.00	372000.00	20.00	37.20	1000.00	4350.00	161.82
18.	Indian Railways Construction Corp	49500.00	134.00	0.27	0.01	1000.00	37393.94	0.50
19.	Indian Telephone Industries	8,800,00	1760000.00	20.00	17.60	100.00	745.00	131.12
20.	Madras Refineries	1141300.00	228260.00	20.00	22.83	1000.00	4900.00	111.85
21.	Mahanagar Telephone Nigam	6000000.00	1200000.00	20.00	120.00	1000.00	16500.00	1980.00

S.No.	Name of the PE	No. of Shares	No. of Shares divested	Shares divested (%)	Paid up value of divested	Paid up value per share shares (Rs. in crores)	Best Value per share (Rs.)	Amount realisable under best value method (Rs. in crores)
22.	Maruti Udyog Ltd	11024000.00	992160.00	9.00	9.92	100.00	250.00	24.88
23.	Minerals and Metals Trd Corp	5000000.00	33500.00	0.67	0.34	100.00	700.14	2.35
24.	National Aluminium Company	1288600.00	350585.00	2.72	35.85	1000.00	2500.00	87.63
25.	National Fertilizers	4905800.00	106946.00	2.18	11.19	1000.00	355.00	3.88
26.	Neyveli Lignite Corp	143582000.00	7179100.00	5.00	71.79	100.00	625.00	448.69
27.	Rashtriya Chemicals and Fertilizers	5516900.00	311153.00	5.64	31.12	1000.00	1592.52	49.55
28.	Shipping Corpn of India	26123000.00	5224600.00	20.00	52.25	100.00	650.00	339.60
29.	State Trading Corp	3000000.00	237900.00	7.93	2.38	100.00	625.00	14.87
30.	Steel Authority of India	39815100.00	1990755.00	5.00	199.29	1000.00	4750.00	945.61
31.	Videsh Sanchar Nigam	600000.00	120000.00	20.00	12.00	1000.00	7600.00	91.20
	Total	-	-	-	889.00	-	-	6356.20

TABLE AI.

Financial Performance of Disinvested Public Enterprises

S. No.	Name of the Company	Sales (Including Excise Duty)			Net profit after tax			Net worth			Paid up capital	
		88-89	89-90	90-91	88-89	89-90	90-91	88-89	89-90	90-91	88-89	89-90
1.	Adrew Yule & Co	122.59	163.45	172.00	2.48	2.94	5.20	38.61	40.29	43.74	9.41	10.57
2.	Bharat Earch Movers	621.68	736.74	787.78	43.30	36.36	39.81	264.51	306.92	350.06	30.00	30.00
3.	Bharat Electronics	496.92	643.82	722.02	24.31	22.11	34.25	214.38	232.93	262.84	75.00	80.00
4.	Bharat Heavy Electricals	2736.39	3036.37	3279.54	87.42	62.86	-39.43	728.50	824.30	836.80	244.76	244.76
5.	Bharat Petroleum Corp	439.07	4919.14	5325.12	115.73	126.75	143.63	433.63	546.20	664.01	27.85	50.00
6.	Bongaigaon Ref.& Petrochemicals	335.96	408.76	415.12	22.80	29.42	48.56	276.76	297.76	336.27	199.82	199.82
7.	Computer Maintenance Corp	104.65	122.45	141.00	0.50	0.85	-6.77	23.09	24.12	17.58	15.00	15.00
8.	Cochin Refineries	1321.75	1507.64	1488.78	40.18	64.44	60.84	150.62	205.42	252.61	68.47	68.91
9.	Dredging Corp of India	48.13	59.41	70.06	5.38	6.84	12.90	84.83	94.18	107.83	28.00	28.00
10.	Fertilizers and Chemicals (T)	438.83	364.79	484.19	7.72	6.17	14.00	352.69	367.58	391.21	322.77	342.77
11.	Hindustan Machine tools	578.31	662.91	773.56	2.27	1.84	10.06	199.28	230.27	252.20	43.56	69.06

S. No.	*Name of the Company*	*Sales (Including Excise Duty)*			*Net profit after tax*			*Net worth*			*Paid up capital*	
		88-89	*89-90*	*90-91*	*88-89*	*89-90*	*90-91*	*88-89*	*89-90*	*90-91*	*88-89*	*89-90*
12.	Hindustan Cables	501.50	408.56	334.25	28.66	6.61	2.32	117.01	122.91	125.40	44.84	45.84
13.	Hindustan Petroleum Corp	5924.73	6710.30	7772.89	162.48	200.31	117.56	495.50	683.38	790.75	63.84	63.84
14.	Hindustan Photofilm Mfg. Co.	155.20	229.42	247.63	5.58	4.62	-14.03	93.91	127.04	142.01	65.53	92.53
15.	Hindustan Organic Chemicals	177.86	205.80	230.22	16.69	29.55	33.13	115.29	141.87	170.63	49.35	49.35
16.	Hindustan Zinc	291.15	425.64	454.40	45.11	80.23	85.81	295.57	393.44	585.12	237.86	265.24
17.	Indian Petrochemicals Corp	1143.88	1295.67	1329.85	97.36	86.18	57.25	587.89	650.53	696.62	186.00	186.00
18.	Indian Railways Construction Corp	153.78	181.15	223.88	13.77	3.60	9.53	130.92	166.06	185.10	4.95	4.95
19.	Indian Telephone Industries	755.92	958.95	978.46	34.23	29.48	36.07	244.37	271.53	304.38	88.00	88.00
20.	Madras Refineries	1382.20	1375.19	1715.81	51.30	49.87	51.16	212.75	239.96	265.74	113.19	114.13
21.	Mahanagar Telephone Nigam	1028.31	1134.36	1330.84	252.18	192.29	95.80	867.93	1060.22	1059.66	600.00	600.00

S. No.	Name of the Company	Sales (Including Excise Duty)			Net profit after tax			Net worth			Paid up capital	
		88-89	89-90	90-91	88-89	89-90	90-91	88-89	89-90	90-91	88-89	89-90
22.	Maruti Udyog Ltd	933.09	1187.86	1512.24	24.71	39.23	39.45	165.55	199.85	239.43	110.24	110.24
23.	Minerals and Metals Trd Corp	3891.10	5113.64	5622.96	30.31	35.72	77.28	247.85	282.78	350.07	35.00	35.00
24.	National Aluminium Company	472.20	885.14	985.00	12.98	172.03	79.94	1253.44	1414.29	1482.23	1288.62	1288.62
25.	National Fertilizers	844.35	808.51	1021.28	4.90	11.60	29.74	677.68	681.79	714.04	490.58	490.58
26.	Neyveli Lignite Corp	424.12	449.93	470.86	77.32	92.61	95.24	1504.94	1889.29	2115.43	1024.82	1315.82
27.	Rashtriya Chemicals and Fertilizers	1258.93	1192.12	932.11	73.62	48.36	38.92	810.06	848.89	878.58	551.69	551.69
28.	Shipping Corpn of India	819.30	1016.59	1119.92	35.87	101.10	95.25	138.69	473.99	569.24	70.19	261.23
29.	State Trading Corp	2698.48	1921.55	1819.97	16.78	72.98	23.13	286.00	311.71	328.84	30.00	30.00
30.	Steel Authority of India	6973.87	7778.04	8446.30	296.79	145.66	223.39	4302.04	4491.73	4138.74	3972.48	3972.48
31.	Videsh Sanchar Nigam	262.43	317.22	375.61	64.22	57.40	73.67	248.55	284.49	345.18	60.00	60.00

Source: Centre for Monitoring Indian Economy, A Statistical Review of Central Government Enterprises, 1990-91, Bombay, April 1992

Notes

1. Visveswaraya, M. Sir, *Planned Economy for India,* Bangalore Press, 1934.
2. Venugopal Reddy, Y., Koteswara Rao, K. and Mishra, R.K., *Public Enterprises – Towards a White Paper,* Institute of Public Enterprise and Booklinks Corporation, Hyderabad, 1990. Pp. 1-19.
3. Sankar, T L. and Reddy, Y. V., *Privatisation: Diversification of Ownership of Public Enterprises,* Institute of Public Enterprise, and Booklinks Corporation, Hyderabad, 1989, p. 126.
4. Kumar, S., "Public Enterprise Policy and Reform Measures in the 1990s", *Management in Government,* Vol. xxii, Nos. 2-3, New Delhi, 1992, pp. 433-9.
5. *The Economic Times,* Bombay, 17 July and 20 December 1990.
6. *The Economic Times,* Bombay, 27 March 1992.

8

ROLE AND RELEVANCE OF STATE LEVEL PUBLIC ENTERPRISES IN 1990s

— T.L. Sankar, R.K. Mishra & R. Nandagopal

The chapter discusses below the origin and growth, pre-profile, classification and relevance of sectoral activities of the State Level Public Enterprises (SLPEs). A three dimensional matrix has been developed to measure the scope for restructuring the SLPEs portfolio by the various state governments. The chapter suggests that the modalities for restructuring will have to be worked out very carefully to get to the essence of the problem.

After four decades of Independence the country is examining afresh the talents of economic thinking which have guided its economic management. The whole efforts is to evolve a more sustainable approach to economic development in the light of the changed international and national economic situation. Among the other things, an intensive debate has started on the role that the state should play in stepping up the rate of economic development by involving itself directly in the various economic activities. There is a view that the role of the states should undergo a shift from the producer state to the facilitator state. The proponents of this argument believe that such a proposition will maximise the rate of economic development by creating a favourable environment for stimulating the individual initiatives. The most recent works on entrepreneurship and its role in the process of economic development have observed a high degree of inter-dependency between the growth of entrepreneurship and rate of economic development. All the reports on public enterprises (PEs) on the efficient conduct of state enterprises to the Arjun Sen Gupta Committee report on the review of policy on public enterprises submitted to the Government in 1984, have pointed out clearly PEs in India have run shot of the expected level of performance. These reports have drawn attention to the inadequacy of the requisite managerial personnel in PEs and the Government. There is need, therefore, being selective in setting these enterprises in stead of encouraging the spread of their operations. To terminal years of the 7th Five-year plan and succeeding period have seen the most depressing phenomena of a severe resource crunch hitting the Indian economy. Realising the import of the situation, the union government has started thinking in terms of private participation in its economic activities in order to mobilise resources of men and money to achieve the planned rate of economic development. Simultaneously, the policy makers are examining the activities which can be retained by PEs and the activities now PEs that can be hived-off in the public interest.

Surprisingly, the scope of this debate has remained confined to the Central Public Enterprises (CPEs); it has not extended to the State Level Public Enterprises (SLPEs). As between the CPEs and the SLPEs, the problems of the later are much more complex and their working is fraught with constraints of several kinds. However, the little discussion on them is confined to their financial performance only. This is understandable. The principals of SLPEs have been presenting deficit budgets year after year net losses incurred by the PEs being a major component of such deficit budgets. There is an felt need to urgently discuss the role and relevance of these enterprises with a view to reduce the financial burden on the union government and state governments in the form of savings on incremental investments and financing of the net losses incurred by the SLPEs.

The purpose of this chapter is to discuss the role and relevance of the SLPEs in 1990s. In order to achieve the end, we discuss below the origin and growth, brief profile, classification and relevance of sectoral activities of the SLPEs. A three dimensional matrix has been developed to measure the scope for restructuring the SLPEs portfolio by the various state governments. The state electricity boards and the state road transport corporations have been excluded from the scope of this paper as their problems are of a different nature and their huge size relative to other enterprises distort the analysis. The requisite data have been collected from the database on the SLPEs set up at the Institute of Public Enterprise at the instance of the Planning Commission. The study spans over the period 1981-82 to 1986-87.

Origin and Growth

The SLPEs have come of age. From a mere 23 in the First Plan period their number increased to 754 as on March 31, 1987. The investment in these enterprises was Rs. 30 crores at the end of the First Plan Period. It shot up to Rs. 13,000 crores as on March 31,1987. Inclusive of the state electricity boards and the road transport corporations, the investment in these enterprises stood at Rs. 46,000 crore and their number ascended to 845. It is interesting to note that the number of the CPEs was 226 and the investment therein stood at Rs. 61,603 crores as on March 31, 1987. Thus, the SLPEs are almost four times the number of the CPEs. They are almost three-fourths in terms of the size of the investment in the CPEs. However, the SLPEs considerably differ from the CPEs in terms of the diversity of operations, origins and objectives. The SLPEs are engaged in a variety of activities ranging from industrial development and financial promotion, trading and marketing, contract and construction services, consumer goods and production of engineering goods to development of backward regions and weaker sections of society, and development and promotion of specific sectors of industry viz., agro-industries, minerals and metals, the small industry and tourism.

The SLPEs owe their rise in numbers to historical factors rather than ideological considerations. Some SLPEs were established by the then princely states and inherited by the new state governments formed after independence. In designing new developmental efforts consideration was given to the fact that there was no local entrepreneurship for taking up large projects. The state governments, therefore, undertook public investments to promote such companies. Many of them started with a view to utilise the locally available raw materials like lime stone for cement or silica for glass works, clay for ceramics, bamboo for paper, etc. Some units were started with a view to meet the local demands for specific goods. In some cases, the state governments were pushed into public investment by the policies adopted by the central government in those days of giving preferential licenses to public sector units. The central government also initiated action in forming joint ventures with the state governments for promotional purposes such as the fisheries development corporations, state finance corporations and state agro-industries corporations. Furthermore, the welfare corporations were started with the explicit objective of helping a particular segment of society which could not have obtained help under the normal market conditions. Many activities which could have done departmentally by the state governments were organised as public enterprises with a view to mobilise investible funds from the national and international financial agencies. An analysis shows that barring a few considered as an instrument of the socio-economic policy of the state governments in a more direct form than the CPEs.

The public policy on approach to economic development differs from state to state. The MSLPEs of varied kinds may have to be set up to prop up the rate of economic development in the case of a newly formed state but where the states have involved themselves for quite sometime directly in the productive activities, there is a need to have a fresh thinking on what should and what should not be retained as a part of the SLPEs portfolio. Viewed from the product portfolio of these enterprise, there can not be a strong defence built up in favour of retaining the manufacturing of soaps, detergents, scooters, textiles , cement and light industrial items. The paper and mining industries get qualified by this norm for retention in the SLPEs portfolio. We may go a step further and even suggest the need for turning over the high-tech MSLPEs to the private sector as by that time sufficient private incentive should be able to forge ahead to take over such activities from the public sector. The acceptance of this suggestion may free funds to the tune of about 3000 crores from the MSLPEs and reduction of losses to be born by the state governments of Rs. 100 crores per annum.

Trading and Service State Level Public Enterprises (TSLPEs)

Theses Enterprises include marketing, trading and service SLPEs. The state marketing corporations, state export corporations, and state civil supplies and essential commodities supply corporations fall under the mould of this category. Their main objectives vary from marketing of goods produced by small producers undertaking production of perishable and durable consumable items, strengthening economic base of producers by providing financial assistance, modernising their production organisation and marketing of their products to achieving economy in execution of construction works. There were 121 such enterprises with a capital investment of Rs. 1588 crores as on March 31, 1987. Their capital investment doubled over the period 1981-82 to 1986-87. In terms of numerical strength Kerala, Bihar and Karnataka have these enterprises in two digit numbers. In terms of investment in three digit numbers, Punjab was followed by Haryana, Bihar, Karnataka, Uttar Pradesh and Kerala. Against 10 per cent of PBIT on the capital invested the rate of return was hovering around 8.32 per cent in 1986-87 and it was low as 1.61 per cent in 1983-84 to these states. In fact Bihar, Maharashtra and Tamil Nadu earned the distinction of earning a negative rate of return although during the period 1981-82 to 1986-87 in this category of enterprises. These Enterprises had a very low turnover to capital employed ratio. The approach followed in this regard related more to selling than marketing. Most of these enterprises suffered from the glaring incidents of bad cash management.

The lingering and increasing overdues and the low inventory turnover ratio coupled with low working capital turnover support this connection. The accumulated losses in these enterprises had eaten away a good chunk of the paid up capital. The handlooms and handicrafts units in the TSLPEs had very low physical achievements, especially in the area of modernisation of looms. They did not export the targeted amount of cotton fabrics although they had a very high export potential. The construction enterprises as a constituent of the TSPLEs were relegated to the status of mere intermediaries as most of these enterprises worked behind the schedules with respect various contracts. The civil supplies and essential supplies corporations were characterized by laxity in procurement and distribution and incurred an extra expenditure on wasteful items leading to losses. In fact, there have been cases when these enterprises embarked upon the schemes without working out their economics and without having any expertise in the connected area. The off-season procurement were made and the style pursued in obtaining the supplies did not reflect commercial performance on their part. However, it may be admitted here that these corporations are fulfilling a major social objective of mitigating food grains shortages in the areas faced with scarcity and providing price-support to agriculturists. It may be difficult to withdraw from this area at this stage. Nevertheless, it will be worthwhile to suggest that these enterprises can hive-off the non-foodgrains procurement activity such as the maintenance of large fleet of trucks, etc. The state warehousing corporations also need to rethink about the relevance of their activities in the present context. It is worth noting that large storage capacities ate being developed in the private sector.

A peep into the performance of these corporations raises the question as to whether the various activities pursued by them qualify anymore for the retention in the portfolio of the TSLPEs. Coming to the construction corporations it can be pointed out that the time and cost overruns disqualify their continuation furthermore as state corporations. To add, there is sufficient private expertise and initiative available on this front which can easily substitute for the public economic initiative. The construction activity, as a specialised task, requires a large number of proficient technical people and their management which can better be left to the private sector.

Though it is advisable to operate the handlooms and handicrafts corporations in the state sector, the export of their products and internal marketing can better be left to the private sector in view of the quick decisional requirements as the basic characteristic of such an activity. The state trading organisations have lost the gloss during the last decade. They have failed to overcome the market failures in order to help the small producers or consumers and are characterized by high rent extractions due to the monopoly in their trading and wind falls of market fluctuation. Most of the state trading organisations have very little freedom in following market trends and taking up entrepreneurial decisions to promote trade either within the country or outside. Their contribution in the total foreign trade is very insignificant. They are not in a position to checkmate the strategies of their counterparts in the private sector. What to talk of developing countrywide outlets, they have failed to manage even their existing small networks. This analysis brings out very clearly that the TSLPEs will have to reorient their working to match the challenges posed by the dynamic market conditions and their counterparts in the private sector. This will impinge on such enterprises to develop suitable systems and procedures, on the one hand, and discontinue the superfluous activities, on the other.

Financial State Level Public Enterprises (FSLPEs)

These enterprises include in their ambit the state financial corporations, state industrial development corporations, state investment enterprises, state leasing companies, chit funds and banks and institutions for financing the panchayat raj bodies. They are involved in accelerating the rate of industrialisation in the state, removing regional imbalances and promoting growth of tiny, medium and small industries. There were 54 such enterprises with a capital investment of Rs. 5055 crores as on March 31, 1987. Maharashtra had a maximum investment of Rs. 831 crores in these enterprises followed by Rs. 616 crores in Uttar Pradesh Rs. 480 crores in Tamil Nadu and Rs. 454 crores in Gujarat and Rs. 437 crores in Andhra Pradesh, one third of the units promoted by these corporations have fallen sick. The disbursements are about 50 per cent of the sanctions in these enterprises. In the case of many such corporations developed regions have received more assistance than the backward regions. They are working mostly as extended arm of the Industrial Development Bank of India engaged in refinancing. Against 9 per cent of the PBIT on capital invested in the years between 1981-82 and 1986-87, their earnings could not exceed 3.29 per cent in any year of the study. Though these enterprises will have to play a great role in the development process, they will have to introduce fundamental changes in their orientation and working. For instance, they will have to formulate speedy disbursement policies to enable them to be eligible for receiving refinance from the Industrial Development Bank of India on their own without approaching the state governments time and again for the renewed equity support. They will have to innovate new schemes keeping in view their clientele. Similarly, considerable effort will have to be made to step up the recovery of overdues. Instead of expanding their work force and depending in toto on their own personnel they will do well to obtain non-essential services from external agencies.

Promotional State Level Public Enterprises (PSLPEs)

The PSLPEs include the forest development corporations, small scale industrial development corporation, tourism development corporations and fisheries development corporations. These enterprises are charged with the responsibility of undertaking the activities assigned to them on promotional basis with both non-commercial and commercial objectives. The small scale industrial development corporations initiated in the 1960s to help the small scale industrialists in terms of supply of raw materials, financial inputs and marketing assistance. These enterprises also take up the manufacture of certain products incidental to their main activities. The forest development enterprises were started it the middle of the 1970s. They have been set up to promote social forestry, conserve and commercially exploit forest produce, develop forest wealth and protect the interests of tribal population living in the forest. The tourism development enterprises also sprung up in the 1970s. Almost all the states in the country have tourism development corporations now. These are engaged in promoting tourism in their respective states by helping private entrepreneurs and taking up many schemes on their own. The fisheries development corporations were set up in the 1960s to help the fishermen engaged in selling fish and allied produce. These enterprises have taken up the manufacture of boats, etc. for the fishermen. In a nutshell, the PSLPEs primarily undertake the non-commercial functions and in the pursuit to do so they have taken up commercial activities to fulfill the role assigned to them. The major objectives of these enterprises include the promotion of economic activities assigned to them through encouraging the private entrepreneurs by direct involvement acting as nodal agencies in their area of operations charged with the responsibility of preparing and implementing the plans for the development of respective activities assigned to them, and continuing to function on a self-sustained basis. As on March 31, 1987 there were 248 promotional enterprises with a capital investment of Rs. 1960 crores. To achieve the ends of public policy, Uttar Pradesh set up 21 such enterprises followed by 20 in West Bengal, 19 each in Karnataka and Kerala, 17 each in Andhra Pradesh and Tamil Nadu and 16 each in Gujarat and Bihar. Andhra Pradesh had a maximum investment of Rs. 263 crores in these enterprises in 1986-87 followed by Rs. 220 crores in Bihar. Rs. 188 crores in Maharashtra and Rs. 157 crores in Orissa. The financial performance of these enterprises was not very promising. The PBIT on capital invested fluctuated between 0.31 per cent in 1981-82 and 1.43 per cent in 1986-87 against the 8 per cent norm for such enterprises. The PSLPEs in Bihar, Manipur, Punjab and Meghalaya had a minus PBIT during the period 1981-82 to 1986-87. These enterprises were involved both in promotional and commercial activities. They did not organise their commercial activities efficiently. However, they will have to play a significant promotional role in the years to come as the development of small industry will continue to be a major plank of the industrial strategy in this country. The forest development corporations in view of the environmental changes and protection of interest of tribal population living in the forest will have a great role to perform in the future. Similarly, the promotion of tourism will be an important economic activity in the state sector in the years to come. The PSLPEs, such as the fisheries development corporations, have a great role and relevance not only in today's socio-economic order. As these enterprises have fallen short of expectations in respect of their non-commercial functions it will be proper on their part to confine their activities to promotional aspects. For instance, there does not seem to be much of the rationale in setting up furniture unit by a small scale industrial development corporation. Similarly, it is worthwhile to ask as to why a fisheries development corporation should set up a boat building plant. Building on the argument further, it will be worthwhile to see as to why the state tourism development corporation should go on building hotel, increasing their fleet of buses and piling up huge assets. These enterprises will do well to exploit the benefits of the networking existing in their own fields of operations.

Welfare State Level Public Enterprises (WSLPEs)

These enterprises are late entrants on the SLPEs scene. Some of these enterprises were set up for the first time during the middle of 1970s by a couple of state governments. However, by the middle of 1980s most of the states of the Indian Union had established these enterprises. The term WSLPEs is omnibus in its nature and difficult to define. In its wider sense, it includes all such enterprises that are engaged in the welfare of the masses of country in general. In the restricted sense of the term it includes only those enterprises which are involved in the upliftment of the scheduled castes and scheduled tribes only. However, for the purpose of this paper the WSLPEs may be said to include the scheduled caste development enterprises, scheduled tribe development enterprises, minority development enterprises backward class development enterprises and area development enterprises. These enterprises have not been set up under a specific form of organisation. A survey of the practices prevailing in different states shows that these enterprises have been established either as the government companies, or cooperative societies or statutory corporations. From a mere 11 in 1975-76 the number of the WSLPEs shot up to 82 in 1986-87. Of the 82 WSLPEs 50 are functioning in 13 states as scheduled caste, scheduled tribe, women development and minorities enterprises. The rest of the 32 WSLPEs are scattered over 8 states as area development enterprises and have been incorporated in the form of government companies. There is no uniformity in the distribution of these enterprises across the states. Uttar Pradesh had a maximum of 16 WSLPEs followed by 12 in Maharashtra, 11 in Madhya Pradesh and 10 in Kerala. The WSLPEs were conspicuous by their absence in Goa, Jammu and Kashmir, Himachal Pradesh, West Bengal, Meghalaya and Orissa. The broad objectives of these enterprises relate to helping the weaker sections of the society to enable them to cross poverty line though a gradual and sustained effort, transforming the economic structure of the weaker sections through the entrepreneurial mode, working for the social upliftment of down trodden strata of the society through working for their educational upsurge, and mobilising the institutional credit for the socio-economic upliftment of the weaker sections of the society. *Annexure-18* shows that the WSLPEs has an investment of Rs. 471 crores in 1986-87. Uttar Pradesh, Andhra Pradesh, Gujarat and Maharashtra had a lion's share in the investment for these enterprises. These enterprises have been although in the red for all the states taken together during the period 1981-82 to 1986-87. Against the norm of 5 per cent PBIT on capital invested, only Andhra Pradesh, Gujarat, Kerala and Maharashtra could keep head above the water. These corporations were set up to take over the departmental activities of the state governments with the view that their conversion into corporate enterprises would help in providing such activities the commercial orientation. But the performance of these enterprises has betrayed the hopes. The overheads in these corporations were exorbitantly high. Many schemes did not register much progress. The disbursement per beneficiary/ scheme was very low. The margin money advanced was not distributed fully. In a give year the recovery of principle and interest had been very low. Further, they were characterised by organisation structures inconsistent with their objectives. Most of these enterprises suffered from the short tenure of managing directors. In that case of the Andhra Pradesh Scheduled caste Cooperative finance corporation in 1988-89 six Managing Directors were replaced within an averaged tenure of about two months. Most of the General Managers and Middle level Managers were deputationists from Government departments with very little corporate understanding. The schemes introduced in a particular year were discontinued very soon. A question may be raised as to why these corporations cannot remove the overlap in their functions and provide better services at reduced costs by curbing down overheads through restructuring. It is worth examining here as to why these corporations should not be reconverted back into government departments in order to bring down the overheads and ensure coordination. Since development of weaker section of society will continue to remain an important concern in years to come, these corporation are expected to play a great role in case they are not reconverted into government departments. The WSLPEs can grow by leaps and bounds and can acquire in that process the requisite commercial tinge if they mobilize considerable finances from the financial institutions.

Restructuring SLPEs

As seen from the analysts, it is urgently necessary to take measures to restructure the SLPEs. In view of the enormous resources crunch that state governments are facing and the rising criticism of the performance of SLPEs, the issue cannot be postponed further. One way of restructuring the SLPEs is to examine each enterprise case by case with reference to three factors. These are:

i. The public purpose served by the SLPE;

ii. The extent of resources mobilised from outside the state budget by the SLPE;

iii. The financial profitability of the SLPE.

Based on these three major factors, we can developed a three dimensional matrix showing high and low for the three components separately, where high means obtaining a positive

Factors

i. Public purpose

ii. Mobilisation of resources of financial institutions

iii. Profitability

It is obvious that if a SLPE has 'High' score on all the three dimensions (H1, H2, H3), it is a fit candidate for existence while a SLPE which has 'Low' score on all three dimensions (L1, L2, L3) will quality for drastic action such as closure or privatisation. But all the SLPEs do not fall into score in regard to that element by an enterprise and vice versa. Any objective which directs the SLPEs to serve a public cause like, say, the weaker sections of the community or fulfil the development role in utilising the local resources or to promote entrepreneurship is taken as a public purpose. The mobilisation of funds to the extent of at least 20 per cent of the total investment is taken as high mobilisation. The profitability of 10 per cent is taken as high profitability and the rest low. These parameters are such that scoring 'high' is not difficult.

The three dimensional matrix for the purpose of arriving at the portfolio for retention can be presented as below:

High	Low
H1	L1
H2	L2
H3	L3

such convenient categories.

An analysis of the results emerging from the three dimensional matrix brings out the following categorisation of the SLPEs and the suggested action for their restructuring.

Category No.	*Categorisation of SLPEs*			*No. of SLPEs*	*Suggested Action*
	Public Purpose	*Resource mobilisation*	*Profitability*	*SLPEs*	
i.	H1 -	H2	H3	75	Continue in the state sector
ii.	L1	L2	L3	200	Closure or Liquidation
iii.	H1	L2	L3	360	Continue in the state sector with increased accent on resource mobilisation and profitability.
iv.	H1	L2	H3	75	Continue in the state sector with increased accent on the resource mobilisation.
v.	H1	H2	L33	-	Continue in the state sector and reorganise internal management
vi.	L1	H2	H3	55	Disinvest
vii.	L1	L2	H3	49	Introduce financial adjustments and then go in for disinvest.
	L1	H2	H3	-	Disinvest

Source: *Journal of Institute of Public Enterprise,* Vol. 19. No. 3 & 4, July-December 1992.

This analysis has been done purely with a view to arrive at the number of industries to be treated in the different ways.

On the whole, the number of SLPEs to be retained in public sector might be around 500 in all the states, while about 250 come for different methods of restructuring. In effect, most of the manufacturing industries among SLPEs qualify for immediate disinvestment. A few of them are doing well financially. A close examination shows that in some cases the preferential purchase facilities afforded by the government departments and monopoly rights over minerals etc. give them a financial advantage. As a first step, the manufacturing companies in the state sector might have to be given very careful scrutiny including those SLPEs who are financially well run. The SLPEs which are to be retained in the public sector will require infusion of large funds for revitalisation. The disinvestment of financially successful manufacturing units can provide funds for them.

The identification of the SLPEs is the first step. Preparing an SLPE for privatisation would take a pretty of effort and time. Annual accounts will have to be completed. A decision would have to be taken for partial privatisation or complete privatisation. The modalities as to whether the transfer will be effected through privatisation, negotiations or flotations or the shares to workers and executives are all decisions which have the political implications. It is, therefore, suggested that a few of the states can get together to work out the modalities and procedures for privatisation.

Through the task of making a case by case analysis appears formidable with respect to each estate, the task will become simpler if a clear priority is observed. In each state there are some public enterprises which are very large and their overall performance affects the whole PE system. For example, in the case of Andhra Pradesh, the two SLPEs viz., Hyderabad Allwyn and Singareni Collieries and in the case of Gujarat State, one SLPE viz., Gujarat Narmada Valley Fertilisers, are the major determinants of the SLPE performance. It is worth mentioning that there are 10 large companies which have major share in the total investment in the SLPEs.

If each state undertakes an analysis in respect of four or

five large SLPEs under their momentum very quickly. The study on restructuring of the SLPEs fully reinforces these findings as it highlight that at least 200 SLPEs which score low in respect of public performance resource mobilisation and profitability. The three dimensional matrix for the purpose of arriving at the portfolio retention decisions clearly points out that only 75 SLPEs qualify for retention in the three counts namely public performance, resource mobilisation and profitability.

Conclusion

The SLPEs form an important segment of the PE system in India. In view of the present debate about the place of PEs in the Indian economy, it is appropriate to rethink about the role and relevance of the SLPEs. The increasing budgetary deficits of the state governments, the burgeoning losses incurred by these enterprises and the death of requisite managerial personnel to manage them reinforces this contention. The sector specific examination of activities of the SLPEs highlight that through they are expected to play a significant role in the years, ahead, there is a need for going case by case in order to decide which enterprises can be retained in the SLPEs portfolio and what activities a particular SLPE should continue to perform. An intensive examination of the MSLPEs has indicated that their performance was below the norm judged in terms of both the physical and financial standards. Further, the objectives for which they were set up initially do not hold much sanctity now. To add, the kind of product range they have does not in any way represent the cutting edge of industries. The TSLPEs are no different from the MSLPEs. They have made a little headway in achieving their objectives of price stabilisation, contravening the monopoly power, undertaking efficient domestic and external operations and effective handling of construction contracts. Their channel management has been utterly dissatisfactory. Moreover, the private sector has been able to bring up much stronger units in this area competing with their counterparts in the public sector. The TSLPEs have missed out their attention on the fact that there is no need for them to take up all the activities necessary for the fulfillment of their end objectives. Many such activities can be hived-off and privatised. The FSLPEs are engaged in the task of providing support to the entrepreneurial development. Their financial performance has remained unsatisfactory. Their systems and procedures have turned out to be grossly inadequate. These enterprises, alike the TSLPEs, can better achieve their objectives by reducing their dependence on the state governments, privatising many of their operations and introducing an element of dynamism in their operating systems. The PSLPEs are very large in number. They undertake non-commercial as well as commercial operations. Their commercial operations have resulted into huge losses. It is suggested that such enterprises concentrate on non-commercial activities and divest their commercial operations to private sector entrepreneurs. The WSLPEs are the latest entrants on the SLPEs scene. They cater to the needs of a very vast segment of the Indian society. Their physical achievements have been very inadequate. Their overheads are very high. Their business portfolio is very narrow. They lack coordination. There is no reason why these enterprises should not be reconverted into government departments. If this is not feasible, these enterprises should corporatise their operations by mobilising a large chunk of money from the financial institutions. The application of the three dimensional matrix only reaffirms these conclusions. About 200 enterprises most of which belong to the MSLPEs, TSLPEs and PSLPEs groups score low on social purpose, profitability and mobilisation of resources from the financial institutions and qualify, thereby, for closure. Nevertheless, it should always be kept in mind that enterprises in the PSLPEs, FSLPEs and WSLPEs categories will continue to serve important social objectives and as a consequence they cannot be closed down straightaway. Restructuring in respect of enterprises in these categories is necessary to find out what activities they should retain and what of their present business they should hive-off. The modalities for restructuring will have to be worked out very carefully to get to the essence of the problem.

Rate of Return in Trading and Marketing SLPEs

		81-82	*82-83*	*83-84*	*84-85*	*85-86*	*86-87*
1	Andhra Pradesh	4.46	-2.03	2.5	4.48	10.6	11.85
2	Assam	NA	NA	NA	NA	NA	NA
3	Bihar	-0.33	-0.18	-0.6	-0.52	-0.052	-0.5
4	Goa	0.98	1.32	0.55	0.99	0.86	0.86
5	Gujarat	84.71	89.34	16.21	35.94	34.68	34.68
6	Haryana	5.36	-1.9	3.59	12.01	12.11	12.11
7	Himachal Pradesh	4.18	5.93	8.86	7.55	7.55	7.55
8	Jammu & Kashmir	NA	NA	NA	NA	NA	NA
9	Karnataka	3.96	4.28	4.9	4.54	5.71	6.35
10	Kerala	2.47	-0.82	3.58	19.46	5.92	12.41
11	Madhya Pradesh	NA	2.95	1.27	2.24	2.24	2.24
12	Maharashtra	-7.82	-5.02	-3.14	-12.83	-2.17	-2.78
13	Manipur	NA	NA	NA	NA	NA	NA
14	Meghalaya	NA	NA	NA	NA	NA	NA
15	Nagaland	NA	NA	NA	NA	NA	NA
16	Orissa	9.94	9.94	28.2	16.76		15.63
17	Punjab	0.53	0.65	-1.88	-3.86		NA
18	Rajasthan	2.12	-5.44	-4	7.57		14.41
19	Tamil Nadu	-3.02	-104.15	-74.36	-65.57		7.84
20	Tripura	NA	NA	NA	NA		5.69
21	Uttar Pradesh	11.38	9.35	4.52	9.92		16.25
22	West Bengal	0.9	5.58	-2.64	-1.9		3.9
23	Meghalaya	40.83	35.68	47.3	47.3		47.3
	Average	6.98	1.99	1.61	3.75	7.42	8.32

Capital Investment In Financial SLPEs

		81-82	*82-83*	*83-84*	*84-85*	*85-86*	*86-87*
1	Andhra Pradesh	18224	21688	26656	30869	38281	43701
2	Arunachal Pradesh	220	231	262	284	310	363
3	Assam	3034	4168	4177	5159	5972	6975
4	Bihar	1821	2048	4665	10085	12060	15805
5	Goa	1990	2260	2610	2840	3200	3589
6	Gujarat	23151	27069	29740	33060	38517	45407
7	Haryana	6100	6800	7714	9860	10560	11394
8	Himachal Pradesh	2450	2800	3650	3900	4200	4600
9	Jammu & Kashmir	4543	5334	6354	7148	8148	9250
10	Karnataka	12468	15717	19626	23619	30037	37334
11	Kerala	9946	11347	12460	14056	15260	16734
12	Maharashtra	40232	44078	50083	63574	76701	83197
13	Manipur	75	83	92	102	108	110
14	Meghalaya	840	950	980	1080	1140	1278
15	Mizoram	510	580	625	740	820	943
16	Nagaland	540	608	680	714	792	847
17	Orissa	6648	9115	14898	16223	18956	20337
18	Punjab	8090	9150	9840	10850	12140	13820
19	Rajasthan	15290	20404	25033	29191	33185	37637
20	Tamil Nadu	30017	33451	36937	40628	45373	48028
21	Tripura	120	132	148	153	158	161
22	Uttar Pradesh	2199	24915	29568	39947	50001	61628
23	West Bengal	9468	11228	13223	15599	17980	18750
	Total	212536	268716	316971	378261	444549	505536

Rate of Return in Financial SLPEs

		81-82	82-83	83-84	84-85	85-86	86-87
1	Andhra Pradesh	5.49	6.47	6.85	7.25	6.78	5.15
2	Assam	NA	NA	NA	NA	NA	NA
3	Bihar	NA	NA	NA	NA	NA	NA
4	Goa	0	0	5.1	5.64	5.34	5.34
5	Gujrat	4.84	6.22	6.93	6.94	7.55	7.55
6	Haryana	0	2.56	2.42	4.12	4.12	4.12
7	Himachal Pradesh	0	0	0	0	0	0
8	Jammu & Kashmir	4.54	4.92	4.94	4.95	4.95	4.95
9	Karnataka	2.48	2.36	0.95	0.83	2.43	3.14
10	Kerala	5.11	3.96	5.24	5.6	5.94	6.65
11	Madhya Pradesh	NA	NA	NA	NA	NA	NA
12	Maharashtra	4.53	3.48	3.7	9.38	8.75	9.85
13	Manipur	NA	NA	NA	NA	NA	NA
14	Mizoram	4.86	4.83	4.86	2.69	2.69	2.69
15	Nagaland	NA	NA	NA	NA	NA	NA
16	Orissa	5.24	6.15	1.82	4.53	3.88	0.97
17	Punjab	7.89	4.21	4.56	2.7	NA	NA
18	Rajasthan	3.21	3.94	0.78	-0.07	-0.16	-0.16
19	Tamil Nadu	6.08	6.4	6.13	5.41	4.41	4.93
20	Tripura	NA	NA	3.06	3.06	3.06	3.06
21	Uttar Pradesh	11.29	5.86	5.9	5.27	5.87	6.46
22	West Bengal	5.31	5.58	6.54	6.14	7.68	7.68
23	Meghalaya	NA	NA	NA	NA	NA	NA
	Average	2.96	2.65	2.94	3.29	3.1	3.13

Rate of Return in Promotional SLPEs

	State	*81-82*	*82-83*	*83-84*	*84-85*	*85-86*	*86-87*
1	Andhra Pradesh	1.66	3.3	3.58	2.81	4.88	5.65
2	Assam	NA	NA	NA	NA	NA	NA
3	Bihar	-0.21	1.61	-2.21	0.72	-0.1	-0.1
4	Goa	NA	NA	NA	NA	NA	NA
5	Gujrat	5.94	10.28	22.78	13.18	7.84	7.84
6	Haryana	5.41	-0.46	3.2	3.56	3.27	3.27
7	Himachal Pradesh	5.14	4.57	4.55	4.36	4.21	4.21
8	Jammu & Kashmir	NA	NA	-2.98	-7.97	-1.74	-1.74
9	Karnataka	1.33	3.03	4.47	5.04	4.37	4.89
10	Kerala	2.3	1.24	-1.64	-1.29	-1.27	1.74
11	Madhya Pradesh	NA	-0.53	3.37	4.38	2.4	2.4
12	Maharashtra	3.24	2.11	-1.98	-1.01	0.71	0.57
13	Manipur	-2.67	-3.2	-3.2	-2.32	-2.32	-2.32
14	Mizoram	NA	NA	NA	NA	NA	NA
15	Nagaland	NA	NA	NA	NA	NA	NA
16	Orissa	-0.69	-3	-4	-2.74	-2.85	-3.06
17	Punjab	-6.71	-4.84	-6.1	-5.76	NA	NA
18	Rajasthan	0.56	0.69	-3.2	4.36	-2.04	-2.04
19	Tamil Nadu	2.31	2.63	6.18	5.87	6.02	8.21
20	Tripura	2.31	2.63	6.18	5.87	6.02	8.21
21	Uttar Pradesh	0.96	1.54	0.64	0.15	0.25	0.59
22	West Bengal	-3.78	-3.07	0.42	0.9	-1.26	1.26
23	Meghalaya	-6.22	-9.58	-4.11	-3.85	-3.83	-3.85
	Average	0.33	0.22	0.33	0.51	0.89	1.43

Capital Investment In Welfare SLPEs

	State	*81-82*	*82-83*	*83-84*	*84-85*	*85-86*	*86-87*
1	Andhra Pradesh	2227	2592	3835	3665	4255	5370
2	Assam	126	199	257	303	404	446
3	Bihar	1985	2195	3441	4995	5040	4721
4	Gujrat	1475	1533	1668	1810	1931	2392
5	Haryana	860	910	991	1080	1240	1615
6	Karnataka	721	1021	1215	1411	1850	2135
7	Kerala	245	334	386	450	650	731
8	Madhya Pradesh	890	820	980	4060	1240	4638
9	Maharashtra	4302	6517	7393	6805	7849	8493
10	Manipur	31	38	47	52	58	63
11	Orissa	0	0	185	235	237	319
12	Punjab	1230	1485	1675	1830	2140	2761
13	Rajasthan	911	960	1068	1154	1274	1308
14	Tamil Nadu	1008	980	1186	1235	1675	1363
15	Uttar Pradesh	6205	8592	9566	11290	12507	13619
	Total	22216	28176	333893	37375	42350	47174

Rate of Return in Welfare SLPEs

	State	*81-82*	*82-83*	*83-84*	*84-85*	*85-86*	*86-87*
1	Andhra Pradesh	3.06	0.63	2.34	1.37	1.27	1.16
2	Assam	NA	NA	NA	NA	NA	NA
3	Bihar	-2.06	14.5	-2.38	-1.91	-1.91	-1.91
4	Goa	NA	NA	NA	NA	NA	NA
5	Gujrat	2.56	2.21	4.41	3.43	8.11	8.11
6	Haryana	-6.76	-5.59	4.75	4.63	4.63	4.63
7	Himachal Pradesh	NA	NA	NA	NA	NA	NA

8	Jammu & Kashmir	NA	NA	NA	NA	NA	NA
9	Karnataka	7.77	14.33	6.9	6.35	10.34	10.6
10	Kerala	-23.29	-16.56	6.77	4.11	3.48	3.08
11	Madhya Pradesh	NA	-6.88	-4.46	3.19	-3.19	-3.19
12	Maharashtra	1.64	1.16	0.89	3.72	4.38	5.56
13	Manipur	-9.04	-4.35	-58	-28.56	-69.89	-69.89
14	Mizoram	NA	NA	NA	NA	NA	NA
15	Nagaland	NA	NA	NA	NA	NA	NA
16	Orissa	NA	NA	-4.62	-4.28	-3.49	-1.84
17	Punjab	1.42	-0.24	0.09	-0.17	NA	NA
18	Rajasthan	NA	NA	NA	NA	NA	NA
19	Tamil Nadu	NA	NA	-6.15	6.21	2.5	7.19
20	Tripura	NA	NA	NA	NA	NA	NA
21	Uttar Pradesh	0.2	3.6	-1.13	-9.58	-5.08	-4.51
22	West Bengal	8.79	-24.14	-15.35	-7.44	-7.82	-7.82
	Average	2.42	-0.97	-3	1.15	-2.58	2.22

Capital Investment Manufacturing SLPEs

	State	*81-82*	*82-83*	*83-84*	*84-85*	*85-86*	*86-87*
1	Andhra Pradesh	3344	4237	4693	5403	6457	7840
2	Arunachal Pradesh	6	7	7	8	8	10
3	Assam	1473	1721	2077	2541	3160	4690
4	Bihar	1632	3725	4576	6270	11038	13435
5	Gujrat	561	1158	1455	2061	2658	3763
6	Haryana	11308	12144	12840	13113	14830	18286
7	Himachal Pradesh	1862	2091	2703	3100	3253	3711
8	Jammu & Kashmir	650	790	834	1109	1615	2179
9	Karnataka	6867	8014	8639	9386	10800	11894
10	Kerala	6867	8014	8639	9386	10800	11894

11	Madhya Pradesh	820	980	1140	1320	1450	1664
12	Maharashtra	820	860	980	1140	1302	1483
13	Manipur	85	91	98	104	110	122
14	Meghalaya	15	16	16	17	21	28
15	Orissa	2092	2381	2810	3050	325	3756
16	Punjab	30460	33790	39175	42140	48650	53954
17	Rajasthan	1715	1765	1782	1885	2990	3203
18	Tamil Nadu	2557	2827	3497	3923	4109	4429
19	Uttar Pradesh	4947	6917	7031	8020	9043	13031
20	West Bengal	110	143	274	327	419	490
	Total	77746	90294	101648	113907	134494	158789

International Resource Generation by SLPEs During 1980-81 to 1986-87

	80-81	81-82	82-83	83-84	84-85	85-86	86-87
Category A							
1 Retained Barings	5551.46	5844.12	7403.88	6720	8317	2706.64	2938.83
2. Depreciation & DRE	1297.14	1364.27	1845.55	2661.57	2501.57	9007.24	9724.95
3. Gross Internal Resources	6848.6	7208.39	9249.43	9381.57	10819.04	11713.88	12663.78
Category B							
4. Retained Barings	-6784.14	-7146.81	-8283.46	-8646.31	-10416.15	-9706.53	-11867.21
5. Depreciation & DRE	8986.81	8145.56	9285.16	10145.64	11286.14	10731.78	16097.68
6. Gross Internal Resources	2202.67	999.75	1001.7	1499.33	869.99	1022.25	4230.47
Category C							
7. Retained Barings	-277779.31	-32553.23	-40553.23	-43154.14	-36336.3	35940.81	-40529
8. Depreciation & DRE	6753.44	7188.44	9589.74	10104.37	15698.94	18643.45	27965.19
9. Gross Internal Resources	-21025.87	-25364.79	-30963.49	-33049.77	-20637.36	-12297.36	-12563.81
Category A	6848.6	7208.39	9249.43	9381.57	10819.04	11713.88	12663.78
Category B	2202.67	999.75	1001.7	1499.33	869.99	1022.25	4230.47
Category C	-21025.87	-25364.79	-303963.4	-33049.77	-20637.36	-17297.36	-12563.81

9

CORPORATISATION AND COMMERCIALISATION OF GOVERNMENT BUSINESS ENTERPRISES IN INDIA

— K. Balaramamoorthy & R K Mishra

Government business enterprises (GBEs) in India are undergoing a great micro and macro transformation as a part and parcel of the new economic policy (NEP) initiated by the government in July, 1991.

GBEs have an enormous width and depth in terms their coverage and activities. They operate in the primary, secondary and tertiary sectors of the economy and are engaged in areas ranging from manufacturing, services and production of intermediate goods to the provision of infrastructure and promotional activities. A large part of public investment since independence has gone to these enterprises. The public investment from India amounts to more than 50% of the aggregate Capital formation in the economy. However, the financial performance of some of the GBEs has not been satisfactory as they have turned out to be net dissavers, on the one hand, and have been incurring cash losses on a year to year basis right from their inception due to a variety of reasons. The country, since the pronouncement of the NEP is engaged in an all round process of economic rebuilding and more than ever today there is a need for these GBEs to give a proper account of their working, in the absence of which the new public investment projects will either not take off or will progress slowly. Having realised this fact, the policy makers in the country have initiated sweeping moves to reform the GBEs. These relate to aspects concerning their micro functioning such as hiring and firing, fixation of wages, raising finances, updated technology. R&D in particulars areas, decisions and fixation of prices. The macro aspects of their functioning also form a part of the reform package.

The new approaches of government business enterprise interface, retention of GBEs' portfolio, and creation of level playing field by effecting changes in the fiscal and monetary policies have become a part of this agenda. In short, there is likely to be a paradigm shift in the existing framework of the working of GBEs and also in the components governing the environment controlling such functioning.

Introduction

The government business enterprise (GBEs) have occupied an important place in the reforms programme pursued by various countries because of their domination in their respective economics. The reforms programme followed by such countries are based on the central philosophy of removing stagnation and reenergising the social, economic and political structures for achieving higher rates of growth in a self-sustained manner. A survey of the rate of growth of India since its independence reveals that it has been very inadequate to satisfy the needs of the increasing population and imparting basic strength to the economy to overcome the inertia. As a part of the reforms programme announced in July 1991; the Government of India reformulated its industrial, trade, financial and public enterprise policies. During the last four years, whereas it has attained an appreciable success in respect of the implementation of the various economic reform policies, its public enterprise policy remains a non-starter. There is a feeling that the reforms have bypassed the GBEs. In its recent assessment of the economic reforms in India, the World Bank has criticised the government for its lack of concern to implement the GBEs reforms and have obliquely suggested that in order to create pressure for such an implementation, it may like to link the aid with the GBEs reforms.

It is necessary that the GBEs are transformed thoroughly so that the fruits of economic reforms are reaped by the Indian masses. The investments in these enterprises are of a gigantic nature. They are even politically significant as they are used as policy instruments by all the three tiers of administration, namely, central, state and local. There is hardly any area of economic activity where these enterprises do not make a contribution. The economic balance of the rests in the hands of these enterprises as they affect the rate of capital information, saying, investment and employment. The capital-output ratio which determines largely the success of any planning effort is also influenced by the working of these enterprises. Further, the intensity of the exports and imports, as also the overall balance of payments position of the country is affected by their efficient or inefficient operations. The purpose of this paper is an attempt to give a brief background of the GBEs in India, portray their performance, provide a brief account of the reform measures initiated to improve their working, and present a new paradigm for their corporatisation and commercialisation. The commercialisation to generate an appropriate backdrop for the various issues that are proposed to be covered here.

What is Corporatisation and Commercialisation ?

Corporatisation and commercialisation are two interconnected terms. There is a wide degree of disagreement about which preceds the other. The process experts opine that Commercialisation proceeds corporatisation, whereas the strategists suggest that for business enterprises to be commercial they should first be corporatised, as the latter sets up the requisite conditions for the successful introduction of commercial practices in an enterprise. In our view, commercialisation and corporatisation are only a means to an end in the context of the GBEs, as they transform the departmental enterprises of the government into companies to finally expose them to privatisation. Commercialisation includes in its gamut freedom about pricing the services or product, separation of the budget of an economic activity from the overall government budget, and introduction of the concept of the element of profit or surplus. The developing countries in their initial stages of development had to rely on the setting up of departmental enterprises to take up directly productive activities. In view of their strategic importance to the economy, such governments did not want them to be exposed to the various public accountability channels. Because of the domination of social objectives, the concept of profit/surplus was given a go by, as a result of which no commercial accounting system could be installed in such enterprises.

The absence of commercialisation resulted in the lack of awareness of important economic and financial variables such as costs, revenues, prices, budgeting, audit, net worth, etc. As such, governments started incurring huge macro-budgetary deficits. The policy-makers in such governments started suggesting new price structures, replacing administrative prices by users' prices, etc. As could be observed from this conceptualisation, commercialisation as a business process reengineering tool creates new conditions for the functioning of a GBE to only a limited extent as it continues to allow the government to perpetuate its rules of business to guide the functioning of such GBEs.

The corporatisation of a GBE leads to separation between ownership and management and provides a variety of alternative to manage an enterprise, besides being run by the government itself. The separation between ownership and management enables an enterprise to evolve its own rules of business which may include enterprise-specific policies about hire and fire, purchasing management, selection of suppliers, setting up a regime of price structures, etc., deciding about product mix and arriving at a specific debt-equity mix. Another salient feature of corporatisation is that it puts a GBE on par with a private sector enterprise by establishing a level playing field. It creates conditions for both sets of enterprises to be controlled by the same bunch of legislations. A hidden but a very vital benefit of corporatisation is the application of the same yardstick for the evaluation of performance of a GBE and a private enterprise which could be nothing else but profit. Finally, corporation provides an all-time recipe for the continued growth of a GBE, in that it stresses on an organic approach to growth instead of artificial stimuli provided by the state intervention to save a GBE from collapse every now and then.

Privatisation is the third and final phase in the life of a GBE wherein the management and control passed on clearly and visibly from the hands of the government to shareholders who run the business through an elected board supported by professional management which should counteracting with the market forces. The government, even after privatising a GBE, could continue to have an oblique relationship through well defined linkages. The privatisation saga of Singapore in the 1980s followed this approach wherein government continued to have its strategic say in the working of the post-privatised undertakings through golden shares. These enterprises in the changed context were functioning as government-linked enterprises. This third stage should happen to be a finality with a sound GBE as in its life-span a time comes when its operations become so specialised and complex that the government loses its grip on its working, and a consequence decides to leave it to the market forces through its privatisation. In some cases, due to ideological constraints, real privatisation may not take place. However, even in such cases it should be possible for the government to introduce the private sector style of management which may act again as a precursor to the full-fledged privatisation of a GBE in due course.

Backdrop

GBEs in India have come into being on account of both the pragmatic and doctrinaire approaches. During the early 1950s the socialistic form of economic management influenced India's policy-makers' thinking action. The economic planning introduced in 1951, therefore, heavily relied initially and subsequently in another two decades on GBEs as the instruments to implement the state policies. These enterprises, therefore, multiplied in terms of number, investment and areas of operation at both the central and state level. However, their proliferation and chronic sub-optimal performance compelled the state to exercise a brake on their expansion in the 1980s and thereafter, but by this time solid foundations had been laid for the growth of GBEs in India and, as a result, they became a very important vehicle for the economic development of the country. The mixed economic regime established at the inception of the planned era virtually leaned in favor of the public sector as GBEs dominated the basic and intermediate industries. This growth of GBEs put them on par with several Asian, African and Latin American counties in whose gross domestic product (GDP) GBEs contributed a share ranging between 10-25%. In fact, India turned out to touch the other extreme where GBEs' contribution ascended to 25% of the GDP (GBEs in the case include not only departmental and autonomous enterprises but also the government departments both at the federal and provincial levels). Today GBEs at the central and provincial levels have touched a mark of 1100. The investment in these enterprises at current costs exceeds a sum of Rs. 3.00, 000 crores (about US$ 100 billion). The number of personnel employed by these enterprises is about 180 million. The output of such enterprises has been estimated at Rs. 2,00,000 crores (about US$ 60 billion). 80% of these enterprise have been organised in the company form, while 10% of such enterprises have been organised under public enactments. The rest have been set up as government boards, government authorities, commissions, etc.

Performance

The performance of these enterprises has come under heavy criticism. A number of tests have been suggested to measure the performance of the GBEs. The profit test tops the list of any such yardsticks. The other tests being suggested include their performance in respect of capacity utilisation, savings accrued, growth in investment, the state of net worth, quality of R & D, quality of services provided, etc. **Table 1** shows the profitability of these enterprises in terms of the different profitability ratios. The combined profitability of these enterprises in terms of the different profitability ratios. The combined profitability of the central and state enterprises pinpoints the fact that put together they have not made any profits in the recent past. However, the aggregates hide some special features of the profitability of these enterprises:

1. The petroleum companies have been earning very high profits. **Table 2** shows that this profitability varied between 20-30% on different scores for the various petroleum GBEs.

2. The sick taken-over private enterprises have been a major drag on the overall profitability of the GBEs.

3. A large number of these enterprises are associated with a positive gross margin, indicating the fact that they have been efficient till the conversion stage.

4. A large part of losses have accrued on account of an imbalanced debt-equity mix and high establishment costs.

5. These enterprises could improve their performance enormously by both better asset and liability management and also through sound cost control and cost reduction techniques.

TABLE 1

Profitability Profile of Government Business Enterprises (Rs. in Crores)

Details	*1984-85*	*1985-86*	*1986-87*	*1987-88*	*1988-89*	*1989-90*	*1990-91*	*1991-92*	*1992-93*	*1993-94*
No. of Operating Enterprises	207	211	214	220	226	233	236	237	239	240
Capital Employed	36382	42965	51835	55617	67629	84760	102084	117991	140110	159607
Gross Margin	7386	8270	9897	11082	13438	16412	18312	22223	25227	276600
Avg. of Gross Margin to Capital Employed	20.30	19.25	19.09	19.93	19.87	19.36	17.94	18.83	18.01	17.33
Depreciation an Deferred Revenue Expenditure	2758	2983	3376	4142	4866	5790	7210	8548	9270	9162
Gross Profit	4628	5287	6521	6940	8572	10622	11102	13615	15957	18438
Avg. of Gross Profit to Capital Employed	12.73	12.31	12.58	12.48	12.68	12.53	10.88	11.59	11.39	11.57
Interest	2529	3115	3420	3587	4167	5367	7601	9673	10881	11894
Pre tax Profit/Loss	2099	2172	3101	3353	4405	5293	3501	4003	5076	6544
Tax	1490	1000	1329	1323	1411	1504	1229	1647	1805	2109

Details	*1984-85*	*1985-86*	*1986-87*	*1987-88*	*1988-89*	*1989-90*	*1990-91*	*1991-92*	*1992-93*	*1993-94*
Net Profit/Loss										
a) Profit of Profit Making Enterprises	909	72	1772	2030	2994	3789	2272	2355	3271	4435
(No. of Enterprises)	2021	2857	3478	3775	4917	5751	5394	6079	7384	9722
b) Loss of loss Making Enterprises	113	119	108	114	117	131	123	133	131	120
(No. of Enterprises)	1142	165	1706	1745	1923	1962	3122	3723	4113	5287
c) No. of Enterprises	92	90	100	103	106	98	111	102	106	117
making neither profit not loss	2	2	6	3	3	4	2	2	2	3
Avg. of Net Profit/Loss to Capital Employed	2.50	2.73	3.42	3.65	4.43	4.47	2.23	2.00	2.33	2.78
Dividends	176	191	297	320	353	323	413	687	792	1014
Retained Profit	733	981	1475	1710	2641	3466	1859	1668	2480	3420

Source: Department of Public Enterprises. Public Enterprise Survey, 1993-1994, Volume 1. Government of India, New Delhi.

TABLE 2

Profit in Petroleum, Sick and Non-Petroleum & Non-Sick-Enterprises (Rs. in Crores)

Details	Petroleum Sector		Sick PSUs in Mfg. Sector		Sick PSUs in Services Sector		Non-Sick & Non Petroleum PSUs		Total	
	92-93	93-94	92-93	93-94	92-93	93-94	92-93	93-94	92-93	93-94
No. of Operating Enterprises	14	14	51	65	14	18	160	143	239	240
Gross Sales (G.S)	56972	59846	2957	7295	1030	1276	86307	89745	147266	158162
Capital Employed	25513	30201	(-)2311	(-)1183	(-)369	(-)828	121357	135738	144190	163928
Ratio of GS to C.E.	223.31	198.16	N.A	N.A	N.A	N.A	71.12	66.12	102.12	96.48
Gross Profit	4424	5757	(-)767	(-)1032	(-)113	(-)153	12413	13866	15957	18438
Ratio of GP to C.E.	17.34	19.06	N.A	N.A	N.A	N.A	10.23	1022	11.07	11.25
Net Profit	2330	3947	(-)2127	(-)3008	(-)499	(-)637	3567	4133	3271	4435
Ratio of N.P. to C.E.	9.13	13.07	N.A	N.A	N.A	N.A	2.94	3.04	2.27	2.71
No. of Total Employees	123	124	226	440	76	70	1723	1431	2148	2065

N.A= Not Available due to Negative Capital Employed.

Source: Department of Public Enterprises. Public Enterprise Survey, 1993-1994, Volume 1. Government of India, New Delhi.

In a production-starved economy, it is a paradox that the GBEs have been bitterly criticised for their low utilisation of capacities. **Table 3** points out that as many as 22% of Iron & Steel Company could use their capacities to 110%, it was difficult to justify underutilisation of capacity in the public sector steel industry. It may be noted that even in the public sector steel industry, the Bhilai Steel Plant produced to the tune of 95% of its installed capacities. The reasons for low capacity utilisation include the lack of balancing facilities, sub-optimal site selection, and in some cases contraction of demand. On the savings front, the GBEs have turned out to be a net dissaver. Most of the savings in the country come from the household sector. The private sector is also associated with a positive record on this score but the public sector has had a negative performance all through during the period 1987-88 to 1993-94. The reasons given for the net dissavings include a higher resource demand and inadequate profit margins. The performance on net worth has been absolutely dismal. The GBEs at both the levels had either a negative net worth or a positive net worth on the margin. The position with regard to R & D and quality of the goods and services provided is also not encouraging. The R & D to sales ratio in these enterprise is very low and less than 1%. Twenty years back the GBEs were the leaders in this field. However, it seems the private sector enterprises have wrested this honour from them. Most of these enterprises still need to receive the ISO 9000. The quality of the services provided has come into conflict. For instance, the State Electricity Boards have been' charged with neither providing adequate power not pricing the power economically. The quality of the exports of Bharat Heavy Electricals Limited have been questioned by the importers abroad. The suppliers made by the State Trading Corporation of India of sugar and rice was commented upon adversely by the Committee on Public Undertakings. As many of the GBEs enjoy monopoly status, many of them never cared for quality. The quality of services provided by the public utilities such as the State Road Transport Corporations, Department of Telecommunications, the Mahanagar Telephone Nigam Limited at Mumbai, Delhi and

Calcutta is poor to say the least. The prices charged by the government monopoly organisations in the field of communications are three times more compared to the prices charged by the similar organisations abroad. In India, one telephone serves about 100 people, whereas the telephone density per 100 people handling 1000 telephones in India is at least twenty times more than the number of people required to handle the same number of telephones in technologically advanced countries.

TABLE 3

Capacity Utilisation in Central GBEs

	1993-94	1992-93	1991-92
(a) Units which have recorded capacity utilisation of more than 75%.	115 (52%)	123 (54%)	118 (56%)
(b) Units where capacity utilisation has been between 50-75%.	59 (26%)	58 (35%)	42 (20%)
(c) Units where capacity utilisation was less than 50%.	50 (22%)	48 (21%)	50 (24%)
Total Units under Production Surveyed	224 (110%)	229 (100%)	210 (100%)

Source: Department of Public Enterprises. Public Enterprise Survey, 1993-1994, Volume 1. Government of India, New Delhi.

Challenges to Public Enterprises

The GBEs are passing through a very crucial period. Today when the entire philosophy of the country's economic development is under questioning, the GBEs cannot escape such a scrutiny. Any analysis of the working of the GBEs during the last four and a half decades would unmistakably point out that there is a gap between their philosophical premises and their current performance. Instead of helping the state, they have virtually become a drag on it. The Indian context is not an exception to what has been found by the policy analysts in the case of developing countries wherein they have pointed out the positive association between the macroeconomic deficits and the public sector loses, and have argued the linking of international aid to public sector reforms. Today India faces the challenge of the involvement of the government in bringing up the infrastructural projects. This could be understood by the fact that the per head availability of power, passenger bus transport, railway lines, telephone lines, medical and health facilities, seats in schools and universities, drinking water and clothing is abysmally low in India. When India won independence it was conceived that as enshrined in the directive principles of the state policy enunciated in the Indian constitution, the government as a welfare state would formulate programmes to overcome these problems but over the years the problems have become much acute as the population has kept on increasing at a menacing pace, whereas the growth of social overhead capital has been very scant and is utterly inadequate. During the last 45 years, both the centre and the states had indulged in schemes which have been populist in nature and far less productive in economic terms. The eyes of all political parties were set on coming to power and hanging on to it. The bureaucracy in the country mostly carried out the orders of the executives. Though they did not collaborate, they also did not display any signs of discomfiture with such moves, but today the masses of the country are looking for a rapid pace of economic development so that they could lead comfortable lives, similar to the citizens in other parts of the world. The policy-makers now are faced with the tough challenge of speeding up the implementation of programmes and folding up of populist schemes. All this requires a thorough overhaul of the GBEs which, as noted earlier, have spread their tentacles to each and every walk of the socio-economic life of this country.

The fulfillment of the challenge of economic development requires the presence of a healthy private sector. The world-over there is a trend towards developing and helping the private sector as a mechanism to take on the developing projects. The success of the private sector depends on their expansion, as well as the support they get from the GBEs. In other sector depends on their expansion, as well as the support they get from the GBEs. In other words, a new mix of GBEs and private sector enterprises is required to be struck in the changed economic scenario. In this era of globalisation, competitiveness would decide the success of any enterprise. The competitiveness depends, among other things, on how an enterprise responds to market signals and the way it transforms its working to innovate radically new ways of running its activities. All this would ultimately require dynamism, quick decision making and new structures for running the businesses. There is now a trend of having flat structures. As mentioned earlier, business process reengineering is also carried out to sharpen the competitive edge of enterprises. Naturally, as a corollary, these strategies would require team-work, cohesion and multi-skilling. Enterprises in such a situation would have to move from formal to informal structures and create conducive climate for flexible ways of thinking to decide upon the various business issues. The GBEs in their existing mould are comparable only to outdated organisations and hence their transformation is very much required to gain the competitive edge.

The outlays to finance developmental programmes present another challenges to the GBEs. The social overhead capital development would require around US$ 300 billion as concluded in the recently held conference of the Asian Infrastructural Alliance at New Delhi in September 1995. The GBEs in their present from are simply incapable of handling a task of this magnitude. They need to tone up their managerial capability and develop administrative systems to deal with a limitless number of consumers.

GBE Reforms

When the policy-makers prepared the blueprint for the economic reforms in July 1991 they did show their resolve to streamline the working of the public sector and redefine their role. It was then professed that no new GBEs would be set up, and that GBEs would remain only in such sectors which were strategic in nature. For the efficient functioning of the Indian economy, cash loss-making enterprises would have to be closed down over a period of time. The sick GBEs would be referred to the Board for Industrial & Financial Reconstruction (BIFR) which would formulate rehabilitation packages for such of the units which in its view could be valid cases for survival. Disinvestments of GBEs would be done, ranging from 1 to 74% to initially finance the fiscal deficits. Capital restructuring would be in the case of such GBEs which were to approach the capital market, and interface of the GBEs with the government along the new lines dictated by the system of Memorandum of Understanding (MOU)[2].

In so far as the bar on setting up of new GBEs is concerned, it is found that during the last four years no new GBE has been set up at the central level. Even the state governments have contained their euphoria of setting up new GBEs. However, some states in the country have been exceptions as they have been late entrants on the development scene. These states are mostly in the north-east part of the country where the normal development scene. The states are mostly in the north-east part of the country where the normal development process has started almost three decades after its initiation in the other regions of the country. However, this does not in itself provide any comfort in the sense that the task of amalgamation and merger has not received any attention, barring a few cases here and there. In Kerala, one of the southern states of the country, holding companies have been set up to regroup their enterprises and then go in for merger, acquisition and closure. This exercise can be replicated even in the case of the GBEs at the centre. For instance, fertiliser companies, the engineering companies and the GBEs in the steel sector could easily be merged, resulting in the reduction of the overall number of GBEs at the centre. It appears that the government's intention about not opening a new GBE has been understood only in letter but not in spirit. Most of the state governments and the government at the centre could conduct a portfolio analysis of the businesses of the various GBEs. This would disclose the possibilities of having off profitable/ unprofitable activities and thereby slimming down the present size of the various GBEs. Different models have been presented on the portfolio which should be retained in the case of GBEs but this debate has not considered any option about the portfolio very seriously. One of the reasons for such an attitude could possibly be found in the impeding elections, indicating the possibilities of strong moves in this direction after the general elections are held by mid-1996. Any discussion on portfolio for retention would not be purposeful until the workers of the concerned GBEs are taken into confidence. Though some enterprises have been identified for a test privatisation exercise, the government has not established a rapport with the workers or the unions of such enterprises. The government has not initiated meaningful discussions on portfolio of GBEs as the general impression gained has given an indication that many important alternatives of privatisation, such as entrusting the enterprise to workers' cooperatives or transferring the ownership to managers are not on the agenda of the government.

The idea of the disinvestment of shareholdings of GBEs was mooted in July 1991 by the then Finance Minister, Dr. Manmohan Singh. Since then, the Comptroller & Auditor General of India has made a detailed report on the disinvestment procedures and outcomes of the initial runs, and the Rangarajan Committee Report has suggested the future approach which government should adopt to implement and monitor its disinvestment programme[3]. The Institute of Public Enterprise at Osmania University, Hyderabad has also had a look at the valuation issue concerning the shares of the various companies disinvested by the government[4]. Eight rounds of disinvement have been completed and proceeds of Rs. 12,000 crores (about US$ 4 billion) have been raised. The disinvestment of shares is a very important public sector reform. It could provide great opportunity to the GBEs by bringing in shareholdings from general investors. It should result in weakening the government controls and transform the GBEs into the mould enjoyed by the private corporate sector enterprise. It should further help the GBEs in enlarging their resource base for receiving equity and debt support as the GBEs going in for disinvestment would get listed on the stock exchanges. In a sense, the government culture in GBEs would be replaced by the corporate sector. This precisely would take shape through the holding of annual general meetings. It is expected that the GBEs in their transformed shape would turn out to be board managed enterprises and such boards would have the government nominees on them only as an exception and not as the rule. The disinvestments have failed to make the promised impact. Though the Rangarajan Committee talked of wholesale disinvestment in non-strategic GBEs, the fact of the matter is that the disinvestment range has narrowed down to 5-40% in the case of the 38 GBEs at the centre forming part of the disinvestment programme raise a number of questions.

While the government has been advocating for disinvestment, it has not divested itself of the disinvestment function. The international experience in disinvestment leads to admission of the fact that the government as an agency cannot do justice to the implementation of disinvestment effort, a continuous availability of date about the share prices, debt-equity ratio, and the timings of disinvestment are essential prerequisites. The method of valuation and the computation of the likely value to be realised are basic input to be fed into any disinvestment model. The government's greed to not entrust this task to an independent body is responsible for the partial success of the disinvestment programme. Though the government has time and again expressed its desire to raise funds through disinvestment to fulfil the short-term goal of meeting the budgetary deficits and the long-term goal of strengthening GBEs and marketising them, the speed at which the programme has been pursued raises doubts about the authenticity of its intention. Even if it is supposed that no new investments would be made in the central GBEs, it would take, at the present rate, about 15 years to disinvest the existing shareholdings of the GBEs. The stage governments have started thinking about disinvestments. The Kerala, Andhra Pradesh, Tamil Nadu and Maharashtra state governments have prepared detailed schemes through. It is, however, important to mention that the State Industrial Development Corporations, the State Financial Corporations, the State Small Industries Development Corporations and the State Industrial Infrastructure & Investment Corporations have been disinvesting a fraction of their investments every year. The long-term development banks in the country, including the Industrial Development Bank of India and the Industrial Finance Corporation of India have also been disinvesting to recycle the money realised from such disinvestments into new projects.

One of the important reform measures has been the referral of the sick industrial enterprises to the BIFR. As of March 31, 1994, 47 central GBEs were referred to this institution. In addition, 47 state-level GBEs were also referred to the BIFR by that date. The BIFR till March 31, 1994 had prepared two rehabilitation packages and had ordered for the closure of five central GBEs, of which three approached the high courts in their respective states and got stay orders. A study done by the Institute of Public Enterprise in the working of the state-level GBEs points out that as many as 68 state GBEs had incurred cash losses continuously during the five years of their operation ending on March 31, 1992. This shows that the number of sick enterprises in the government sector is much more than the cases reported to the BIFR. Whether the institution of BIFR has helped in the closure of unviable GBEs, the answer is indicative. The BIFR and the government are both responsible for this. While the BIFR takes too long a time in giving its verdict, the government is responsible for this phenomenon as it reports about sickness only when it is in its last stages. One of the reasons responsible for the failure of this reform is its ostensible non-approval by the work force of these enterprises. In a country like India where it is very difficult to get alternative employment, any reform measure resulting in mass unemployment could not be expected to have the tacit approval of the work force. Giving due consideration to this, the central government set up a National Renewal Fund (NRF) for providing a social safety net to workers to facilitate retrenchment and reduction in the work force. However, the money put into the NRF has been so scant that it has been able to take care of the retrenchment package of only 75,000 workers connected to the textile, jute and engineering sector. The retrenchment package has not been very attractive and does not compare favourably with similar packages offered in countries around India, let alone the developed countries. Further, the NRF has not been strong on retraining and providing insurance for guarantee of employment. If these have to be provided by the GBEs, the central government would require to put a colossal sum of at least Rs. 30,000 crores (about US$ 10 billion) as against Rs. 2000 crores presently at the command of the fund. The setting up of the NRF has been a good idea but the functioning of the board managing and controlling the fund, the pace at which centres have been selected to implement the programmes of the fund, and the money at its disposal, have turned out to be weak links in the chain. The non-association of the state governments which own about 1000 GBEs, which are four times the number of central GBEs, has also whittled down the importance of the fund[5].

The government-GBEs interface has been very complex and dysfunctional. The GBE has to continuously interact with a number of agencies, has to have occasional interactions with another few such organisations, and has to maintain sporadic touches with the parent ministry which could veto any of its proposals. It could be said that the various kinds of interactions take away the precious business time presently at the disposal of a GBE and detrimentally affects its business culture.

MoU Approach

As a reform measure, the central government decided to strengthen the working of its MOU programme in July, 1991. The number of enterprises having MOUs has shot up to 102 in 1993-94 as shown in **Table 4.** Of these 44 enterprises received "A" grade, which means outstanding performance. The number of enterprises receiving "A" grade is on the rise year after year. The MOU is a reform exercise directed to improve the GBEs-government interface. Its major aim is to provide autonomy to GBEs and at the same time increase their accountability to the government. On the government side, it expects a one-time intervention annually and a consensual agreement at the time of signing the MOU. The MOU exercise in India is modelled on the basis of the French pattern and the Pakistani and African patterns centering around the signalling aspects of the performance. A typical MOU between a GBE and the central government covers description of the objectives, targets for the year, support to come from the government and the mechanism to evaluate performance. The last part of the MOU document states the dynamic and non-dynamic criteria and the weights provided to each criteria, and the methodology of assessing scores. This system initially received very high kudos. However, during the last two years it has lost much of its shine. It is appropriate to mention here that as many as 100 enterprises has not started their MOU exercises till July-August 1995 for the financial year 1995 –96. The basic idea of introducing MOU was to present the GBEs have observed that the MOU is an agreement has between two unequal partners. To add to this, it could be said that the government has very frequently behaved like an irresponsible partner in the exercise as it has hardly fulfilled the promised support to the GBEs recorded in the MOUs. The GBEs have also not given a fair account of themselves as a number of such organisations have manipulated their scores by understanding the targets or revising them downwards in the course of time. One of the pitfalls of the MOU exercise appears to be the lack of imagination in regard to providing efficient evaluation criteria which requires continued fresh thinking. Incidentally, India adopted MOUs when they failed to deliver the goods in France and had achieved mixed results in Pakistan. The administrative arrangements for the monitoring of MOUs have also attracted severe criticism. In the entire exercise the bureaucracy has been able to establish an upper hand. In South Korea where MOUs have succeeded as a mechanism to transform the government-GBEs interface it is noted that the politicians monitor the working of the MOU system.

TABLE 4

Performance of Central GBEs with M.O.U

Performance	1990-91	1991-92	1992-93	1993-94	1994-95
1. Excellent	14	25	34	44	Under Evaluation
2. Very Good	8	21	35	30	-do-
3. Good	8	21	35	30	-do-
4. Fair	-	3	10	7	-do-
5. Poor	1	-	2	6	-do-
6. Not evaluated	-	13	1	2	-do-
	23	71	98	102	106

Source: Department of Public Enterprises. Public Enterprise Survey, 1993-1994, Volume 1. Government of India, New Delhi.

One of the items of the agenda for the GBEs has been the reduction of the budgetary support. Government has gone a long way in such reduction in the case of the central GBEs. In 1986-87, the central GBEs financed internally to the tune of 32.3%. through external budgetary resources a magnitude of 20.8%, and out of the government budgetary resources to the tune of 46.9%. In 1994-95, the share of budgetary resources came down to a mere 11% and it is expected that in 1999-2000 the budgetary resources will form about 5% of the total financial needs of the central GBEs. In the case of the state GBEs similar trend has been discerned. The central and state GBEs have been able to mop up funds through public deposits, flotation of equity and bonds and issue of commercial paper. GBEs such as the Indian Petrochemicals Limited, Steel Authority of India Limited, Hindustan Organics & Chemicals Limited, Balmer Lawrie & Company Limited and a host of other enterprises have very successfully approached the capital market. Some enterprises have even raised money in the international capital markets through Euro issues at highly competitive rates because of their high credit rating. In the state sector, the State Financial Corporations and Industrial Development Corporations have been raising money through the floatation of bonds. SICOM (State Industrial & Investment Corporation of Maharashtra) capitalised funds through floatation of equity. Some state governments have been trying to get their undertakings rated by the credit rating organisations in order to prepare them to have an access to the Indian capital market. However, a study of the eligibility of the GBEs for the various sources of finance clearly underscores the vast possibilities for them to raise funds both internally and externally. It is understood that some 80 GBEs are eligible for the issue of commercial paper. However, it was only the Balmer Lawrie & Company Limited which took the lead in 1990. Not many enterprises followed this good example afterwards. In the case of public deposits, the central GBEs could raise 35% of their net worth through this means. The total money raised by way of public deposits is about Rs. 15,000 crores. If 35% of net worth is taken as a yardstick, the GBEs in the central sector could raise something like Rs. 40,000 crores. Another important instrument of funding the working capital requirements could be a well with cash at hand on March 31 to the tune of at least Rs. 15,000 crores, on which they receive a small interest of 5-6% per annum. There are some GBEs which have to obtain cash credit, on the other hand, at a very high rate of 20-25% per annum. Then, there are some GBEs who mobilise large sums through advance deposits and keep them in current account or savings bank, earning a partly interest of 5-6% per annum. These enterprises as well could lend this sum to the needy ones who have a vision of the range of sources, their costs and the duration for which such sources could be utilised.

Privatisation

Though no precise policy of privatisation exits in the country, there is an implied understanding that the GBEs should be privatised either wholesale or in parts through the hiving off or selling of their profit/loss-making activities/divisions/

plants. Whereas closure or selling of GBEs may create some tough political problems, it should be possible to unbundle their activities and then stick to only those ones where the GBEs have their core competencies. For example, the State Transport Corporations (STCs) in India can find out the scope of privatisation of their activities in terms of unbundling their sub-activities in the realm of ownership, financing and management as shown in the diagram below.

Privatisation of STCs

Ownership	Financing	Management
Bus Routes	Share Capital	Constitution of Boards
Bus (fleet)	Debt	Recruitment
Bus Building	Public Deposits	Management Services
Bus Stations	User Contributions	Employee Services
Workshops	Reduction in Taxes	Management Audit
Printing Presses		
Roadways		

It is clear from the diagram that they would only stand to gain by adding to their bus fleet, bus routes, bus stations, etc., by private participation. A lot of good could happen to them if they could withdrawn from activities such as running of printing presses or building bus stations[6].

New Framework for Commercialisation and Corportisation

The success of any new endeavour for having the way for greater commercialisation and corporatisation of GBEs in India would rest on covering the left out GBEs, on the one hand, and speeding up the ongoing reform process in the identified enterprises, on the other.

Commercialisation has to make inroads in the departmental enterprises. Such enterprises operate at all the three levels, namely, central, state and local sector. These departmental enterprises are in very strategies areas, including the provision of public utilities and defence production and printing of currency notes. In India there are about 100 factories producing arms and ammunition for the defence ministry. An equal number of departmental enterprises are involved in printing currency notes, working as mints, providing drinking water facilities, bus services and handling the production of narcotic goods. They undertake commercial activities but are being run like a typical government department. Some of them have great scope for growth and expansion but on account of dysfunctional controls accountability procedures they have been deprived of good business opportunities. Recently, an ordnance factory at Jabalpur, producing vehicles for the army, has gone commercial and is now manufacturing light and medium range automobiles. Its out turn have been received very well in the market and it is likely to earn huge profits. It is high time that the departmental enterprises in India have a user price system and maintain their accounts on a double entry mode instead of on a single entry basis. These enterprises should be given enough latitude to price their goods and should be allowed to buy their supplies through the open market or even from markets abroad. The curb that they should buy their goods from the Directorate General of Supplies & Disposals should be abolished. They should be allowed to have access to commercial banks and have their own hire and fire systems. The enterprises where Corporatisation is in progress should make efforts to further strengthen the process. Corporatisation in the Indian context in so far as GBEs are concerned has been restricted to merely the conversion of public corporations into government companies. The Oil & Natural Gas Commission, Air India, Indian Airlines, Industrial Finance Corporation of India, and the Industrial Development Bank of India are cases in point. Further, corporatisation has thrown open to them vast possibilities of competing with their counterparts in the private sector in India and similar organisations abroad. These other enterprises which are also working as government companies have yet to take the lead to rewriting their Articles of Association and Memorandum of Association. The government has yet to decide to finally withdraw its interference in the activities of such GBEs. These enterprises need to profesionalise their activities and tone up their internal organisation by installing appropriate checks and balances through suitable working and control systems. The performance evaluation, budgeting of expenses and revenue, quality consciousness, development of core competencies, instilling team work and appropriate culture for the growth of leadership could well from a part of such systems.

Corporatisation would require all types of GBEs to get organically linked completely with the investors and market. This would help them to become proactive to face the market challenges and to constantly improve upon their efficiency. The strength to meet the challenges emanating from corporatisation would come essentially from the corporate culture which is the missing link in the GBEs. Such corporate culture would embody a distinct vision of the enterprise in the minds of the employees who would own it just because they have contributed substantially to its creation.

Conclusion

The GBEs form the backbone of the Indian economy. Their activities range from the very small to the most important facts of the Indian economy. The investments in these enterprises are substantial and almost 50% of the GDP. They lead the economy in terms of capital formation. However, due to continued loss-making they have turned out to be net dissavers. Today when the country is faced with the challenge of increasing substantially the investment in the social overhead capital, these enterprises could not be allowed to incur losses any more. The financial turnaround of these enterprises requires their complete overhaul. The economic reforms programme announced in 1991 contained a reform agenda for the GBEs also. As a part of such an agenda, since July 1991 steps have been taken to disinvest GBE shareholdings, reduce budgetary support to them, introduce MOU as a new technique to streamline the government-GBE interface, retain only such GBEs in government portfolio which operate in strategic sector of the economy and privatise/close down such GBEs which have outlived their importance. A number of steps have been taken to corporatise and commecialise the GBEs. However, an intensive study of the pace of reforms affected in GBEs points out that the success has been very limited and rigorous and renewed efforts would be required to contest the opinion that the economic reforms in India have bypassed the GBEs.

References

1. Mishra, R.K., "Performance Evaluation of Public Enterprises in India" in Wettenhall, Roger L., and Nullain, Colm O., *Performance of Public Enterprises : Seven Country,* International Association of Schools and Institutions of Administration, Brussels, 1990, pp. 1-35.
2. Mishra, R.K., "Privatisation in India", *Institute of Public Enterprise Journal,* Vol.17 (1&2), Hyderabad, pp. 1-31.
3. Mishra, R.K., (ed.) (1995), *Disinvestments in Public Enterprises,* Institute of Public Enterprises, Hyderabad, Mimeo.
4. Mishra, R.K., et al, Disinvestments in Public Enterprises: The Indian Experience, *The International Journal of Public Sector Management,* MCB University Press, Bradford (England), Vol.7, No.2, pp. 69-87.
5. Mishra, R.K.,(1995), "Safety Net, National Renewal Fund and State Level Public Enterprises in India" in Association of Management Development Institutions in South Asia and Friedrich Ebert Stiftung (ed.), *Redeployment of Labour in South Asia,* Hyderabad, pp. 68-77.
6. Mishra, R.K., and Nandagopal, R., Privatisation of State Trasport Undertakings in India in Gouri, Geeta., Jayashanker, R., and Fadahunsi Olu (ed.), *Efficiency through Competition in Public Utilities-Policies for Restructuring,* published by Commonwealth Secretariat and International Centre for Public Enterprises in Developing Countries, Ljubljana, Slovenia, 1993, pp. 127-137.

10

MEMORANDUM OF UNDERSTANDING AND PUBLIC ENTERPRISES IN INDIA

— P. Geeta & B. Navin

Introduction

Public Enterprises (PEs) in India are the result of planned economic development. The policy makers of independent India wanted to provide equal employment opportunities through the establishment of PEs and the State took up the issue of 'social justice' and 'public good'. Contrary to this design, the PEs over the years have become overextended and a number of problems have cropped up in these enterprises. They are unable to make return on the investments made on them and at this point the Government of India is thinking of ways to make the enterprises work profitably. Various reform measures have been taken from time to time to improve the performance of the enterprises.

As a part of the reform measure, Memorandum of Understanding (MoU) was introduced into the Central Public enterprises (CPEs) in 1987. The objective of the MoU system as per the Public Enterprise Survey 1996-97 is to:

- Introduce a performance improvement system that would simultaneously increase autonomy and accountability in the public sector.

- Remove the fuzziness in the goals and objectives of the enterprises.
- Set up an objective performance evaluation system and introduce a performance incentive system.

Problems and Issues of PEs

The study discusses the problems and issues in PEs, which are directly, or indirectly affecting the performance of the enterprises. The following observations have been made:

- ❖ **The problem of entry of PEs into non-core sectors:** PEs were initially set up in the infrastructure area (core sectors). But in the due course of time they were entering into areas which did not suite them. Heavy investments have gone into sectors where PEs have failed to perform and which are now difficult to retrieve.
- ❖ **Uncertain tenure of the Chief Executives:** The common problems, which the PEs face, is that their chief executives are hardly given a tenure of 1-2 years with each enterprises. By the time the officer sets the tone and tunes himself to the environment he is shifted to another enterprise. This has created a general apathy among the officers, and the officers in turn see that their involvement with the enterprise is not a serious one.
- ❖ **Varying interests of the Chiefs:** There is a tendency of the chief executives of the enterprises to pursue certain ideas, which they believe are very important for the growth of the particular enterprise. They pursue them with great interest, generate a lot of interest in their staff too, for the particular idea. Lot of investments is made for pursuing the policy. When the chief leaves the organization, and another one replaces him he comes with a new set of priorities for

the enterprise. The investment in both ways i.e. resources and manpower goes waste as there is change in idea at the management level.

- **Political interventions and interests:** PEs are known to be hot beds for political combats. The political parties have their interests going high in appointing the top management. For example the senior member who could not be given a ministerial birth is accommodated as the chairman of a public enterprise. Thus the political parties have always found the PEs as areas of vested interests. Of late there is growing awareness regarding this issue and the PEs themselves have ceased to be lucrative and the political chiefs have found better pastures and now are talking about their privatization.

- **Lack of operational autonomy and accountability:** The major problem that the PEs face is lack of operational autonomy for them. Number of efforts have been done in order to overcome this problem. The Navratana package was announced for the blue chip companies and it gave them the necessary operational freedom to work for a better performance. The MoU is also a similar exercise, which was undertaken by the government in 1987-88 in order to induce professionalism into the PEs working.

- **Cyclic performance of enterprises:** Another major problem with the PEs enterprises is that there is a cyclic pattern of performance in these enterprises. They work successfully for a certain period of time and then there is a gradual decline in their performance. The insiders as well as researchers have observed this trend.

- **Lack of flexibility & adaptability:** The PEs are lagging behind in all the major areas of changes i.e. technology, novel management techniques, advanced information system. At the same time the private enterprises make the best use of these developments. The PEs are stuck with outdated technology and techniques, which forces them to show bad performance and end up with a sense of defeat.

- **Changing role of the State:** The State had initially taken up the role of a welfare state with an agenda to provide equal opportunity to all. With the changes in the socio- political and economic conditions, the State decided to pull out of it's responsibilities and restrict itself to activities in a select few sectors where it could give a better performance. The State realizes that it is no more competent to give profitable results in many areas, which are otherwise taken over by the private sector. Almost all the countries with large PEs have opted for privatization in the late 80s and early 90's. The initiation of MoU in India was also a step in this direction. The system of MoU was formally introduced in the year 1988-89 following the recommendations made by the Arjun Sengupta Committee report of 1985.Almost 110 CPEs have signed the MoU in the year 1996-97.

Government's Policy on Performance Evaluation

The Industrial Policy Resolutions of 1948 and 1956 broadly classified the role of Government vis-à-vis the private sector undertakings. The Government of India assured to take the responsibility for industrial and economic development of the country. Accordingly all strategic industries were to be set up, developed, strengthened and diversified under government ownership. But nothing was discussed in these Policy Resolutions about the performance evaluation of PEs. Mostly ad-hoc measures were introduced from time to time. Further, 1977 Industrial Policy Statement focussed on its package of development of rural industries and strengthening the agrarian sector. But no attention was focussed in regard to performance evaluation.

However, the 1980 Industrial Policy Statement did not pay

much attention to the problem of performance evaluation of PSU's. Only ad-hocism governed the performance evaluation and techniques of evaluation differed from enterprise to enterprise and ministry to ministry. Government did not go for any comprehensive package of performance evaluation for PSU's. A significant development that took place prior to the announcement of the New Economic Policy in 1991 was the appointment of Arjun Sengupta Committee in 1985. The Committee was entrusted with the task of suggesting suitable performance evaluation mechanism for the Indian PEs. Based on the experience of other developing countries with regard to performance evaluation of PEs, the Committee made detailed recommendations in regard to performance evaluation of PEs through the MoU system and the same was accepted by the Government and adopted to the PEs.

In 1991 Industrial Policy Statement (Public Enterprise Survey, 1996-97) aimed at improving the portfolio and performance of public sector. The salient features of the policy include,

- Portfolio of public sector investments will be reviewed with a view to focus the public sector on strategic, high-tech and essential infrastructure, whereas some reservations for the public sector are being retained, there would be no bar for areas of exclusivity to be opened up to the private sector selectively. Similarly, the public sector will also be allowed entry in areas not reserved for it.
- PEs which are chronically sick and which are unlikely to be turned around will for the formulation of revival or rehabilitation scheme be referred to the Board for Industrial and Financial Restructuring (BIFR), or other similar high level institutions created for the purpose. A social security mechanism will be created to protect the interest of workers likely to he affected by such rehabilitation packages.
- In order to nurse resources and encourage public

participation, a part of the government's share holding in the public sector would be offered to mutual funds, financial institutions, general public and workers.

- Boards of public sector companies would be made more professional and given greater powers.

Adoption of MoU System

Arjun Sengupta Committee Report in 1985 dealt with the issue of improving the performance of the CPEs. The contractual system, which India adopted for the PE performance, was named as the "Memorandum of Understanding". The MoUs have been in operation in Indian PEs since 1987, commencing in an experimental way with 4 PEs. The number of PEs, which signed the MoU's, has gone up to 109 in the year 1997-98. The system has remained so far confined to the CPEs and has not percolated to the State Level Public Enterprises (SLPEs).

The Industrial Policy Statement 1991 (Public Enterprise Survey, 1996-97) regarding the system of MoU clarified that,

1) There will be greater thrust on autonomy through MoU systems through which manufacturers would be granted greater autonomy and will be held accountable. Technical expertise on the part of the government would be upgraded to make the MoU negotiations and implementation more effective.

2) To facilitate a fuller discussion on performance, the MoU signed between government and the PE would be placed in Parliament. While focussing on major manufacturing issues, this would also help place matters of day to day operations of PEs in their correct perspective.

As per the Public Enterprise Survey, the following observations are made for the reason for implementing the system of MoU to CPEs:

1. Widely held perception that the PEs are less efficient

than their private sector counterparts.

2. PEs are unable to perform because there are a variety of agencies that feel that they have a mandate to run the PEs. These organizations keep setting different objectives for the enterprises, which are often conflicting.
3. No one in the PEs is accountable for the performance of the enterprise.
4. PEs are handicapped in their operation due to absence of functional autonomy.

Contents of Performance Contracting

Ingredients of a Performance Contract

Performance contracts are adopted as tools by the PEs to improve their performance. Based on the contents, the contracts are broadly classified under two systems a) the French based systems b) the Signaling system.

The main difference between the two types of contract is that the typical French Contract Plans don't allocate weights to the targets. This adds to a high degree of subjectivity to the evaluation process. This system is followed in France, Africa (Senegal, Benin and Morocco), and Latin America. In the signaling system signals are sent to the managers in order to monitor the results of the contacts. This system originated in Pakistan and Korea is popular in Asia (Pakistan, South Korea and Bangladesh), Africa (Ghana, Nigeria and Gambia) and Latin America. There are countries like India, which practice both the systems. Initially MoU in India was based on the French System, while those signed more recently follow the Signaling system.

The enterprises contracts essentially comprise of, the mission of the enterprise, the objectives of the enterprise, the criteria selected, the weightages assigned to each criteria, the period of contract and the mode of evaluation.

Organizational Environment

Every organization has a number of different types of plans for improving its performance. They can be generally classified on the basis of the, Purpose or Mission, Objectives of the enterprise, Strategies, Policies, Procedures & Rules, which the organization must follow to reach the goals. The Programs & budget would be the basis on which the enterprise would pursue to achieve the goals. In the same way, performance contracting of an enterprise comprises of a number of components, which can be arranged in a hierarchy.

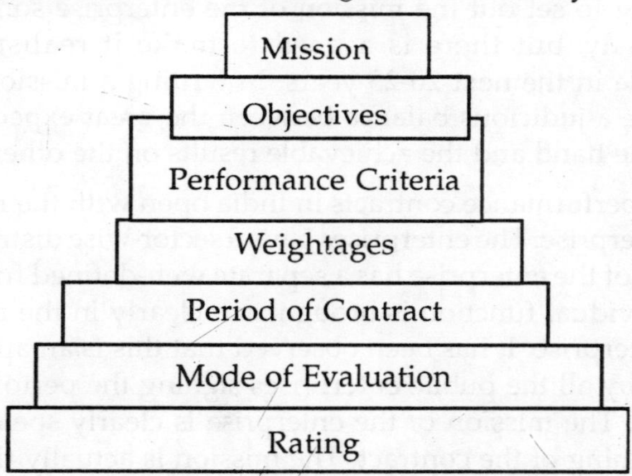

The Hierarchy of Performance Contract

Mission

The mission or purpose identifies the basic function or task of an enterprise. Every kind of organized operation has, or at least should have if it is to be meaningful, a **purpose or a mission.** In every social system, enterprises have a basic function or task, which is assigned to them by the society. The purpose of a business is generally production and distribution of goods and services. This can be accomplished by fulfilling a mission of producing certain types of products. It is generally thought that the mission of an enterprise is to make surplus. This is absolutely necessary for the enterprise to survive and to perform the task that the society has entrusted to it. But this basic objective is achieved only by undertaking certain activities as per the clearly defined directions and accomplishing the mission.

All the PEs are presumed to serve the public. There is a tendency therefore to state the mission in very broad terms and in a way that anything that is considered good for the public is included. There is also a tendency to describe the mission in grandiose terms. For example, the mission of a PE, which is in the consultancy business, is set out **'to be the most important international consultancy organization in the world.'** It is not wrong to set out the mission of the enterprise somewhat ambitiously, but there is a need to make it realistic and achievable in the next 20-25 years. In writing a mission there should be a judicious balance between the great expectations on the one hand and the achievable results on the other hand.

The performance contracts in India open with the mission of the enterprise. The enterprises have a sector-wise distribution and each of the enterprise has a separate well-defined function. This individual function is brought out clearly in the mission of the enterprise. It has been observed that this is an approach adopted by all the public enterprises signing the performance contracts. The mission of the enterprise is clearly spelt out at the beginning of the contract. The mission is actually the long term planning for the enterprise. It highlights what the enterprise is aiming at in the long run and intends to achieve through undertaking certain activities.

Objectives

The objectives are the goals towards which the activity is aimed at. They represent not only the end point of the planning but also the end towards which organizing, staffing, leading, and controlling are aimed. While enterprise objectives are the basic plan for the firm, a department may also have its own objectives. These goals would certainly be congruent to the goals of the enterprise as a whole. Objectives state the end results and the overall objectives need to be supported by the sub-objectives. Thus objectives form a hierarchy as well as a network. Moreover organizations and managers have multiple goals which are sometimes incompatible and may lead to conflicts within an organization, within a group or between individuals.

As presented in the diagram below the objectives form a hierarchy ranging from the broad aim to specific individual objectives. In this hierarchy first there is the purpose of the society. It involves the organization to contribute to the welfare of the people by providing goods and services at reasonable costs. Second there is a purpose of the business, which might be to furnish convenient, low cost transportation for the average person. The next level of hierarchy contains more specific objectives, such as those in the key result areas. These areas are the ones in which the performance is essential for the success of the enterprise.

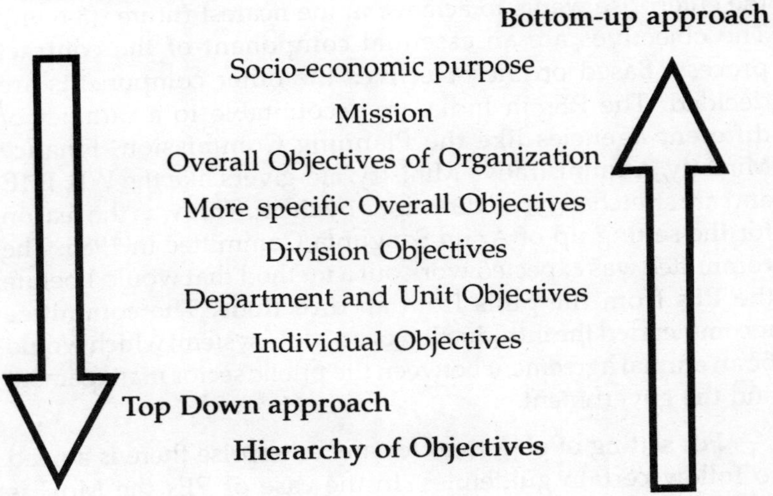

Bottom-up approach

Socio-economic purpose

Mission

Overall Objectives of Organization

More specific Overall Objectives

Division Objectives

Department and Unit Objectives

Individual Objectives

Top Down approach

Hierarchy of Objectives

Management by Objectives

Management by Objectives (MbO) is now practised round the world. MbO in the words of George S. Odiorne is defined as,

"Management by objectives is a comprehensive managerial system that integrates many key managerial activities in a systematic manner and that is consciously directed towards the effective and efficient achievement of organizational and individual objectives."

Fredrich V. Malek, a former special assistant to the President of United States, recognized the need for Management by Objectives (MbO) in government. For any government enterprise, in order to be managed efficiently, it clearly needs a system for setting priorities, pinpointing responsibilities requiring follow-through, and generating feedback that could be monitored and evaluated from the top.

As the PEs being government run organizations were also made a part of the system of controls by objectives. Objectives of the enterprise are the major feature of the performance contract in India. The objective of the enterprise is actually the short-term reachable goals of the enterprise. It highlights what the enterprise wants to achieve in the nearest future (3-6 yr.). The objectives are an essential component of the contract process. Based on the objectives the other components are decided. The PEs in India are accountable to a number of different agencies like the Planning Commission, Finance Ministry, Administrative Ministry, aid givers like the WB, IMF, and are stretched on all directions by them. This was the reason for the setting up of Arjun Sengupta Committee in 1985. The committee was expected work out a method that would liberate the PEs from the pulls from all directions. The committee recommended the introduction of an MoU system, which would be an annual agreement between the public sector management and the government.

For setting of objectives for any enterprise there is a need to follow certain guidelines. In the case of PEs the MoU is formulated on the basis of guidelines supplied by the Department of Public Enterprises. The specific guidelines are issued at the beginning of the financial year to all the enterprises and the contract is designed based on theses guidelines.

There are a number of benefits of introducing a system of assessment based on the objectives set for the enterprises. With the introduction of this system there are possibilities of improving the management and clarification of organizational goals. It also enhances the encouragement of personal commitment to work and at the same time increases the effective controls over the system. The two features of autonomy and accountability are achieved at the same time with the introduction of MbO.

There are a few disadvantages with the system of MBO. It is generally seen that there are serious possibilities that the goal setters themselves might not be very clear about the ideas of the real objectives of the enterprise. This might lead to failure to give guidance to goal setters and difficulty in goal settings. The lack of clarity of goals is considered as one of the major reasons for the failure of the public sector, in India. With the introduction of objectives there is very little room for flexibility for the mangers. The objectives also have the drawback of emphasizing only the short-term benefits of the organization, as they seldom reflect the enterprises long term plans.

Criteria

The next major component of the contract is the performance criteria or indicators. Criteria are decided before entering into the contract and based on the criteria, weightages are assigned to them. The selection of proper criteria is considered to be as important as the selection of an appropriate measure. Prajapathi Trivedi (1988) spelt out certain prerequisites for selection of criteria. He says that regarding the performance criteria there are a few preconditions, which have to be fulfilled for the contracts to be a success. Performance criteria included in the contract must be clearly defined and understood. The mission of the enterprise, the objective of the enterprise, the criteria should be clearly spelt out. Only then will it be possible to decide whether the enterprise has covered the target, which it was expected at the end of the year.

Performance criteria should be 'fair' to the manager and it should encompass only areas within the control of the PE management. If the criteria decided is beyond the control of the enterprise manager it would be practically impossible for him to reach the targets that have been specified.

Performance criteria should be fair to the country. The performance criteria decided should be in accordance to the ideology of the nation. If the country is following a mixed economy pattern where it has not given itself to the commercial forces the assessment also should accordingly. At the same time if the country is totally a privately managed one it can opt for harsh financial targets and lead the enterprises towards achieving them. It is not sufficient that the contracts are made keeping in mind the criteria for measurement, it has to also look into the necessary institutional arrangements, which are available, for fulfilling the contract terms. The institutional arrangements need to be compatible with the purpose of the enterprise, which would ensure positive results.

Suresh Kumar in his observations on the Indian MoU system and particularly highlighting upon the selection of criteria has given the following as very desirable, Performance criteria , like Corporate Objectives should be limited. There should be congruence between the objectives and the performance criteria. There should not be any duplication in the selection of criteria. Selected performance criteria's should be measurable and their evaluation method pre-determined and laid down in the MoU.

The corporate objectives should sharply focus the ideology of the enterprise. There is a need for the objectives to be unambiguous and clear. Based on the goals of the enterprise, the criteria have to be selected. There has to be a complete congruence between the objectives of the enterprise and the performance criteria. The criteria selected must be clear and must not be overlapping, as this will hamper the results and the actual performance of the enterprise will not be highlighted. The criteria selected for the evaluation process must be verified and measurable. They should be properly laid down in the MoU. Pakistan signaling system aims at motivating management to maximize return on the capital. In order to attain this objective, attempt is made to evolve primary criteria of evaluation, which reflects the improvement in real productivity, which in turn leads to an increase in socially relevant profit. The Pakistani Signaling system has the important feature like the profit (real). This is a factor, which is not the basis for foundation of the PEs as their objective is achieving the social profitability. Public profits are private profits adjusted for those elements not deemed relevant to a public enterprise. Pakistanis Signaling system is based on the principle that public enterprise management should be appropriately guided to aim at improving real productivity. Its efforts should be acknowledged and rewarded by an incentive system. Deciding on the performance criteria is a crucial exercise for the enterprises. The success of any contract depends on the type of criteria that has been selected. The true performance of an organization is reflected only when proper criteria are selected.

Target- Setting Process

Targets

Performance contracts set targets for all goals and indicators of a PE, and these may include targets in non-financial areas apart from the financial ones, such as personnel; marketing and technological development, which are covered by a corporate plan but not usually by a budget. Targets are based on what the enterprise can reasonably achieve, given the expected policy environment, market prices, planned capital expenditures, and the level of management autonomy where there is a performance variable. For each indicator a rage of values is set so that performance can be graded, e.g. as excellent, good, fair, poor or bad).

Targets are individual to an enterprise and to a particular period. The same targets for profitability should not be applied to all PEs, or even to a group of similar enterprises. Targets, should be set which reflect each enterprise's exogenous conditions, such as inherited plant and equipment, labour force and local infrastructure.

A typical Indian performance contract will have the

following elements in it; (fig-approx.)

1) Physical Factors-55 2) Project Implementation-3

3) Energy-5 4) Environment-5

5) MoU related-0 6) Financial -25

7) HRD-7

A typical Indian MoU would contain components like the physical factors which would include production, exploration, distribution, sales etc. It comprises the major part of the contract. The project implementation is also spelt out in the contract, as to how successful the enterprise has been in completing the projects assigned to them. Factors relating to energy consumption and its effect on the environmental conditions also figure out in the contract. The financial performance of the enterprise i.e., profitability, productivity etc. is brought in through these parameters. The financial factors spell out the real performance of the enterprise. There are other non-financial parameters like the HRD related issues and MoU related issues, which highlight in the MoU.

A typical Pakistani performance contract negotiates the three agreed criteria as shown below. The concerned parties may give relative priority to these criteria in terms of weights as:

Production : 30%

Profit : 50%

Project implementation : 20%

The weights may be specified as percentages when they should add to 100. Alternately, the weights may be fractions adding up to one, like 0.03, 0.50, 0.20, which adds to 1.00.

Pakistan signaling system aims at motivating management to maximize return on the capital. In order to attain this objective, attempt is made to evolve primary criteria of evaluation, which reflects the improvement in real productivity. This in turn leads to an increase in socially relevant profit. The

Pakistani Signaling System has the important feature like the profit (real). This is a factor, which is not the basis for foundation of the PEs as their objective is achieving the social profitability. Public profits are private profits adjusted for those elements not deemed relevant to a public enterprise. Pakistani Signaling system is based on the principle that public enterprise management should be appropriately guided to aim at improving real productivity and efforts acknowledged and rewarded by an Incentive System. Deciding on the performance criteria is a crucial exercise for the enterprises. The success of any contract depends on the type of criteria that has been selected. The true performance of an organization is reflected only when proper criteria are selected.

Target level

Targets should be neither too low that they are achieved without effort nor so high that manager considers them as unachievable, resulting in a counter-productive effect. Managers often complain that if they achieve a target, it is raised the next year. The target-setters should distinguish between targets, which can be raised without limit, such as profitability, and targets, which have physical limits, such as capacity utilization. Otherwise this may lead to the tendency for the enterprises to set targets in such a way that it is very much within the reach of the enterprise. This distorted feature has been noticed in the enterprises during the study and this happens to be one of the reasons for the failure of the system. Asymmetry of information between an enterprise and target-setters (the information superiority of those who are choose to the production process) allows the enterprise to get the targets it wants through selective disclosure of information.

For each indicator there should be a target value to motivate the managers. The government has a great interest in each target because it represents the enterprise's intended contribution to a public goal. The Ministry of Finance, for instance, will be concerned with profit and how much of that it will receive as income tax, interest, dividend, etc. It is also concerned about what subsidy the enterprise will need. The government is concerned that the targets are challenging and that they, as owners of the enterprise, get value of money spent. Larger and stronger PEs may be able to negotiate lower targets. Government negotiators should aim to be equally tough with all enterprises.

The targets should be set in such a way that they are compatible in the contracting system as a whole. It is generally observed that the target levels assigned to each criteria depends on the past performance on that particular criteria and the expectations of its performance on that particular criteria in the coming years. This process is greatly influenced by the information flow between the government and the PE. There is a tendency to give lower targets and get away with better performance.

Efficient target setting should be carried out in a participatory process. Without this approach, targets tend to take the form of formal directives, which are often overtly accepted and covertly resisted. Targets should be clear-cut. Targets should neither be too low or too high. This would give wrong signals to the managers. Each enterprise must be looked at in its own unique environment which must be taken into account. The targets must ensure that generation of surplus is significantly more than distribution by way of bonus. Targets must take into account the social tasks, which are taken up by the enterprises.

The target setting exercise in Pakistan is done by the Expert Advisory Cell. It ensures that the targets are clear cut and neither too high nor too low. The targets are set keeping in mind the environment in which the PE is working. It is ensured by the cell that the targets take care of the surplus factor which would go as a bonus at the same time consider the social accountability of the enterprise.

Fundamental For Target Setting

In principle, there are three possible bases for setting future enterprise targets.

Inter-firm comparison: the recent performance of comparable firms, adjusted for differe ce in circumstances and expected future exogenous change.

Inter-year comparison: past performance of the enterprise, adjusted for exogenous change.

Inter-year method: The production engineering or work-study estimate, applying "reasonable" standards to each cost and revenue element in each activity and expected values of exogenous variables. A mixture of methods may be used, and the same mixture should then apply to all public enterprises in each period. Qualitative indicators are usually assessed retrospectively, using the inter-year method.

Comparison with other firms is not usually possible for monopoly enterprise, except where they are broken up regionally and the regional bodies can be compared. International comparisons of firms are rarely easy, because differences in cost condition, markets, and fiscal and regulatory requirements are not readily known as adjusted for.

Past performance is a poor indicator of potential performance. Nevertheless, trend analysis may still be used as a basis for assessing performance improvement, on which incentives can be based. If performance contracting is conceived as an instrument for progressive improvement of performance, then past performance adjusted for exogenous change is a sufficient standard.

The Korean performance contracts make extensive use of regression analyses of past data. Seven-year time series analysis is made for most of the quantitative indicators. From these it is possible to project the expected targets for the following years, and also the standard deviation. This method is said to simplify target setting and reduce controversy. However, it rests on the assumption that the future will be a simple projection of the past.

Yardstick competition is applied by a target-setter knowing

the unit costs in similar enterprises. In Bangladesh, for example, a detailed system of comparing cotton textile mills is used by the Bangladesh Textile Mills Corporation. The target is set by reference to the average enterprise, or the most efficient enterprise, taking the best performance on each activity. The United Kingdom Audit Commission has a tradition of "inter-firm" comparisons of local authority performance, which indicates that such comparisons may be valid and useful, despite disputes on their interpretation.

Work study and management audit is also used to set up targets, which represent reasonably efficient performance. Though this method is slow and costly. The United Kingdom Monopolies and Mergers Commission carries out in-depth review of efficiency as required by the Department of Trade and Industry. The MMC examines the trend of performance indicators, such as unit costs and quality, and management processes. For want of valid international or intra-national comparisons of performance indicators, it tends to conform to widely accepted standards of management practices.

Management Participation

One technique that has been given strong support as the result of motivation theory is the increased awareness and use of participation. In addition to this most people in the center of an operation have knowledge both of problems and of solutions to them. As a consequence, the right kind of participation yields both motivation and knowledge valuable for an enterprise success.

Targets should be negotiated between the government and management and should not be imposed. Certainly, the government is in a position to set whatever targets it likes and to apply sanctions. The principle of negotiation is the principle of participatory management under another name. PE managers are encouraged to participate in setting their targets so that they "internalize" them and are more committed. In fact, most contracting systems require initial targets to be proposed by the management. Korea is an exception where the

Task Force sets targets in a top-down fashion. The mode of target setting is very much affected by the information of the parties.

The benefits of participation are not confined to the government management interface. It is apparent that improvement of performance can arise only by changes in behavior at the operating level. Therefore, there should be an internal dialogue through all levels of the enterprise extending the corporate goal and incentives to divisions and sections of the enterprise.

Period of Contract

The key to choosing the right planning period lies in logical planning. Planning encompasses a future period of time necessary to fulfill through a series of actions and commitments made. Since the capital which is the lifeline of an organization is normally limited in relation to the firm needs. Its expenditure must be accompanied by a reasonable possibility of recovering it, plus a return on investment, through operations.

Targets may be set for each year in a multi-year agreement or for a single year only. Irrespective of the period of agreement, it is better to set short-period targets. If targets are set for a number of years ahead, they are likely to be soon outdated by events. So they may be updated and revised each year as in a rolling plan. The performance contracts in Kenya provide examples of this.

Early French contracts were made to terminate with the National Plan. The Sixth Plan in 1975 and the Seventh Plan in 1980 were seen as instruments for the implementation of National Plan targets. in several countries, only the first year's targets are used for purposes of performance evaluation, and subsequent year's targets are reset on an Annual Rolling Plan basis.

In the case of India targets are made annually coinciding with the Annual Plans of the enterprises. During the survey of 109 MoU signing enterprises it was noted that the enterprises varied in their views on the period of the contract. While production companies accepted the time span of one year the companies which were in the construction and exploration business were of the view that the contracts should be for a longer period. They suggested that the period should be at least for 24-36 months, which is minimum time period for completion of a project.

Pakistani contracts made under the signaling system were initially for one year. However, this reflected the lack of corporate plans at that time, and it was anticipated that longer time horizons would be adopted with the development of corporate planning by enterprises.

In Gambia, for instance, performance contracts have been for four years. They spell out the goals of the enterprise, and autonomy for the management. The targets are separately negotiated each year and signed at the technical level. These are the basis on which annual performance is evaluated and rewarded or penalized.

Ideally targets may be set for each year only. Irrespective of the period of the agreement, it is better to set short-period targets within a medium-term-planning framework. If targets are set for a number of years ahead, they are likely to be soon outdated by events, so they may be updated and revised each year.

Monitoring and Control

The managerial function of controlling is the measurement and correction of performance in order to make sure that the enterprise objectives and the plans devised to attain them are accomplished. Planning and controlling are closely related. Without objectives and plans, control is not possible, because performance has to be compared against some established criteria. The basic control process, wherever applied and whatever is being controlled involves three steps:

Establishing standards: plans are yardsticks against which manager's device controls. Standards are actually the criteria for performance. They are selected points in the entire planning process. Based on these measures of performance are made so that managers can receive signals about how things are going.

Measuring performance against the standards: The next step in control process is the measurement of performance. If standards are appropriately drawn and if means are available to determine the progress, the appraisal of performance can be done.

Correcting variations from standards and plans: if the performance is measured correctly, then it is possible to straighten the deviations. Performance contracting is a cyclical process in which results are fed back to the government and public enterprise. This is done in order to make correction for short-term variances form contract and this process is called monitoring. This could be represented by the feed back loop of control as below.

Desired Performance	Actual Performance	Measurement of actual	Comparison of Performance against standards
Implementation of Corrections	Program of corrective action	Analysis of causes of deviation	Identification of deviations

Feedback Loop of Management Control

In the case of the Indian MoU process, the monitoring and control over the contracts is done at the Bureau of Public Enterprises. This institution is responsible for preparing the contracts, getting the contracts signed and monitoring the contracts as well. Public Enterprise Information Systems are usually organized around accounting systems. There is a need for standardization, so that data is comparable. In many countries, public enterprises are required to use the same accounting standards as applied to private businesses. The International Federation of Accountants (IFAC 1989) has recommended this, i.e. that public enterprises follow National Accounting Standards where these exist, otherwise the IFAC/

IASC International Accounting Standards.

Evaluation

Evaluation is to put a value on the performance for the period. This is done by comparing actual performance with the contract goals and targets and analyzing the reasons for shortfalls and over-target achievements. Most governments see this entirely in terms of enterprise performance, not their own. In other words, performance contracts are thought of as extension of budgets. An exception is India, where a High-Power Committee, chaired by the Cabinet Secretary, examines performance of both sides impartially.

After expert analysis, there should always be a final evaluation meeting between the contracting parties to discuss performance and draw out lessons that can be applied in future periods. In the popular mind, PEs are evaluated largely on financial profitability, for want of any other clear criterion. Profit is not only a means of survival traditionally it is the way the score is kept. Even when performance contracts are set out there is a strong tendency for the public to misinterpret the resulting score as a proxy for profitability, or perhaps efficiency. In Korea, however, there appears to have been wide public acceptance of the performance indices coming out of the evaluation process, and the ranking of PEs each year.

Let us consider the example of evaluation of a PE with the following performance:

Criteria	*Unit*	*Weight*	*Score*		
			1.0	*0.8*	*0.25*
Production (tones)	Thousand	0.3	>>22	20	<<15
Profit	Million (currency units)	0.5	>>25	20	<<18
Project imple-mentation	Million (currency units)	0.2	>>30	25	<<20

Source: A Handbook for Performance Contracting, UN Publication, 1995.

Production	26,000
Profit	12 million currency units
Project Implementation	26 million currency units

The scores will be calculated as,

If the actual production lies anywhere between 20,000 tones and 22,000 tones, the score will be only 0.8 (or 80 %). Only when it exceeds 22,000 tones will the value jump to 1.00 (or 100 %). In the above case, for production the achievement of 26,000 tones is above the score target for 1.0. So the score value is 1.0 x weightage = 1.0 x 0.3 = 0.3.

For profit, the score is 0.25 as the achievement is below the score target of 18 million for minimum score. The score value is 0.25 x 0.5 (weightage) = 0.125.

For project implementation the score is 0.8 as the actual is between 250 million and 300 million. The score value is 0.8 x 0.2 = 0.160.

The composite score = 0.3+0.125+0.160=0.585. In other words the entire enterprise has obtained a total of 58.5 % marks in overall performance.

Audit & Accountability

Audit closes the circle of public accountability. PEs are normally subject to independent and expert audit, but audit institutions typically confine the scope of their audit to the accuracy of the financial records and accounts and compliance with laws and regulations. Auditors cannot audit the efficiency or effectiveness of a PE without an operational definition of goals. Auditors welcome performance contracting, as it provides the necessary basis for performance audit of PEs.

Performance contracting raises the stakes for enterprise managers, especially where their pay depends on the final score. Internal monitoring and reporting systems is subject to increasing pressures. An effective system of internal control is the first line of defense. It is also necessary to guard against management increasing their apparent profit by changing their accounting practices; any such changes should be separately disclosed in the accounts or auditor' report.

In some countries there are parliamentary committees which review PE performance. These bodies should also welcome contracts as bases for their review. Other channels of accountability may be opened up. The success of the Korean system has been due not only to its technical features but also to the interest and support shown by the President and the Deputy Prime Minister and the media publicity attending the system. The secrecy that surrounds the performance of PEs in many countries may be dispelled through open and transparent publication of performance contracts and evaluation reports for PEs in competitive markets, confidential data may be edited out.

Rewards & Penalties

The PE managers are paid the same for poor performance as for good performance. Pay is usually based on civil service scales, which in many countries are significantly lower than those of their counterparts in the private sector. Non-pecuniary rewards do exist but are small and uncertain. PE managers are seldom removed for incompetence. Even criminal activity is seldom punished. The result is management weakness, characterized by low morale, feeling of frustration, failure to apply management skills and techniques, and dysfunctional attitudes.

Summing Up

The performance contracts contain a number of features, which encompass the various facets of PEs, like the mission, objectives, performance criteria, weightages, target values. The contracts must be made meticulously and properly evaluated if the real performance of the enterprise has to be reflected through it. During discussions with the senior officials of the enterprises dealing with the MoU it was observed that it is a highly confidential exercise. The purpose with which the system of contracts was started in India and other countries was to improve autonomy and strengthen accountability simultaneously. But the system seems to have made little impact regarding the two important issues of autonomy and accountability, which left the functionaries dissatisfied. If the system of MoU were to be implemented as per the design it would have certainly shown positive results. The problem lies at the implementation level of the system and not at its conception.

References

1. Bureau of Public Enterprise, *Annual Survey Report,* GOI, Part 1. 1996-97 and various issues.
2. *Estimates Committee,* Second Lok Sabha, 23rd Report, p. 12.
3. Geeta, P., *Memorandum of Understanding in Central Public Enterprises: A Study of Select Public Sector Undertakings in India,* Doctoral Thesis, Dept. of Business Management, OU, Hyderabad, 2000.
4. Gupta, K.R., *Economics & Management of Public Enterprises,* Atlantic, New Delhi, 1984, p. 192.
5. Jones, Morris, W.H, *The Government and Politics in India,* pp. 195-96.
6. Kapur, A.C, *Select Constitutions,* S. Chand & Company, New Delhi, 1983, 11th Edition, p. 250.
7. Narain, Laxmi, *Public Enterprise Management,* S. Chand & Company, New Delhi, 1988, p. 260.
8. Narain, Laxmi, *Public Enterprise Management,* S. Chand & Company, New Delhi, 1988, p. 280.
9. Narain, Laxmi, *Public Enterprise Management,* S. Chand & Company, New Delhi, 1988, p. 254.
10. Shrivastava, Mohan, *Problem of Public Accountability of Public Enterprises,* Uppal, New Delhi, 1986, p. 144.
11. Thomas Peters and Robert Waterman, *In Search of Excellence,* New York, Harper & Row, 1982.

Appendix – 1

REPORT OF THE COMMITTEE TO REVIEW POLICY FOR PUBLIC ENTERPRISES (ARJUN SENGUPTA COMMITTEE REPORT)

1.1 The foundations of the public sector in India go back to the early years of planning. The Industrial Policy Resolution of 30th April 1956, which is still the basis of present policy, proposed that all basic and strategic industries and public utilities should be in the public sector given the objective of a socialistic pattern of society and the need for planned and rapid development. The intimate connection between planning and growth of public enterprises was spelt out more clearly in the Second Five Year Plan which stated that "The use of modern technology requires large scale production and a unified control and allocation of resources in certain major lines of activity. These include exploitation of minerals, and basic and capital goods industries which are major determinants of the rate of growth of the economy. The responsibility for new developments in these fields must be undertaken in the main by the State, and the existing units have also to fall in line with the emerging pattern. Public ownership, partial or complete, and public control or participation in management are specially required in those fields in which technological considerations tend towards a concentration of economic power and of wealth."

1.2 In terms of the objectives specified in the Industrial Policy Resolution, public enterprises have certainly established their dominance in basic and strategic industries like coal, petroleum, steel, non-ferrous metals, heavy engineering, etc. which are listed in Schedule 'A' of the Resolution and a substantial presence in industries like machine tools, fertilisers, basic and intermediate chemicals, drugs, etc., which are listed in Schedule "B'. Public enterprises have achieved a great deal in terms of their contribution to quantitative targets of production, to the establishment of a modern industrial structure, to balanced regional development and to the formation of technological skills. They have become principal instruments of planning in India, occupying commanding heights of the economy, controlling and directing in a large measure the whole course of its development.

1.3 Over the period of last 30 years of more, the growth of the public enterprises has been phenomenal in terms of investment and production as well as the scope of activities. At the end of 1983-84 the capital employed in the central public enterprises alone stood at Rs. 32,202 crores having a total turn over of Rs. 46,777 crores. From only 5 Enterprises on 1st April 1951, they have grown to 209 by April 1983, employing more than 2 million people. It has spread over all parts of India. Its coverage has extended beyond the basic and heavy industries into light manufacturing, variety of consumer goods, electronics, high-tech products, construction, consultancy services and even tourism and hotel industries.

But in spite of this phenomenal growth, the overall performance has remained unsatisfactory especially in terms of their contribution to the generation of resources and financial profitability. For example, the Sixth Plan assumed an overall net rate of return of 8 percent per annum increasing to 10 percent in 1984-85 for all public enterprises in constant prices. This has not been achieved and the profitability of the enterprises has declined over time. The provisional results for the year 1983-84 indicate that in aggregate terms public enterprises have made a net profit of Rs. 32.2 crores as against a profit of Rs. 617.9 crores in 1982-83 and Rs. 445.9 crores in 1981-82. Consequently, the net contribution of public enterprises to the requirement of funds for their investment proposals is small, resulting in pressure on budgetary resources. The ability of the budget to finance further public investment has been seriously eroded because of low returns on past investment and rising burden of Defence and other non-plan expenditure.

1.4 The rationale of the operation of public enterprises and the expectation that the management should be run on commercial and business lines, that they should earn profits to contribute to the revenues of the State, that they should be judged for their total results and subject to these performance criteria they should have full freedom of operation, were clearly set out in the Industrial Policy Resolution of 1956 as quoted below:

"With the growing participation of the State in industry and trade, the manner in which these activities should be conducted and managed assume considerable importance. Speedy decisions and a willingness to assume responsibility are essential if these enterprises are to succeed. For this, wherever possible, there should be decentralisation of authority and their management should be along business lines.

> It is to be expected that public enterprises will augment the revenues of the State and provide resources for further development in fresh fields. But such enterprises may sometimes incur losses. Public enterprises have to be judged by their total results and in their working they should have the largest possible measure of freedom......"

In accordance with this rationale most of the activities of the public sector were organised in the form of corporations or companies set up either under the Statute or under the Companies Act while some activities continued to be organised within the framework of departmental undertakings or statutory boards; their numbers are few and operational methods are dictated by specific requirements of the Government. For this Report, the recommendations will pertain only to public enterprises set up as corporations or companies, which as mentioned above were supposed to function "along business lines".

1.5 The expectation that public enterprises as commercial ventures should "augment the revenues of the State" and provide a return which can be used for further investment and growth has not been fulfilled. Even for units which were making losses because of the nature of products or because of their serving some specified social objectives, the efficiency of operation has often deteriorated. In actual practice, the freedom of operation of the management has been quite often curtailed or interfered with by formal or informal Government intervention. While the public enterprises were to be judged by their "total results" the monitoring and evaluation system of the Government has not been adequate to the task. The strict enforcement of performance standards on public enterprises would entail having a closer look at the constraints of the operation. While some of these arise from the general nature of our economic structure and some from incorrect investment decisions of the past, others stem from poor managerial practices within the enterprises and formal and informal interference by Government.

1.6 The primary objective of this Report is to consider these constraints and to suggest measure to change the whole environment of operation of public enterprises so that their performance can effectively improve. A new look at Government – Public Enterprise relations is essential if performance standards are to be enforced, as it would not be realistic to expect results without giving necessary autonomy to the enterprises with regard to the decisions which affect such results. Moreover, the size and pattern of public sector is now such that the modalities of instructions which may have been appropriate with a few pioneering enterprises, may not be as useful when enterprises have grown both in numbers and in size as well as in their scope of operation. A different approach to the role of public enterprises in plan development is now required and that is the task the Committee addresses itself to in the rest of the Report.

II. Public Enterprises and National Planning

2.1 Public enterprises in India have to function within the framework of planning and, in many areas they are in effect the principal instruments for the realisation of plan objectives. Hence, the relationship between the Ministries and Departments of Government of India and the enterprises cannot be reduced to the usual annual interaction between shareholders and corporate management. A more active interaction between the Government and the enterprise is unavoidable in critical areas like strategic planning, setting up of investment priorities and formulation of large projects. Moreover, public enterprises are not islands unto themselves and decisions taken by one enterprise affect the fortunes of others. Therefore, some arrangement for coordination becomes necessary of the production and investment decisions as well as wages, employment, pricing and technology policies of the different enterprises. However, it would not be desirable to subject all decisions to scrutiny and approval of the Government. Direct intervention, to be effective, has to be limited and the crucial task would be to define clearly the areas where compulsions of planning require close coordination of economy-wide and enterprise-level plans.

2.2 Public enterprises in India operate in a large number of sectors; while some are in the core sector, others are not. In our opinion, a careful dovetailing of all the plans of public enterprises and the National Plan is required only in a few core sectors which are critical for the planned development of the country because they are closely linked with other sectors. In fact, in these sectors, a measure of central intervention is required not merely in the case of public enterprises, but also in similar private enterprises. However in practice in most of these core sectors, public enterprises account for the bulk of available capacity and have a near monopolistic position. These sectors generally operate in a non-competitive environment, with a few producers, and in many cases, with price and/or distribution controls. Most of the large projects in the industrial fields also fall within this core sector.

2.3 We would suggest that for the purpose of defining Government Public Enterprise relations, the following sectors be considered as core sectors:

Coal and lignite

Crude oil, petroleum and natural gas

Power

Primary steel production

Primary production of aluminium, copper, lead, zinc and nickel

Fertilizers

Primary production of petrochemical intermediates

It may be noted that in national planning, apart from these, the concept of the core will also include other sectors like agriculture, irrigation, railways, etc. But in these, investments are generally not undertaken by central public enterprises. These are, therefore, not taken into account in our report.

2.4 Public enterprises operating in the core sector will naturally have to interact intensively with the Ministries or departments of the Government of India with regard to matters like investment planning, price fixation and financial management. Their plans will have to be integrated into the National Plan as is the case at present. However this would not preclude modifications in the present procedures to allow for a greater measure of autonomy. As for public enterprises in the non-core sector we would recommend that their plans be integrated into the National Plan only in an indicative sense and such units would continue to be governed by the indicative and regulatory framework of planning as applicable for all similar private sector units. Even in the non-core sector, it will be necessary to distinguish between units which are financially viable and others which incur losses, hence imposing a draft on budgetary resources.

2.5 Thus, from the point of view of planning and budgetary management, public enterprises may be grouped as follows:

a) Enterprises operating in the core sector as defined in paragraph 2.3 above;

b) Financially viable enterprises in the non-core sector, and

c) Enterprises in the non-core sector incurring losses

This broad grouping has to be taken into account in defining the policy framework for regulating interaction between the Government and the public enterprises.

2.6 As we see it, this interaction, where the Government's policies are determined by the priorities and compulsions of planned development and public enterprises are to serve as instruments of implementation of these policies, the central issue is to find the right balance between autonomy and accountability of the enterprises. Autonomy, in this context, would mean the ability of an enterprise management to take decisions freely based on economic consideration, on matters for which they are to be held responsible. Accountability itself has to be defined in terms of well-specified performance criteria and the degree of success in the fulfillment of specific task assigned to public enterprises. In our view this would require changes in:

- The organisational structure of public enterprises and their relations with the Government;
- The procedures and regulations which determine the degree of autonomy of public enterprises;
- The system of performance evaluation and accountability;
- The code of conduct that governs the exercise of authority in the Government and in public enterprises.

2.7 In what follows we deal specifically with these areas and suggest certain changes which in our view will increase the degree of autonomy of public enterprises, enforce accountability for performance effectively and contribute thereby to its better performance.

III. Organisational Structure of Public Enterprises

3.1 The Committee has discussed the issues regarding the appropriate organisational structure of Public Enterprises which would ensure their autonomy and also facilitate their efficient functioning. The Committee's recommendations on this subject are submitted below.

3.2 The autonomy of Public Enterprises consists in the ability of its management to exercise the freedom of action in day-to-day operations, in taking all decisions affecting their performance without being restrained by any external authority, such as the Government. It should, however be recognised that in our situation there are some inherent limitations on this autonomy.

3.3 First, the Government of India is responsible to Parliament and if questions are raised in Parliament about the policies, performance and operation of any public sector enterprise, the Minister has to provide answers and accept the responsibility for the functioning of that enterprise. Because of this accountability to Parliament, public enterprises cannot be completely free from governmental scrutiny, not only of their general policies but occasionally also of some aspects of their day-to-day operations, where some lapses or abuse of public funds may be involved. Parliament's authority in such matters is supreme but it may be necessary to evolve a convention by which Members of Parliament accept some self-imposed restraints on the nature of questions they ask. The Committee has considered these issues in a later chapter.

3.4 Further, in our framework of economic planning, the policies of public enterprises, their investment decisions, their programmes for growth, expansion, etc. have to be dovetailed to national priorities and mobilisation and allocation of resources. Even when the investment and expenditure decisions of some of these enterprises do not depend upon the government's budgetary support, their claim on the total economic resources, especially in the core sector. Etc. may be so important as to require their reconciliation with the national plan objectives.

3.5 Similarly, wage and employment policies of different public enterprises would have implications for other enterprises and the national economy and, hence, will have to be subjected to some overall coordination.

3.6 There are also several enterprises which are making losses and which come to the Government for financial support in order to survive and it is not always possible for the Government to allow the companies to be liquidated as in the private sector. It will, therefore, be necessary for the government to go into not only the broad policy decisions of these companies but also their day-to-day operations, so that their performance can be improved and losses reduced.

3.7 It will, therefore, be unrealistic think that the public enterprises could be made completely autonomous and independent from Government's supervision. Most Chief Executives of public enterprises recognise this fact of life and it appeared from the discussions the Committee had with all concerned that the basic problem was not that the Government's supervision or guidance was avoidable, but that it was often excessive and not based on well established rules and conventions. More often, they are not related to efficient functioning or for achieving the objectives of the Enterprise.

3.8 The need is, therefore, to evolve a set of rules and conventions by which the Government can help in the better functioning of the public enterprises and work out an organisational pattern which would reduce the points of intervention by the government in the management of the enterprises, without minimising the Government's right to have needed information for evaluating performance. It is recognised by all that, on paper, managements of public enterprises enjoy large autonomy, sometimes much more than even by the private sector managements. However, in practice, information and formal involvement of Ministries and Departments take place in areas wholly within the decision making powers of public enterprise management.

3.9 The Committee attaches considerable importance to devising a proper organisational structure for public enterprises in the belief that certain forms of organisations, rather than others, can be more conducive to the efficient functioning of the public enterprises through a proper division of authority and responsibility between the Government and the public enterprise management. Given this division, the system should run by established rules and not by arbitrary exercise of discretion.

3.10 In our approach Government should be primarily concerned with overall strategic planning and policy rather than with day-to-day functioning of the public enterprises. Government's responsibility is to ensure that public money invested in these enterprises earns an appropriate rate of return, and that the functioning of these enterprises earns an appropriate rate of return, and that the functioning of these enterprises is consistent with plan objectives, including those related to employment, fair pricing regional dispersal of industries and efficient use of scarce resource. Once the goals have been mutually agreed to, the enterprises should be allowed to operate without further intervention by the Government in day-to-day functioning. The enterprises should, however, be held strictly accountable for their performance in relation to the goals set and there should be an appropriate mechanism for evaluation of their performance.

3.11 The Committee discussed, the length, alternative models of organisational structure for public enterprises, under which there will be a clear division of responsibility between the Government, as represented by the Ministry or Department, and the management of these enterprises, as represented by Board of Directors or the Chief Executive. In short, the Ministry should be responsible for the implementation of that policy, and the interaction between them should be such as to facilitate the exercise of overall Government supervision, without impairing the efficiency of operation of the enterprise. Such an organisational structure should keep the operations of an enterprise at "arm's length" from the government and promote decentralised decision-making within the enterprise.

3.12 One such form of organisation, widely practiced in many European countries is that of a "Holding Company". While there are differences in models prevailing in different countries, basically Government's interface with the public enterprises takes place under these models at the level of the Board of the Holding Company which is responsible for day-to-day operations of a number of subsidiary companies. The Government in turn sets the goals and targets for the Holding Company and receives periodical performance reports regarding the overall efficiency of the latter's operations. The administrative responsibility in respect of individual companies is that of the Holding Company and the Government itself does not come in day-to-day contact with the individual companies.

3.13 Currently, a Ministry in-charge of a number of public enterprises, which are mostly unitary companies, not only gets involved with the Management of the enterprise but also in the coordination of decisions and activities of the different companies. The logic of "Holding Company" structure is to introduce an intermediate level of management i.e., the Board of the Holding Company between the Ministry and the Companies, reconstituted as subsidiary companies. The Board of the Holding Company also takes up the job of the coordination between the subsidiary companies. As a result, the interface between the Government and the subsidiary companies is minimised without sacrificing the essential need for coordination of the operation of the companies.

3.14 The Committee considered also the possibility of reorganising the existing unitary companies into what can be called Apex Companies with a Board of Directors, at the Apex level, about a number of Divisions or Units which would be either profit or cost centres. The objective would be to have centralised policymaking with decentralised operation and administration. A local management committee in each division or unit may control the operation of the division or unit with adequate delegation of authority by the Apex Board.

3.15 While the Committee recognised that uniform structure for all public enterprises may not be either feasible or desirable it felt that the concept of Holding Companies provided a reasonable framework of organisational structure. Where a Holding Company cannot be formed it, recommended structuring the Unitary Companies as Apex Companies on the lines as defined above. The relationship between Holding Companies and the Government should equally apply to apex Unitary Companies. The Government will ensure that the policies of the Holding or Apex Company are in line with the national plan objectives and general policies of the Government. But will have no direct dealings with the Subsidiary Company or Divisions of the Holding or Apex Company as the case may be.

3.16 The relationship between the Holding Company or the Apex Company and the Subsidiary Companies or Divisions would be based, as mentioned earlier, on the principle of decentralisation. The subsidiary companies or divisions concerned would be delegated all the authority needed for ensuring the fulfillment of targets and operational efficiency. The Boards of the Holding Company or the Apex Company as the case may be would evaluate their performance on the basis of well defined criteria and performance parameters. The Board of the Apex or Holding Company will coordinate the operations of Subsidiary Companies or Divisions under their charge and supervise their functioning as well as employment, recruitment, wages, financial and pricing policies.

3.17 In this framework, whether public enterprises will be reorganised in the form of Holding Companies with Subsidiary Companies or in the form of an Apex Company with divisions as profit or cost centres will depend upon the size of the enterprises concerned, the technological interdependence between enterprises and the need for effective coordination of the decisions at different levels of management. If interaction between the Government and the public enterprises is limited, as suggested, only to the overall policies and performance evaluation as agreed with the Board of the Holding Company or Apex Company, leaving the subsidiary companies or Divisions to interact only with the respective parent organisations, the autonomy of the public enterprises may not be affected.

3.18 The Committee considered that the Holding Company structure is more useful both for an effective evaluation and monitoring of the performance of the enterprises and for a greater decentralisation of operation. The Board of the Holding Companies can evaluate the performance of the subsidiaries terms of definite performance norms while the Boards of the Subsidiary Companies can do similar evaluation of the operation of the units or divisions under them. As the subsidiary companies will be independent companies, under the Company Law, there will have to be a decentralisation of the decision making process between the Boards of the Subsidiaries. The Government would be involved with only the evaluation of the performance of the Holding Company in terms of a few selected criteria, fully assured that the performance of the different subsidiaries of the Company has been effectively monitored by independent Boards of different levels.

3.19 A suggestion has been made that there is no need for representation of Government on the Board of Directors of the Public Enterprises. The Committee recommends that the institution of Government Directors should continue as, in general, they are a positive source of help and mediation between the Government and the enterprises. It should, however, be ensured that officials nominated as Government Directors and adequate experience of public enterprises. Where this is not so, such officials, before being nominated to the Board, should be given orientation for a sufficient period in one of more public enterprises under the charge of the Administrative Ministry concerned. In our view, wherever Holding Companies are being formed, the appointment of Government Directors should be restricted only to the Board of Directors of the Holding Company. The subsidiaries of the Holding Company need not have Government Directors on the Boards.

3.20 On baiance of consideration, the Committee felt that public enterprises in the core sectors such as steel, coal, power, fertilizer and petroleum should be reorganised into Holding Companies funrtioning under the administrative control of the concerned sectoral Ministries. If a single sectoral Holding Company becomes too large, it may be necessary to set up more than one such Holding Company. It would facilitate coordination if major public enterprises which supply inputs, machinery and equipment to the producing units, and related consultancy organisations also are brought under the sectoral Holding Companies, for example, HEC and MECON for steel, MAMC for coal, EIL for petroleum etc. IN the petroleum sector, it may perhaps be necessary to have more than one Holding Company. We are not going into details, which should be worked out carefully.

3.21 The financing of investments for the core sectors would be mainly through the budget and, therefore, the present modes of scrutiny and controls would by and large continue. Holding Company would act as a link between the government and the public enterprises and the areas of authority and responsibility between the government and the Holding Company would be clearly defined. The Government's involvement would be limited to:

i) appointment of the Chief Executive and other members of the Board of Directors;

ii) investment financing and project appraisal;

iii) target setting, budget, performance evaluation; and

iv) broad policy guidelines

In all other matters the Holding Company and its subsidiaries would be subject to the same controls and procedures as in the case of private sector units.

3.22 The responsibility to the Parliament would be discharged by the Minister with the assistance of the Chief Executive himself who would assist in the answering of Parliament questions, debates, etc.

concerning enterprises under his charge. The Secretary of the administrative ministry would not be concerned with these matters. The Board of Directors of the Holding Company would enjoy all authority consistent with their responsibility.

3.23 The Holding Company would also specify its plans for investments, production, capacity utilisation, profits, dividend, etc. for a 5 year period and, therefore, enter into Memorandum of Understanding with the Government on mutually agreed basis. Certain obligations would also be cast on equity, price level etc. This Memorandum of Understanding would be reviewed each year and updated and the performance of the Holding Company judged on this basis, making due allowance for the failure or otherwise of the Ministry or Department to fulfil its part of the Understanding.

3.24 For the Companies in the non-core sector, an exercise should be done to reorganise the enterprises into a few Holding Companies and some Apex Companies (i.e. Unitary Companies with Apex Board and Subsidiary Profit Centres) depending upon the nature of the products, the location and the other linkages. The Committee also felt that all these non-core sector units should be under the sectoral Ministries. The enterprises in the non-core sector generally operate in a competitive environment with a substantial private sector presence. The sectoral Ministry will formulate sectoral policies which will apply to both public and private sector units. But unlike in the Core Sector the Ministry's involvement here will be limited only to administrative supervision including appointment of the Chief Executives and members of the Boards of Directors and evaluation of their performance according to some well-defined norms and criteria.

3.25 There are a few promotional corporations set up in the public sector like the Indian Dairy Corporation and the National Research Development Corporation of India. The Committee suggests that promotional corporations should be more appropriately set up under an Autonomous Board or as a registered society. These promotional corporations would have to remain within the charge of the concerned sectoral Ministries since they are primarily instruments of public policy.

3.26 The Committee observed that many of the taken over units from private sector were located in sectoral Ministries which were not appropriate. The grouping of small public enterprises in to larger ones, particularly from among the Engineering and Pharmaceutical enterprises also needs urgent attention.

3.27 The Committee, therefore, recommends that a Working Group be formed by the Government to go into and make recommendations on the following:

i) transfer of existing public enterprises, or any of their constituent units, to the appropriate sectoral Ministry:

ii) merger of existing public enterprises into smaller number of companies by appropriate grouping;

iii) formation of Holding Companies and Apex Companies under the sectoral Ministries from among the sectoral public enterprises;

iv) based on the reorganised Holding and Apex Companies, suggest, where necessary, transfer of certain subjects for nodal responsibility from one Ministry or Department to another.

IV. Autonomy of Public Enterprises

4.1 The objective of setting most of the public enterprises

as corporate entities was to provide the maximum autonomy in their day to day management. However, in practice, the decision making powers of public enterprises and its Board of Directors are restricted to a great extent due to specific clauses in their Articles of Association, Bureau of Public Enterprises and Government guidelines and directions, the procedures followed for scrutinising investment funding, choice of projects, wage policy, etc., issued from time to time in addition to all other controls and regulations which are common to both the public and private sectors. We feel that the division of decision-making power on commercial matters between enterprises and the Government needs to be examined and modified in what follows we do this for some of the major areas where decision-making powers of public enterprises are limited by the requirements of prior approval of Government of India or by having to be in conformity with specific guidelines.

A. Investment Approvals and Capital Budget

4.2 The present system of investment financing for public enterprises integrates their plans fully into the total public sector plan. As a consequence, the investment activities of public enterprises are subject to Government approvals and several stages. Certain consequences of this system of investment financing are worth noting:

- Since internal resources of public enterprises are a part of plan resources, the outlay provides for a planned investment programme irrespective of whether the outlays are financed by internal resources or from the budget;
- The extent to which public enterprises mobilise resources from capital market directly is very limited and they obtain the bulk of their finances through the budget;

- There is a virtual guarantee of investment finance to cover cost and time overruns.

4.3 The intimate links between public enterprise investment plans and the budget has led to a complex system of governmental approvals for individual proposals. In order to integrate their plans with the national plan, an enterprise has to interact with Government at several stages.

- The investment proposal must form a part of the Five Year Plan and therefore must be included in the recommendations of the Working Group on the particular sector. The investment proposal has to be included in the concerned Ministry's plan and the plan as finally approved.
- The investment proposals are formulated in consultation with the Administrative Ministry and other Government Departments for certain crucial parameters like location, size, technology, etc.
- If the proposals are beyond the financial powers of their Board of Directors, these have to be scrutinised by the Public Investment Board (PIB) or Expenditure Finance Committee (EFC) and the approval of cabinet is also necessary in some cases.
- Even after the investment proposal is approved, the public enterprises has to obtain approval annually for its capital expenditure programme.

4.4 Despite such rigorous scrutiny and Government interventions, in practice, the system does not really provide greater leverage in regulating the public sector's draft on resources. Unforeseen cost overruns, which have to be financed, losses which require budgetary support and delays in implementation of projects actually increase the uncertainty with regard to formulation of budget whereas excessive government intervention prove to be time consuming and at the same time erode the autonomy and responsibility of the public enterprise management in implementing the projects. While the enforcement of plan priorities though detailed and project by project, scrutiny on public enterprise investment may work in a few sectors where the public sector dominates, it is of limited utility in other sectors. The Government cannot really exercise its responsibilities as a lender since public enterprises are sometimes required to undertake unremunerative projects. Thus, in practice the present system does not really facilitate the processes of budgetary control or investment on plan priorities. At the same time, it probably leads to a measure of financial irresponsibility in the public enterprises.

The Proposals

4.5 The direction of reforms in the present system of investment financing has to be in line with the importance of public enterprise investments in the national plan. In this regard, a distinction has been made in the previous chapter between (a) core sector enterprises (b) financially viable enterprises in the non-core sector and (c) enterprises in the non-core sector which are incurring losses. The Committee was of the view that in the case of core sector enterprises, the existing system of fully integrating their plans with the total public sector plan must continue since in most cases the public enterprise plans and coterminus with the national sector plans. Many of the core sectors are highly inter-linked and, therefore, this calls for coordination with other sectoral plans. The resource requirements of these sectors is also very large and, therefore the present system of scrutiny of all their investment proposals, whether financed through national budget or through the funds raised by the enterprises themselves, has to continue.

4.6 In the case of the financially viable non-core sector, there does not seem to be any need for such detailed scrutiny and the public sector investment plan should include only the flows through the budget. To the extent, these enterprises can finance their investment requirements, by raising funds from the public through deposits or debentures or by borrowing from the financial institutions, they need not be subjected to any process of governmental clearance.

4.7 This approach is linked to certain changes in procedures for investment approval. In the core sector the nature of scrutiny and approval at the Government level will, if anything, have to be made more effective. Since the commitment of the Government here will not be only for equity but for the total project cost, and because the cost of failure from a wrong investment decision is very high, the system of Government approvals for these sectors should be built around the two-stage clearance procedure of PIB. The first stage which gives approval in principle and sanctions preliminary expenditure should be the stage at which basic questions about plan priorities, project parameters, investment decisions, etc. should be settled. The second stage would really be for scrutinising the details with regard to technology, costs, etc.

4.8 AT the first stage itself discussion could be started between the user industry and the manufacturers of equipment. PIB should set up a 'task force' for this purpose consisting of, inter alia, representatives of both the producer and the user. This 'task force' would go into all aspects relating to internal availability of equipment, capability of public enterprise to manufacture the equipment, the need for import, the quantum of import, etc.

4.9 At the second stage the projects should be considered on a detailed project report, adopting the procedure of a single window clearance. PIB could take a view whether equipment will have to be imported or order should be placed on indigenous manufacturers. Foreign exchange clearance should also be tied up especially by incorporating capital goods clearance procedures. Any question relating to price preference could also be settled by PIB on the basis of the recommendations of the 'task force'. Where, however, certain investment proposals are tied to available credits from external sources, this exercise would have to be performed as usual, in consultation with the Finance Ministry. Since all the Ministries are represented on PIB, this second stage could thus combine the usual PIB clearance with the approval for financing packages, external credits, collaboration agreements, capital goods imports, locational and environmental aspects etc.

4.10 At present proposals which fall beyond the delegated powers of the public enterprise but are estimated to cost Rs. 10 crores or below are brought before the EFC for approval. Investment proposals costing above Rs. 10 crores require the approval of the Cabinet and these are brought before PIB. It is suggested that these limits be raised as below:

- EFC – Investment proposals costing above Rs. 5 crores but not above Rs. 25 crores.
- PIB – Investment proposals costing over Rs. 25 crores.

4.11 We would also suggest that EFC/PIB should be served by a single Appraisal Agency which should be the principal point of contact between the public enterprise and the various agencies which scrutinise the investment proposals. All these various agencies should be required to provide their comments to the single modal agency which should integrate them into a comprehensive appraisal report to be submitted for consideration of EFC/PIB. We feel that the Project

Appraisal Division of the Planning Commission should be this nodal agency, and for this purpose it should be suitably strengthened.

4.12 Currently the public enterprises submit their investment proposals to the PIB through the Administrative Ministries, which invariably introduces delay. When an investment proposal is cleared by the Board of a Holding or Apex Company, the same would be sent simultaneously to both the Administrative Ministry and PAD for appraisal. If the Administrative Ministry does not bring up the case before the PIB within three months, PAD may do so and comments of the Administrative Ministry, like those of any other Ministry, should be examined as a part of the normal PIB procedure.

4.13 In the case of *enterprises in the non-core sectors* which are financially viable investment projects usually are not very large and, therefore, it should be possible to mobilise bulk of resources for these investments outside the budget. In these sectors, therefore, the flow through the budget can be restricted to the contribution towards equity and such enterprises should be expected to mobilise the rest of their resource requirements through –

a) Internal resources generation;

b) Project finance from term lending institutions; and

c) Director mobilisation through public deposits and/or non-convertible debentures, without Government guarantee.

If this reform is accepted the plan ceiling for these enterprises may relate to only the equity contribution from the Government which will be sanctioned through the PIB procedures.

4.14 These changes suggested in the modalities of financing public enterprises, imply certain modifications in the role of the Government machinery in project approvals. In the non-core sectors, enterprises will be expected to mobilise funds through financial institutions and capital markets. This will generally mean that investment proposals will be subject to some form of external scrutiny and appraisal. The main difficulty will be that financial institutions and capital markets will be mainly concerned about the bankruptcy of these projects rather than their impact on the economy as a whole. The Government may, however, wish to use some of these enterprises as agencies for the establishment and development of a new technology or for the development of a backward area observe some other social objectives which may not be commercially profitable. In such cases, either the Government has to make substantial equity contribution or some mechanism has to be developed to reimburse the additional net cost of such activities. This kind of projects would go through the normal procedures.

4.15 Therefore, some form of Government approval for the investment programme of even non-core enterprises will be required if they required additional equity contribution from the budget. The Five Year Plan will indicate the amount of investment byway of equity that Government would be willing to make, the rest of investment being loans raised by debentures, public deposits, and from public financial institutions. Therefore, as and when particular projects one formulated such projects will be appraised, by the public financial institutions in association with central appraisal agency of Government. On the basis of such appraisal, funds will be released by Government and by the institutions without passing through any further procedures or processes in Government. Contribution by Government in whole, or in substantial part, will be subject to usual approval, above Rs. 25 crores by the government (Cabinet). This modality of raising funds partly through Government (equity) and through external sources/banks and public financial institutions will be open only to those non-core public enterprises which have a dividend record of at least 9 percent on net worth or 50 per cent of net profits, whichever is lower, distributed over the past three years. One of the existing financial institutions like the Industrial Development Bank of India would service such public enterprises. For this purpose, a specific allocation would be made to the earmarked financial institution for a period of 5 years.

4.16 The Committee considered the possibility of some public enterprises raising funds from the public through sale of shares. It was felt that only companies which were performing well may be in a position to raise funds from the capital market through the sale of shares, which they could do as well through raising deposits or floating non-convertible debentures. While raising loans involves a fixed liability, selling shares may create problems of ownership without giving the public sector enterprise any greater advantage. The Committee, therefore, did not recommend selling of shares to the public by existing public sector companies.

4.17 An important corollary of the liberalised investment procedure is that restrictions on the borrowing powers of the enterprises based on the Articles of Association of Government guidelines, if any, would have to be removed in respect of the financially viable non-core enterprises. They would, of course, continue to be subject to the normal guidelines applicable to all enterprises, public or private. It must also be emphasised that such borrowings of these enterprises through public deposits of issue of debentures should not be guaranteed by the Government. For any borrowings based on Government guarantee prior approval of the Government would be necessary.

4.18 The third category of loss making units poses certain special problems. The appraisal of their investment projects and the mechanism of approval will have to be linked to programmes to make them viable by reducing their losses and improving their performance. These are dealt with fully in a subsequent Chapter.

B. Wage Policy in Public Enterprises

4.19 Workers in public enterprises are governed by the Industrial Disputes Act and their remuneration levels and patters are determined by a collective bargaining process, except in a few industries (like Textile and Cement) where these are settled by industry-wise Wage Boards. In respect of some industries, wages are determined on the basis of bipartite machinery consisting of the management of the public and private sector enterprises on the one hand and the workers' representatives on the other. Historically the long-term settlement between the enterprises and the workers' unions has been a period of three to four years.

4.20 In the sixties, the Government of India as such was not deeply involved in the negotiations. Limits were set in terms of percentages within which the managements were expected to negotiate. The management would keep the Board of Directors fully informed of the progress. The Government representatives on the Board, both in the Administrative and Finance Ministries, were expected, in turn, to keep the Government informed of the progress. However, no final commitment by the management could be made to the workers without obtaining the concurrence of the Secretary and the Minister of both the Administrative and the Finance Ministries.

4.21 Nowadays, in practice the managements clear with the Administrative Ministries and the Bureau of Public Enterprises the global limits within which they could negotiate, as well as the individual components of the package like House Rent Allowance, Transport Subsidy, etc. Once consensus is reached the managements feel that they have carried the workers with them, formal proposals are sent to the Administrative Ministries and after obtaining the approval of the Minister concerned, sent to the Bureau of Public Enterprises to process the case for the approval of the Finance Minister. Formal agreement between the management and the unions is concluded only thereafter. In many cases Memoranda of Settlement have also been signed by the management and the workers incorporating a clause to the effect that the provisions of the Memoranda of Settlement would be subject to the approval of the Government.

4.22 Apart from the basic pay, dearness allowance linked to the cost of living index, HRA, CCA, Transport Subsidy, Shift Allowance, etc., there are two other components of workers' remuneration. These are the Annual Bonus according to Section 20 (i) of the Payment of Bonus Act, 1965 or Bonus linked to production in lieu of profit sharing under Section 31 (A) of the Bonus Act, 1965 and Production Incentive Schemes operated on an integrated basis outside the provisions of the payment of bonus Act.

4.23 Payment of bonus under Section 20 (i) of the Payment of Bonus Act is applicable to those enterprises which derive not less than 20 per cent of their income in competition with units in private sector. They are allowed to disburse bonus as per provisions of the Act on the basis of determination of allocable surplus based on audited figures. Public enterprises not governed by Section 20 (i) of the Payment of Bonus Act but coming within the purview of Sub-Section (ii) of Section 20 are authorised ex-gratia payment equivalent to the amount they would have been entitled to the amount they would have been entitled to get as bonus had the enterprise fallen within the purview of the Bonus Act, 1975. Executive instructions are being issued to the managements from 1976 onwards in this regard.

4.24 Productivity linked incentive payment schemes have been introduced by several public enterprises either under Section 31 (A) of the Bonus Act which envisages payment of bonus linked to productivity over and above the minimum statutory bonus or outside the framework of the Act. Public enterprises are required to get the approval of schemes introduced by them. They are also required to review the existing schemes in the light of some guidelines.

4.25 At present there is a feeling among the public enterprises that they have very little autonomy in the matter of wage negotiations since Government approvals are required for virtually all components of the wage. They would like greater degree of freedom in arriving at a settlement with workers as part of the collective bargaining process. However, there are certain difficulties inherent in letting each enterprise negotiate independently. Competitive bargaining is not always based on the performance of the enterprise itself, but on what has been conceded to workers in another enterprise either in the same location or which is similar in technology, size, etc. This comparison does not confine itself to the total benefit but also to individual components like minimum wage, HRA, CCA, washing allowance, education allowance, LTC, etc. In this situation some suitable compromise between bargaining at the enterprise level and a wage policy dictated from above is necessary. At the same time a clear link with productivity is also needed for the health of not only the public sector but also the organised sector as a whole.

4.26 It is, therefore, suggested that the basic wage structure of the employees of public enterprises (covering basic pay, dearness allowance and certain standard allowances like HRA and CCA) should be determined on industry basis or on industry cum region basis. This can be done either by a Wage Commission or through the mechanism of industry-wise wage boards and settled for a period of five years.

4.27 In addition to this basic wage, there should be a component which should be linked with productivity which may be negotiated by each enterprise with its employees within the constraint of a certain amount specified as ceiling for the total annual cost of such incentives. The amount may be determined in consultation with the government on the basis of profits earned by the enterprise or substantial reduction in the losses. In some sectors, adequate cushions must be provided for factors relating to administered prices, increase in input costs on policy grounds, etc., so that the lack of profits does not impinge on the ability of the workers to earn what they should on the basis of total productivity improvements achieved.

4.28 In devising the above scheme, the Government would give the broad guidelines and the Board of Directors of the enterprises should be given fully authority to take decisions which, if they are within the guidelines, should not require the prior approval of the Government. Such a scheme would fulfil the twin objectives of increasing productivity of the existing capital assets, at the same time giving incentives to the workers to earn higher wages than they would otherwise have.

4.29 With regard to the payment of bonus, we do not suggest any change in the present procedure. It may, however, be desirable not to expand this scheme very much in the future, so that most of the increases in wages, over and above the basic wages and the minimum bonus, re-granted to the workers through the productivity incentive schemes.

C. *Executives' Appointments and Remuneration*

4.30 The power to appoint and dismiss Chief Executives and full-time Directors vests at present with the Government. This is as it should be and even in the private sector such appointments have to be approved by the general body of the shareholders. However, this particular power of the Government can lead to the erosion of autonomy by the exercise of informal interference in decisions which, otherwise, do not require its prior approval. Hence, we would like to suggest certain changes which will help to safeguard the autonomy by the Chief Executives and the full-time Directors in the exercise of the powers which are theirs under the rules and yet subject them to the test of performance.

4.31 The present practice of giving the Chief Executives and the full-time Directors a tenure of two years include probationary period of one year is acting as an inhibiting factor in their performance. In respect of large organisations these officials could not be reasonably expect to bring about any noticeable changes or improvements within a spell of two years. Therefore, with a view to improving organisational efficiency, it is recommended that the tenure of the Chief Executives and full-time Directors should be 5 years subject to a probationary period of one year and removal at three months' notice for unsatisfactory performance. The top management of public enterprises must have the security of knowing that, provided they perform well, they will have a tenure long enough to show results. We would also suggest that non-confirmation of dismissal of a Chief Executive of Functional Director should be decided by the Appointments Committee of the Cabinet (ACC) only after taking into account the views of the Public Enterprises Selection Board. In the case of resignations by the Functional Directors/Chief Executives, acceptance thereof will be with the approval of the ACC.

4.32 The authority to appoint part time Directors also rests with the Government. However, we would suggest that the concerned department should always consult the Chief Executive before finalising the list of part-time Directors. The non-official Directors should have a tenure of 3 years. The Committee feels that vacancies on the Board should not be left untilled for a long time.

4.33 The power to create Board level posts rests with the Government and we would not suggest any change in this. However, in some cases, the Articles of Association also limit the power of enterprises to create posts above a certain limit but below Board level. We would suggest that, in such cases, the Articles of Association be modified to give the Board full authority to create posts with a pay scale below Board level.

4.34 Recruitment to posts below Board level is within the powers of the Board of Directors. However, recently it has been decided that even if a post is below Board level, if it carried the pay scale of a Board level post, recruitment will be in consultation with the PESB. We feel that in consonance with the concept of autonomy of the public enterprises, appointment to such posts also may be left to the Board of Directors of the enterprise.

4.35 Board level posts in public enterprises are categorised into four schedules and the authority for doing this rests with the Government. We would not recommend any change in this except that the categorisation should take into account the specific needs of each company along with indicators like investment, profitability, number of employees, number of independent divisions etc. Sometimes Chief Executives of Functional Directors may be required at a level higher than indicated by their category in sick or high technology units. In such a case the Chief Executive or the Functional Directors, as the case may be, could be given a higher scale on a personal basis. In other cases, upgradation of posts on personal basis should be permitted only under the most exceptional circumstances.

4.36 There is presently considerable gap between the remuneration of Chief Executives/Functional Directors of public enterprises and private sector companies. The Committee felt that there is a strong case for narrowing this gap. This can, however, be considered only after the recommendations of the Fourth Pay Commission are received. A Working Group may be set up at the appropriate time to specify salary scales and perquisite. The committee suggests that executives should be entitled to participate in the productivity-linked bonus schemes.

4.37 The Committee felt that as far as the housing was concerned, public enterprises should go for either construction or purchase of flats. In the meantime, the Chief Executive and Functional Directors could be provided with houses, the rental ceiling being raised to the equivalent of their basic pay, without changing the provisions regarding the plinth area. As regards Executive Directors, the salary ceiling of hiring a house may be raised to 75 per cent of their basic pay. The Working Group suggested in para 4.36 may also look into this.

4.38 Disciplinary proceedings against Board level appointees is the responsibility of Government which is the appointing authority. However, in respect of below-Board level executives, in certain cases, the intervention of Central Vigilance Commission is necessary according to present procedures. We feel that this can be dispensed with and disciplinary proceedings against employees below the Board level should be entirely within the powers of the Board of Directors.

4.39 The Committee recommended that the performance of the Chief Executive of the enterprise as evaluated according to agreed parameters should form his performance record for the year. In the case of Functional Directors there is no need for a review of the Annual Confidential Report written by the Chief Executive. However, wherever an adverse report is given, the Functional Directors has a right to appeal to the Secretary of the Administrative Department.

4.40 One of the most vital but neglected areas in public enterprises has been the training or retraining of workers and supervisors, managerial development at induction and at middle levels as well as succession planning for the top posts. It is not possible to give a common prescription for all types of public enterprises. Firstly, the emphasis over this area must increase. Further, it is desirable that each enterprise management must submit to its Board of Directors, once a year, a manpower budget, the training or retraining plans for all category of employees, particularly the managerial cadres. These plans to be submitted before the start of the financial year must contain details and contents of well designed training or development courses and should be debated extensively by the Board of Directors. It is important for the Boards to approve such promotion policies that more competent managers move to higher positions relatively faster so that it is ultimately possible to fill the top management positions from within. Persons below the level of the top positions must undergo advanced management training in and outside the country. In large Holding Companies and Apex organisations, inter-disciplinary in-plant management development courses should also be organised in order to improve the competency of managers in general management, financial management, commercial and marketing operations, production and productivity management, etc. Personnel policy of a company must provide for management development training input to be provided for a predetermined number of days or weeks training on an average to each executive. Induction level training of one year's duration which is given to executives in many organisations should include adequate training the technical discipline for which they are earmarked.

4.41 Mobility of managerial personnel between the public sector enterprises should also not be discouraged. However, on completion of long term training course or on induction to an organisation, on a higher position or on promotion within the organisation the concerned executive must continue to serve the organisation for a period to be specified in the personnel policy.

V. Accountability of Enterprises

5.1 We have dealt in the previous section with measures which will enhance the degree of autonomy enjoyed by public enterprises. In our view we also need to make public enterprises more accountable for their performance. Hence the present processes of accountability which operate through the evaluation of performance in the Government, through audit and through Parliamentary scrutiny needs to be modified and strengthened. In what follows we deal with these three channels of accountability.

A. Performance Evaluation

5.2 The organisational changes and the expansion of autonomy that we have suggested require that the accountability for performance should be strictly enforced. In order to do this, performance criteria and procedures for reporting and evaluation have to be specified.

5.3 In discussing the organisational structure we have discussed the possibility of a Memorandum of Understanding being arrived at between Government in the Administrative Ministry and the Public Enterprise Management well before the commencement of the financial year. In these cases, the evaluation of performance has to be in terms of the extent to which such an understanding has been fulfilled. Due allowance will of course be given to any part of the Memorandum of Understanding which the Government has not fulfilled and which impinges on the performance of the public enterprise. Such a Memorandum of Understanding, however, could cover only a few enterprises where the details of tasks of either partly could be specified. So, it is necessary that a more general set of performance criteria is evolved.

5.4 Public enterprises pursue a number of objectives simultaneously and a single measure of performance is difficult to specify. However, there are certain objectives which are common and these should form the basis for general performance criteria. These general criteria may fall into four groups:

1. Financial performance
2. Productivity and cost reduction
3. Technical dynamism
4. Effectiveness of project implementation

B. Financial Performance

5.5 In our view, the criteria for financial performance are the most important, in that, public enterprises are expected to play an important role in the mobilisation of resources and they can do so only if they are financial viable. We would recommend three basic criteria:

i) Gross margin on assets (for all enterprises)

ii) Net profit on net worth (for core sector and profit making enterprises)

iii) Gross margin on sales (for service enterprises)

5.6 The standards against which financial performance has to be evaluated will have to vary for: (a) core sector enterprises; (b) financially viable enterprises in the non-core sector; and (c) loss making units.

5.7 Enterprises in the core sector are generally subject to price control and their financial performance is affected by this fact. However, some normative rate of turn is often implicit in price fixation procedures and can provide a standard for comparison. In any case, an inter-firm comparison of performance is always possible within each sector. In general, after allowing for distortions inducted by lags in price adjustment, the rate of net profit, as defined above, should be at least a stipulated per cent which can be fixed for each enterprise at the beginning of the year. The gross margin on assets should be improving over time.

5.8 In the non-core sector, manufacturing enterprises in the public sector generally operate in a competitive environment with a substantial private sector presence. Some of them (e.g. cement, drugs) are subject to price control. In general, for these enterprises, the criteria for comparison should be the industry average both for gross margin on assets and the rate of net profit. This will of course only apply to profit making units.

5.9 Many service enterprises in the public sector operate as monopolies or have special privileges which allow them to function on a cost plus basis. Moreover, the capital base on these service units is very different from what it is in manufacturing enterprises. In service enterprises, it may be more useful to focus attention on the direction of change in the gross margin on sales, through the other measures of financial profitability should also be examined. Wherever service enterprises operate in a competitive environment, a comparison with private sector units would also be useful.

5.10 In the third category of loss making units, it is clearly not possible to examine measures of profitability. However, the gross margin should be positive so that the loss making unit is at least covering operating costs. In addition, it may be useful to monitor the direction of change in a few other measures like (a) the ratio of loan liabilities to assets (b) the ratio of wages to value added per worker and (c) cash loss per worker.

C. *Productivity and Cost Reduction*

5.11 Monitoring performance in terms of financial profitability has to be supplemented by some simple monitoring of productivity and costs which, in manufacturing enterprises, can be done by examining the direction of change in indicators like capacity utilisation, raw materials costs (at constant prices) per unit of output, value added per rupee of wages etc. Wherever possible, an overall index of the cost of production should be worked out to provide a measure for monitoring changes in costs and productivity. It is particularly important to undertake such monitoring changes in costs and productivity.

It is particularly important to undertake such monitored by looking at the direction of change in the utilisation of fixed assets, number of days of inventory and manpower per unit of turnover.

D. Technical Dynamism

5.12 The third group of performance indicators relate to technology development. In this case a simple quantitative indicator is difficult to define. However, a rough indication can be provided by the number of product or process innovations introduced or patents obtained during the year. Such an indicator is undoubtedly subject to vagaries of interpretation of what constitutes an innovation and has to be supplemented by a qualitative assessment by technical experts (say, the Science Advisory Committee attached to the Ministry) or the quality R&D technology adaptation and quality control in the enterprises. Additional indicators are reduction in cost of production as a percentage of its total cost, efficiency level of the product, export competitiveness, sale of know-how, etc.

E. Project Implementation

5.13 The fourth set of performance indicators relates to project implementation. At present, there is an elaborate system of progress reporting; but it is too detailed to provide a simple measure of the quality of performance in project implementation. Therefore, some simple indicator of project implementation status is required. In the case of core sector enterprises, at least an attempt can be made to assess performance in terms of (a) percentage utilisation of plan funds and (b) average slippage in ongoing projects, the weights for the average being defined by the cost of each project, and (c) percentage cost revision for the approved investment programme relative to the previous year.

5.14 The four sets of performance indicator that we have suggested may have to be supplemented by other indicators to cover specific special tasks, if any, assigned to enterprises by the Government. These special tasks should really be treated as a type of understanding between the Government and the enterprise and appropriate performance indicators should be specified at the time the task is assigned and the Government may be required to compensate for the extra cost.

5.15 The method of performance evaluation that we have suggested may require the monitoring of ten or so indicators for core sector enterprises and a very much smaller number for non-core enterprises. These indicators should be reported on a quarterly basis by the Holding Company, or the Apex Company for the organisation as a whole. An annual performance evaluation report should be prepared on such enterprise by a group constituted by the Administrative Ministry with representatives from the Ministry, the Planning Commission and BPE and made available before the Annual Plan discussions for the next year and also to the Public Enterprises Selection Board. We suggest this because performance evaluation will lack bite unless it is taken into account in investment decisions and in appointment, promotion, confirmations and extensions for top management.

5.16 The performance indicators and the procedures that we have suggested are very much simpler than the present Management Information System instituted by the Bureau of Public Enterprise vide their O.M.No.BPE/GL-003/75/I&R/16($)72 dated 11 March 1075. This system collects a vast amount of information and envisages an elaborate system of quarterly performance review meetings. The Planning Commission also holds a parallel set of review meetings. We feel that our approach to autonomy and accountability requires a less intensive form of interaction. In fact, the primary concern of the Government should be to exercise the responsibilities of an owner who should concern himself not with details of all operations but with the results in terms of a few indicators. An excess of monitoring dilutes not merely autonomy but also accountability since in a welter of figures and meetings, an overall assessment of performance becomes difficult. We would therefore, suggest that the existing Management Information System and the quarterly monitoring by the Planning Commission be abandoned. Enterprises which need the assistance as and when necessary. The Government Secretariat can also obtain specific information, when the need arises, from the enterprises. The only element in the existing system that may need to be retained is a system of production reporting on major projects costing more than Rs. 100 crores.

5.17 Detailed monitoring should be the responsibility of the Holding Company or the enterprise. The Government should insist that in each public sector unit, there should be a well defined Management Information System (MIS) linking all cost or profit centres to the top. In fact, this MIS should be the basis on which top management reports performance indicators to the Government so that they are in a position to provide any clarifications that may be required in the evaluation process. The items which should be covered in the MIS should be left to each Holding Company or enterprise. However, it is our expectation that the performance indicators we have suggested will induce top managements to monitor a wide range of production, productivity and cost variables and thereby generate pressure for improvements in efficiency and profitability. On the basis of the performance evaluation criteria evolved, a Working Group would go into the MIS requirement.

F. Role of the Comptroller and Auditor General

5.18 At present most public enterprises are subject to 'two audits', one by the chartered accountants and the other, a supplementary audit, by the Comptroller & Auditor General (C&AG). The first is a requirement under the Companies Act and the second is a consequence of the fact that these enterprises have been financed out of public funds. The chartered accountant's audit deals mainly with questions of regularity i.e. whether accounts are correctly maintained, expenditures and receipts correctly booked, etc. C&AG does not carry out a repetitive audit over that of the statutory audit but only some test checks where necessary. Besides, he also looks at the propriety of the transactions.

5.19 Besides, the supplementary audit, the Auditor General also caries out a periodical performance audit of the public enterprise through the medium of an Audit Board which includes industrial specialists and experts on general management.

5.20 The general consensus in the Committee is that the performance audit of the Auditor General should be continued. These reports serve a very useful purpose and have generally earned the respect and admiration of the legislator and the discerning public.

5.21 It is, however, a moot point whether supplementary audit on the Annual Accounts of Public Enterprise should continue. A large number of Chief Executives have suggested doing away with this audit. In their view certificate of a firm of Chartered Accountants regarding " the true and fair" view of a company which is in accordance with the statutes of the country should be acceptable in the case of public enterprises also. In their view, therefore, the additional certificate presently given by the Auditor General in the case of public enterprises was superfluous.

5.22 The Committee noted that in public enterprises common accounting policies and accounting standard have not yet been evolved. This is very essential and we would suggest framing of common accounting policies and standards for the public enterprises without further delay. Once this is done, the Committee recommends that supplementary audit by C&AG may not be considered necessary in respect to profitable non-core companies. Necessary amendment to the Companies Act is, therefore, suggested in this regard.

5.23 For large enterprises in the core sector, supplementary audit as at present may be continued by C&AG. The Committee would, however, recommend that attention be focussed on major lapses. The Committee noted that in statutory corporations like Air India, Indian Airlines, etc. regular audit by the Chartered Accountants is not carried out and the audit is done by C&AG. If, therefore, in the large core sector enterprises, it is necessary to avoid "two audits" it is suggested that the regular audit by Chartered Accountants may be dispensed with and only audit by C&AG provided for by suitable amendment to the provisions of the Companies Act.

C. Relations with Parliament

5.24 The normal Parliamentary practice of the accountability of the Minister-in-charge to the Parliament involves answering questions by Members of Parliament, debates on particular issues, debate on the Demands for Grants, etc. In a Parliamentary form of Government these matters are normally left to conventions and, ultimately, to the authority of the Speaker. The late Speaker, Shri G.V. Mavalankar had also envisaged in a letter to the then Prime Minister that "asking of questions or raising discussions on the working of such bodies by the whole House is neither desirable nor practicable. The corporations must be left free in their day to day administration and the Ministers should not be called upon to answer detailed questions or discussions in the House, except on such occasion when questions of some general policy has to be raised or discussed".

5.25 Accountability to Parliament is a major reason for continuous surveillance and involvement by the Ministry or Departments of the Government in the operations of public enterprises. This involvement sometimes relates to matters which are wholly within the powers of the Board of Directors of the enterprise. The informal involvement dilutes the autonomy and impairs the efficiency of operation of these enterprises. A convention must be evolved by which this is avoided.

5.26 The Committee recognised that in general Parliament's intervention in regard to the overall performance of public enterprises had a very beneficial impact. However, the accountability of the enterprises should be for performance and results. We would, therefore, submit for consideration the following suggestions which would help to enforce accountability of public enterprises more effectively:

i) Parliament questions on day to day operation and management of the public enterprises may be avoided.

ii) Committee on Public Undertakings (COPU) can examine and probe the working of public enterprises in depth and in direct contact with public enterprise management.

iii) The debate on the Demands for Grants of the concerned Administrative Ministry could be used for purposes of a debate on the performance of public enterprises under the control of the Administrative Ministry. The tabling of the Annual Report and the Accounts of the enterprises can also provide on occasion for a general discussion on the performance of the enterprise.

VI Technology Upgradation

6.1 Studies have shown that a number of public enterprises have not made sufficient efforts to absorb imported technology or in some cases at adaptation to the Indian environment. This has led to considerable losses in both output and productivity, high rejection rates, lowering of quality standards etc. The transfer of know-how of imported processes and designs to suit Indian environment should take into account availability of strong product design and engineering manpower as well as production engineering group of a high caliber. It is only through the efforts of such personnel that continuous efforts are required to be made to modify the designs and processes to suit new material inputs and environments and to develop new products more appropriate for Indian conditions. In the absence of such personnel, transfer of "Know-why" from a collaborator does not take place and the implementation of an agreement is confined to "Knowhow" only. In some cases, there are only one or two enterprises in the country, in public sector, which use the output of products of producing organisations. In cases of such monopoly users they should concur the selection of imported technology, product size and design. These designs and sizes should also not be changed very frequently because in doing so, the unit cost of production, many a time becomes higher leading to a burden on the economy not justified by corresponding higher productivity etc.

6.2 The Committee felt that appropriate mechanisms should be established in the enterprises linkage wherever necessary and to ensure prompt absorption of imported technology as well as its adaptation and, wherever possible, further improvement. The product design and R&D personnel should be involved from the beginning of the process of import of technology, at the stage of the formulation of the proposal. Fullest use of overall national capabilities, and planning out the technology planning and development of the domestic equipment manufacturers to meet the long-term technology requirement of the public enterprises, should be considered carefully before a decision is taken on importing a particular technology. The committee also recommends that in addition to strengthening of product design, process engineering, production engineering groups etc., adequate investment should be made on R&D centres in the enterprises to facilitate such technology absorption and upgradation.

6.3 All major enterprises should periodically do an assessment of world status and trends of their respective technologies. Further, they should have technology adaptation and development programmes explicitly indicated, budgeted and approved by the Board of Directors. A component in the investment proposals towards application and absorption of technology may be allowed as an element of grant from the Government to the enterprises.

VII Financial Viability of Loss Making Units: Capital Restructuring and Closure

A Capital Restructuring

7.1 In this section, only one aspect of the problems of loss making units is taken up. At present, apart from investment approvals, other proposals for capital restructuring, or moratorium on interest on lone repayments, subsidies for cash losses, etc., are also subject to prior approval by Government. Loss making enterprises are a burden on the public exchequer, and therefore, they cannot expect the same degree of antonomy as financially viable units. In fact, it would often be necessary to have a tighter Government scrutiny of not only investment and other financial decisions but also many of the operations of such enterprises.

7.2 Normally, commercial enterprises can face a year or two of losses; but if they are basically sound, they should have the capacity to tide over such difficult periods. What we are concerned with is enterprises which are unable to cover even their actual cash expenses and show a cash loss for several years in a row. In many of these cases, the problem has become worse as cash losses for long periods of time continue to be financed by interest bearing non-plan loans. An analysis of the operating results of public enterprises producing and selling goods and which have deficit showed that in 1980-81, the interest to turnover ratio in respect of 30 enterprises was over 20 percent. In 1981-82, the corresponding number was 27 and in 1982-83, it was 20. The reduction in the number of companies with an interest burden of over 20 per cent is more due to grant of interest holidays, interest waiver, etc. As against this, the interest burden turnover ratio for all industries was 4.82 per cent according to the ASI data for 1979-80.

7.3 It is recommended that Government may not take a rigid position in its approach to the capital structure of such enterprises. While it would be difficult to restructure capital automatically without taking into account its effect on its operation, it is suggested that where a company suffered cash losses for a number of years, the Government should consider such cases for capital restructuring. It is, therefore, recommended that the Bureau of Public Enterprises could initiate a *suo moto* examination of the *pros* and *cons* of capital restructuring of a number of such loss making companies and make appropriate recommendations for covering debt into equity or writing down of capital as appropriate.

B Closure

7.4 There are many public enterprises incurring cash losses continuously over a period of years and in many of these cases the average value added per employee per month is even less than the average monthly emoluments per employee. Whatever steps are taken such enterprises can seldom break-even or make good. Such enterprises, particularly when they are not in the core sector, could hardly justify their existence by eating into the Government resources.

7.5 It is therefore, considered that the Bureau of Public Enterprises should *suo moto* take up special studies of the operations of such enterprises if need be, with the help of consultants. The general criteria for taking up such examination would be as below:

a) Such units should have incurred cash losses over a continuous period of not less than 5 years;

b) Value added per employee per month should be less than the average monthly emoluments per employee; and

c) Equity capital should have been wiped out by mounting deficits.

7.6 If such a study of the BPE reveals that capital restructuring would help the enterprise in avoiding the cash losses, the same can be undertaken. It should also be examined if modernisation would help the unit get out of its present situation. If the present position is due to any peculiarity in the pricing of the company's products, remedial measures should be suggested.

7.7 These comprehensive reports should then be brought before PIB. In PIB, both the Secretary of the Administrative Ministry as well as the Chief Executive of the public enterprise can represent their points of view should they contend that the enterprise should not be closed down. Taking into account all facts of the cases, including the cost of the closure of the unit, the PIB would make suitable recommendations to the Cabinet regarding the closure of enterprise or any constituent units thereof.

7.8 No specific proposal from a loss making unit will be considered unless the above exercise has been undertaken by the Bureau of Public Enterprises and a suitable package of measures considered and approved by the Government. In cases where healthy public enterprises are willing to voluntarily take over a sick public enterprise, such take over must be encouraged by a suitable package of measures in favour of the volunteering public enterprise. The present Government procedures for such takeovers may be smoothened out for this purpose.

7.9 Once closure is recommended, a scheme should be devised for liberal retrenchment compensation to the workers concerned. The compensation should be on liberal terms so that a substantial position of their wages could be earned by them by investment of the capital sum, which would include their normal provident fund dues, gratuity, retrenchment compensation, etc.

7.10 Such compensation schemes could equally apply in the case of units which are viable but have sizeable surplus labour. In these cases the managements can come up to the Government with suitable proposals. This would in many cases prevent companies becoming sick over time.

7.11 Many loss making units in the public sector are those taken over from the private sector as sick units. It would be difficult to resist the social pressures for take over of such units in future. However, such take over should be considered only if the substantial number of workers, say; more than 2000 are affected. Even in such a case, a like procedure as for closure should be followed. The Bureau of Public Enterprises would study all aspects of the operation of the concerned unit and bring up the matter before PIB. After considering these aspects, PIB may make suitable recommendations to the Government including, in exceptional cases, payment of suitable grant to the State Government to meet the expenditure towards compensation of retrenched workers where it is felt this would be advisable.

7.12 In the light of the above proposals where retrenchment of workers consequent upon closure or being rendered surplus becomes essential, it would be necessary to devise a method by which such retrenchment compensation can be financed through the creation of a fund to which contributions could be made both by employers and employees. The Government can also contribute to such a fund. Alternatively, an insurance scheme could also be explored to cover the contingency against retrenchment. These schemes should cover workers of all factories with a strength of over 500. The Committee recommends that an Expert Group consisting of representatives of the Labour Ministry, General Insurance Corporation, the Bureau of Public Enterprises, etc. be set up to consider the feasibility of evolving a suitable scheme.

VIII Pricing in Public Enterprises

8.1 Some of the public enterprises operate under a regime of administered prices as in the cases of Coal and Oil Sectors. In some, like steel, even though statutory price control is not applicable price increases generally require the approval of the Government in view of the impact such increases would have on the economy as a whole. In certain areas like Fertilizer and Cement where public enterprises operate along with the private enterprises the scheme of retention price operates.

8.2 In the last few years, there has been considerable improvement in the pricing policy adopted by the Government in respect of public enterprises. By and large, prices have been fixed at levels which take into account costs at normative levels of efficiency. However, occasionally there have been delays in revising prices in line with increases in costs, which have tended to erode profitability in certain crucial sectors. It is important to ensure that where a public enterprise functions under the administered or retention price regime, the periodicity of revision of such administered/retention price is reasonable so that the profitability of the enterprise is not affected because of the rise in input cost. Where price- fixation is dependent on the recommendation of the bodies like the Bureau of Industrial Costs and Prices (BICP), decision on the same should be taken within a reasonable time or an additional element in price must be added to allow for the delays.

8.3 The Committee also believes that price control by the Government should be retained only in areas where the nature of the product justifies such control, and not because a particular product happens to be produced by public enterprises. The areas where public sector is operating in competition with private enterprise and where there is no price control on the latter, the public enterprise should also be left free to fix prices of their products purely on the basis of commercial considerations. Unless the public sector share of the market is such that the concerned public is the price leader, there is no point in the public sector alone charging a price lower than those of other producers. In areas, where prices are uncontrolled, as a rule, the Government should avoid getting involved in formally or informally approving of fixing prices.

8.4 The Committee also believes that in fixing prices, the Government should explicitly take into account the need to provide incentives for improvement in efficiency as well as for replacement of equipment. In our price policy, there are instances where an increase in operating efficiency leads to reduction in price granted to the enterprise, while a deterioration in efficiency automatically leads to an increase in the price. In such a situation, there is no incentive at all for controlling wasteful expenditure or to improve efficiency in energy use, etc. The Committee would recommend that henceforth BICP should be explicitly asked to take this aspect into account in making its proposals for a revision in prices.

8.5 A number of public enterprises are operating under monopoly conditions. In respect of such enterprises, it is important to ensure that prices fixed by them or by the Government are not arbitrary and do not hide cost inefficiency or economic unviability of the enterprise. For such enterprises, a measure of Government surveillance is necessary as their pricing behaviour can have an economy-wide impact. It has also to be recognised that our tariffs are generally high, and the combined effect of a monopoly operating under high tariffs walls can be to artificially increase our prices and perpetuate operational inefficiency and technological backwardness. The Committee suggests that in fixing prices of such items, particularly intermediates, specific attention should be paid to ensure international competitiveness and reducing costs. Tariffs, and landed costs, should not be used as a guide to fair domestic prices.

Price Preference

8.6 The Committee considered the existing price preference system where a 10 per cent price preference is being given to public enterprises vis-à-vis the private sector, this being 15 per cent where imports are involved. While there are valid reasons for extending price preference to public enterprises, it has to be recognised that the gain of the seller is a cost to the purchaser. To the extent that capital costs and raw material costs are increased because of price preference, the competitiveness and profitability of the buying public sector enterprise is eroded. After careful consideration of the issues involved the Committee recommends that such price preference should be phased out over a period of 4 or 5 years (except where imports are involved). The elimination of price preference may cause problems for certain public enterprises whose costs are high because of various historical reasons. In such cases the Committee recommends that an explicit subsidy, upto 10 per cent, of the tender price may be given by the Government for a period of time. For the Government as a whole, the replacement of the system of price preference by subsidies, will not have any overall financial impact as the cost of subsidy will be offset by reduction in capital costs or operating costs of the enterprise that purchases their products.

IX Other Issues

9.1 Apart from investment and personnel policy there are certain other types of decisions which presently require the prior approval of the Government. Our suggestions on these are as below:

A Award of Contracts

9.2 An important area of interaction between the public enterprises and the Government relates to award of contracts. In general these are within the powers of the Board of Directors for any approved scheme. However, contracts involving an expenditure of more than Rs. 2 crores in foreign exchange are submitted to the Government for approval. We would suggest that this procedure be reviewed specially when the contract is against an approved scheme with necessary foreign exchange allocation. The enterprise should process such cases directly, without the intervention of the Administrative Ministry of the Finance Ministry, through the relevant organisation which will handle similar cases from the private sector like the Capital Goods Committee, the Foreign Investment Board, the Reserve Bank of India, Chief Controller of Imports and Exports, etc. As a general rule the enterprises should be totally autonomous with regard to flotation of tenders, negotiations and contracts provided they operate within the framework of approved schemes, capital budgets, foreign exchange allocations and the existing regulatory framework which apply to the public and the private sectors equally. Even though on paper the enterprises do enjoy complete autonomy in these areas, in practice, however, interference from the Ministry of Department of the Government does take place. We suggest that suitable convention be evolved to ensure that such interference are avoided.

B Expenditure on Township and Residential Quarters

9.3 There are certain restrictions on the power of the Boards to spend money on construction or acquisition of residential accommodation and on townships. We would suggest that in this matter instead of case by case approval, BPE should draw up guidelines on percentage of employees to be covered, housing norm, nature of facilities to be provided in townships and residential colonies, broad norms for construction standards, etc. Enterprises which operate within the framework of these guidelines should be free to take decisions on capital and revenue expenditure without prior approval by Government. The capital expenditure would of course be subject to the limits of delegated powers for investment approvals in general and to the constraint of the approved capital budget.

C *BPE Guidelines*

9.4 At present some of the BPE's instructions are issued on the basis of recommendations of COPU which have been accepted by the Government. Sometimes when Notes on Performance of Public Enterprises are put upto the Cabinet Committee on economic affairs, or the cabinet, certain directives are issued by these bodies. These are, in turn, issued as instructions by BPE. These will continue and observance of such instructions would be mandatory for public enterprises. Another set of guidelines issued by BPE relates to norms and standards in various areas of operation and the Committee suggests that these may be reviewed by BPE. Sometimes Government issue economy instructions like ban on recruitment and filling up of posts, reduction in advertisement expenses etc. These are at present being applied to public enterprises also. Having regard to the fact that requirements of public enterprises are not identical with those of the Ministries or the Departments of Government, it is considered that a more practical view should be taken in this matter. The Committee would, therefore, recommend that the Government may not *ispo facto* make all economy instructions applicable to the public enterprises.

9.5 At present no accounting policies or standards have been evolved for public enterprises. We would suggest a Group, consisting of the representative of C&AG, professionals in the field including public enterprises and BPE, should be formed to evolve these without further delay.

9.6 At present, creation of new companies, merger or closures requires prior Government approval. Similarly powers for the processing of Memorandum of Articles of Association and amendment thereto are vested with the Government. The Committee is of the view that these areas of controls could be retained by the Government.

Appendix-2

REPORT OF THE COMMITTEE ON DISINVESTMENT OF SHARES IN PUBLIC SECTOR ENTERPRISES (RANGARAJAN COMMITTEE)

1. Introduction

1.1 It has been decided by the Government of India that the scheme of disinvestment of equity in Public Sector Enterprises which commenced in 1991 – 92 would continue through 1992-93. In view of the above, the Ministry of Finance, Department of Economic Affairs vide their Office Memorandum No. 14/1/SE//92 dated 26.2.92 had appointed a Committee with Shri V. Krishnamurthy, Member, Planning Commission as its Chairman, with Sarvashri K.P. Geetha Krishnan, Montek Singh Ahluwalia, Suresh Kumar, Ashok Desai, S.S. Nadkarni as Members and Shri Kamal Pande of Department of Economic Affairs as its Member Secretary. The terms of reference of the Committee are as follows:

(i) To devise criteria for public sector Enterprises for disinvestment during 1992-93

(ii) To advise on limits on the percentage of equity to be disinvested in respect of such public Sector Enterprises;

(iii) To suggest the target clientele including Mutual Funds, Financial Institutions. Banks, Employees,

Resident Investors, Nor-Resident Indians, Foreign Institutional investors etc.

(iv) To make suggestions on the modus operandi of disinvestments, whether through public offer or private placements.

(v) To laid down the criteria for valuation of equity shares of Public Sector Enterprises.

(vi) To make recommendations on any other subject matter germane to the disinvestment plan.

1.2. The committee held three meetings on March 31st 1992, April 24th 1992 and May 13th 1992. On the advice of the then governor of RBI, the committee temporarily co-opted Mr. D. Basu, Deputy Managing Director, State Bank of India as a member because of his expert knowledge on the subject. The committee also had the benefit of detailed analysis done by the officers of the Department of Economics Affairs and Department of Public Enterprises.

1.3. The Government reconstituted the committee in November 1992 with Dr. C. Rangarajan, Member, Planning Commission as Chairman and Dr. Y Venugopal Reddy as member secretary. The chairman and member secretary held informal meetings with some members of the committee discussed issues with selected managers of PSUs pursued recent publications, reports of seminars, letters/suggestions received from individuals, institutions, trade union leaders at Ministry of Finance obtained the advice of chairman, SEBI in the light of subsequent development sought advice of Dr. L C Gupta of the secretary for the capital market research and development and drew upon the research work already conducted by the Institute of Public Enterprise, Hyderabad. The Committee then met on December 31st 1992 and January 1st 1993 for detailed discussions

1.4. In its general approach, the committee was guided by several important factors such as

(a) The contributions made by the public sector in general to economic development, and entrepreneurial skills.

(b) The institutional, technological and fiscal compulsions that have led to a review of Public sector investment.

(c) The exercise gained in disinvestment in the recent past, taking into account the unusual circumstances in capital markets.

(d) The need to enhance the competitive strength and ensure expansion of these enterprises while protecting the interest of workers and

(e) Above all, the requirement of constituency with the on going economic reforms in the areas of industrial licensing, foreign trade and investment and financial sector

Criteria for Selection of Public Sector Enterprises Disinvestment During 1992-93

2.1. The committee noted that the government disinvested its shareholding in 30 public sector enterprises during 1991-92. The extent of disinvestment worked out to 8 percent of the government shareholding in these enterprises and the total amount realised was Rs. 3038 crores.

2.2. The present status of disinvestment during 1992 –93 may be summarised as follows

(a) Advertisement was given inviting tender for purchase of shares of 8 central PSUs, namely, Steel Authority of India Ltd, Bharat Petroleum Corpn. Ltd. Hindustan Petroleum Corpn. of India Ltd., HMT Ltd, National Aluminium

Company Ltd. and Neyveli Lignite Corpn. of India Ltd. The last date for receipt of tenders was extended to 14.10.1992 to enable a wider response.

(b) A minimum reserve prices fixed on the basis of recommendations of three merchant bankers-Industrial Credit and Investment Corporation of India, Industrial Development Bank of India and SBI Capital Market Ltd.

(c) Having this criterion, the bids eligible for acceptance amounted to a total share value of Rs. 681.95 crores for 12. 87 crore shares in eight companies.

(d) Advertisement was again issued on November 28, 1992 for disinvestment of shares 14 PSEs. The extended terminal date for reviving the bids was December 22, 1992. The bids for 12 of this companies for a value of Rs. 1183.3 crores were accepted. The average price realisation per share disinvested in the second round was subsequently lower than the price realised in October 1992.

(e) The government invited a third round of bids for sale of equity in 15 PSEs for a total of 533 million shares in March 1993. While bids were received, it was decided to accept bids for a total of 10.1 million shares only aggregating to Rs. 46.73 crore. The referral price was fixed as earlier on the recommendations of the three agencies.

(f) The government has also decided in principles in disinvest shares in selected companies in favour of employees during 1992-93.

2.3. The committee further noted the following features relevant to the policy of disinvestment for the rest of the financial year.

(a) The financial year 1992-93 is about to end.

(b) The listing of shares of many PSEs has been completed, there is a little or nc trading in most of them. In fact, many of the mutual funds and financial institutions which have acquired PSEs shares have not been able to sell them in the market. This could adversely affect fourth coming trances of disinvestment.

(c) The weaknesses in stock markets such as low trading volumes and non-transparent trading practices have come to the fore. The stock market themselves have shown unusual volatility.

(d) As of now, it has to be recognised that there is no trading history for most public enterprise shares.

(e) The restricted tendering and handling of shares had to be resorted to in the past due to unusual circumstances but more recently, enterprise – specific bids have been invited and financial limits for bidding have also been lowered.

(f) It is generally agreed that a public issue by way of an offer to the members of public would be the most desirable option. However, if time and market circumstances do not permit it, bid mechanisms close to a public offering should be devised.

(g) By the time this Report was finalised and submitted, the new financial year has commenced.

3. Limits on the Percentage of Equity to be Disinvested

3.1. The Committee recognises the need to broadly indicate the objectives that are sought to be achieved through disinvestment in public sector equity:

a) As an immediate objective to mop up resources

of non-inflationary character to meet the budgetary needs which include requirements of developmental activities and social obligations.

b) To subserve, in the medium term, the overall fiscal objective of gradually reducing the fiscal deficit and bringing about a positive overall impact on future liabilities and income flows to Government.

c) To improve the overall economic efficiency by bringing about a more competitive atmosphere with emphasis on the cost and quality of product and service to the customers of public enterprise sector.

d) To enhance the efficiency of individual enterprises by imparting a new dynamism in the management of these enterprises through diversification of ownership and control as also larger and freer access to the expanding capital markets in India.

e) To realign the extent of ownership, control and regulation in different activities consistent with the technological needs and developments in Industrial Policy.

3.2 The Committee, therefore, recommends that limits to the level of disinvestment should be derived from the target level of government ownership in each enterprise in the medium term. Thus:

a) The target levels of ownership could be zero; 26% to ensure limited control over special resolutions brought in general body ;meetings of the enterprise; 515 to have effective control and 1005 for full ownership.

b) While determining the final level of government ownership, it must be recognised that there may be group specific or enterprise-specific intermediate levels of disinvestment depending on the state of preparedness of each enterprise, stock market conditions and the requirements of government.

c) The desirable levels of public ownership may be reached with greater advantage to PE concerned and government by expanding the equity base through public offering than disinvestment.

d) The economic efficiency and financial gains to government through disinvestment in respect of leach tranche in leach enterprise need to be continuously assessed so that there is no compulsive disinvestment merely to reach the target levels of ownership by government.

3.3 The Committee recommends the following considerations in determining the target level of disinvestment:

a) Target level of disinvestment for the medium term (say 5 years) should be derived from desirable level of public ownership in an activity or unit consistent with Industrial Policy

b) Target level of ownership should be attained through disinvestment after fully recognising the preparatory actions ;mentioned in para 3.6 below.

c) The target level of ownership in respect of all units reserved for public sector should be 51% to enable control over management. A target level of 26% of public ownership may be considered in exceptional cases. Such cases may include enterprises which currently have a dominant market share or where separate identity has to be maintained for strategic reasons. In others, it could be zero.

d) There should be a set of specific reasons for continued government ownership of enterprises except in sectors which are reserved for public ownership. In all other sectors, government should justify its continued holding of equality on considerations as fan investor and not as owner. The government may hold more than 26% of the total equity in enterprises with outstanding prospects, but the investment would need to be justified on the basis of growth potential and the scope for larger realisation and not on the basis of desirability of government control. The effort should, therefore, be to disinvest the holding at the best available price at the opportune time.

3.4 Arising from the above, the Committee considers that the percentage of equity to be disinvested should be generally under 49% in industries reserved for the public sector and over 74% in other industries.

3.5 In realising such target levels, no year-wise target for disinvestment need be rigidly prescribed but action plans have to be evolved as indicated in para 7 of the Committee's Report.

3.6 The Committee strongly recommends the following preparatory steps:

(a) Where the PSE is not in a company form, (i) determine whether it should be converted into a single or multiple companies; (ii) decide upon the capital structure differentiating between debt and equity; and (iii) evaluate whether an independent Regulatory Commission should be established for the concerned sector and, if necessary, put such a Commission in place.

(b) Estimate firmly the ongoing investment plans for

expansion or modernisation or technical collaboration.

(c) Project the pattern of financing of such expansion through additional debt or expanded equity.

(d) Review existing debt-equity structure including scope for bonus issue to government to capitalise accumulated reserves where the reserves are disproportionately large in relation to the paid-up capital; where loans are disproportionately high, review scope for conversion of such loans into equity or consider other ways of distributing/lowering the burden of debt so as to keep the equity base at a level attractive to the capital market.

(e) Examine the feasibility of issuing convertible bonds as a measure of raising adequate resources for the PSEs.

(f) Decide in the light of the above, the desirable level of equity base land the targeted level of government ownership.

(g) Settle the modalities and accounting procedures for settlement of large arrears, if any, of dues payable receivable between PSEs and the government, among the PSEs or between PSEs, government and financial institutions.

(h) Appoint a merchant banker for each of the PSEs to assist in initiating some of the preparatory measures mentioned above.

(i) Arrange to create a market-friendly image for PSEs by projecting and publicising the strong points of each PSEs among the investing public in advance of the next disinvestment exercise.

3.7 In making the above recommendations, the Committee explicitly recognised the following:

(a) The introduction of Golden Share as in UK, where government holds a share with special voting rights amounting to veto in some matters of importance was considered. The Committee felt that there may be constitutional problems of discrimination and did not pursue it further. Instead, 26% ownership is suggested wherever such control is necessary.

(b) The current organisational structure of the enterprise viz., whether it is departmental or statutory corporation or company, by itself is not material for determining the target level of ownership. In fact, organisational change where needed, is part of preparatory work for disinvestment. Similarly, the strategic importance of a unit should not be determined by the nature of the Ministry to which it is affiliated.

(c) It is possible to visualise asset stripping (i.e. sale of either non-income generating assets or one of the production units in a multi-unit company) by a PSE. This may be one of the preparatory exercises before disinvestment in the case of some enterprises.

(d) In some cases, it may be necessary to put a regulatory framework in place. In some other cases, the regime of administered prices may have to be altered. Further, the procedures for evaluation of bids for large value contracts by PSEs may need to be changed in some cases so as to let PSEs reap the entire benefits of any credit package for the contracts instead of government sharing such benefits. It is necessary to complete such vital actions before and not after disinvestment.

(e) The existing status of profitability (or loss) is not material as long as it is ensured that the price realised for shares offered represents a net gain in terms of future cash flows to the Government.

4. Modus Operandi of Disinvestment

4.1 The procedure of bundling share, combining different public enterprises in lots and restricting the disinvestment in favour of public sector mutual funds, was adopted in 1991- 92 as this was the first exercise in disinvestment. For the year 1992 – 93, the sale of shares was made enterprise-wise and to a wider clientele in order to get optimum benefits.

4.2 There are two acceptable and transparent processes for divestiture of government's shareholding:-

(a) Offering shares of public sector enterprises at a fixed price through the medium of recognised market intermediaries.

(b) Sale of equity through auction of shares amongst predetermined clientele whose number could be as large as necessary or practicable. The reserve price for the public sector enterprises' equity is determined with the assistance of merchant bankers.

4.3 In addition, a third method practised worldwide for disinvestment is to transfer the controlling interest in an enterprise to a specific firm or group of persons based on a negotiated price, the entire process being finalised based on certain pre-determined objective criteria.

4.4 Two important considerations for the government in deciding the precise mode of disinvestment are the best means to realise the highest price and the best course which would save the highest number of jobs in the enterprise disinvested.

4.5 All the above methods have their own merits and demerits. In the first alternative of 'offer for sale', difficulties may be encountered in estimating and determining the 'fixed' price if it is offered for the first time and the shares have not actually been trading in the stock exchange. On the other hand, this method has the advantage of spreading the ownership widely amongst the general public and in a transparent manner. A pre-requisite for the method is to list the shares of enterprises in the stock exchange and establish a track record of trading. In the case of those PEs for which the first sale of equity is yet to be made, or those where the track record of trading in shares is yet to be established, the tender system would be advantageous. The last method of negotiated sale has the advantage of direct interface with potential new owners so as so specify the manner of future operation of the enterprise to achieve the best social objectives. But it has the demerit of the potential for long drawn out negotiations and allegations of favouritism.

4.6 The committee, in the light of experience gathered to date recommends the following modus operandi:

(a) Once a reasonable market price is established in a normal trading atmosphere over a reasonable period of time and a public enterprise completes the preparatory work, the fixed price method would be appropriate. In any case, for expanding the equity base through capital markets, the fixed price method has to be adopted.

(b) In all other case, the auction method with wide participation may be adopted.

(c) Close and continuous involvement of public enterprises concerned and the merchant banker appointed for the purpose of devising the modus operandi is essential. In fact, disinvestment should be planned and implemented for each enterprise separately and not in groups.

(d) PEs should have the freedom to engage merchant bankers and other intermediaries to ensure effective and efficient exploitation of market opportunities.

(e) Where employee-takeover is involved, appropriate modus operandi would have to be devised, essentially through negotiations.

(f) Where it is proposed to offer equity stake to existing technical collaborators in the PSEs, it needs to be ensured that such equity link-up is based on strategic considerations. The choice of partner, extent of equity stake, terms of offering, timing etc. would need to be based on objective criteria such as access to newer technology, scope for increasing export turnover and possibilities of setting up third country operations. The modus operandi would thus have to be uniquely devised.

(g) In respect of PEs which are operating as holding company structures (for example, SAIL) or companies with multiple production units (like the Cement Corporation of India), the modus operandi could be similar but the processes have to be devised in detail and actively implemented by the PE concerned.

(h) An enterprise-specific approach in the modus operandi, including timing of issue and choosing intermediaries, is essential to meet the needs of the government, the enterprise concerned and stock markets.

(i) Costs of flotation have to be explicitly assessed, and reasonableness of costs ensured.

4.7 The Committee recommends that 10% of the proceeds appears a reasonable amount to be set apart by the government for lending to the PEs concerned on concessional terms to meet their expansion /

rationalisation needs. The Committee recognises the need to use a part of the proceeds of disinvestment for effecting improvements in the PEs concerned in a manner similar to earmarking a part of the gross proceeds for the National Renewal Fund. Such an approach provides incentives to the PE management to augment receipts from disinvestment.

4.8 The Committee also recognised that disinvestment of government equity could be tailored to an informed process of management of external debt of the country. By allowing PEs to swap the entire or a portion of their outstanding external debt with lenders for an equity stake at negotiated prices, the twin benefits of reduction in debt service obligations to the country as well as to the enterprise concerned and a better debt equity gearing for the entity may be achieved.

4.9 The Committee, however, recognised that there are practical limitations to such an approach. Debt equity swaps have been practised as part of privatisation in certain countries with acute problems of debt overhang and servicing. Especially countries which have defaulted on external payment obligation and whose debt is traded in secondary markets at substantial discounts have resorted to this option.

4.10 The Committee concluded that the above factors are not relevant in the Indian context. There is no comparable external debt problem for India. Therefore, there is no practical utility in encouraging recourse to debt equity swaps in the context of privatisation. However, it is recommended that where in individual enterprise finds unique advantages in adopting this approach, such enterprise could be enabled to do so.

5. Criteria for Valuation of Equity Shares of Public Sector Enterprises

5.1 Valuation of shares in the past was generally based on the guidelines formulated by the Controller of Capital Issues. Currently, however, these are no longer in vogue. In general, three methods for valuation of shares are adopted, viz., Net Asset Value method, Profit Earning Capacity Value method and Discounted Cash Flow method. While the NAV would indicate the value of assets, it would not be in a position to indicate the profitability or income to the investors. The profit earning capacity is generally based on the profit actually earned or anticipated. The discounted cash flow is a far more comprehensive method of reflecting the expected income flows to the investors. However, in the context of valuation of shares of public enterprises, none of the traditional methods would by themselves be adequate. The special circumstances that require to be assessed in the context of valuation of shares of public enterprises are:

(a) In the management of the public enterprises, the focus has been on discharging economic and social responsibilities indicated by the government rather than on projecting profitability to the investor.

(b) In regard to valuation of some of the assets, the book value might reflect land and other facilities provided to such enterprises at lower than market cost.

(c) The structure of the debt and equity of public enterprises had not necessarily followed commercial norms.

(d) Many enterprises have had gains or losses in the past due to the effect of administered prices. Further, recent policy measures are also affecting immediate business prospects of some PEs (e.g.

STC due to decentralisation).

(e) A number of public enterprises have been already invested heavily in projects under construction and some of them have ambitious expansion programmes.

(f) No effort has been made to project in the public eye and in the market, the strengths of these enterprises in the past for a variety of reasons.

(g) While in some activities such as cement, there are private enterprises whose shares are listed and traded in the market, there are certain other activities where there are no private enterprises involved in the same activity to provide appropriate basis for valuation.

5.2 The Committee wishes to record the following relevant factors in the context of valuation of shares:

(a) Valuation is a difficult exercise, whether in the private or public sector, in India or in other countries; and more so when there are wide divergences in valuation by different merchant bankers in respect of the same public enterprise.

(b) The price at which a share can be sold is determined more by investor perception of the worth rather than any mechanical measure of intrinsic worth. Hence the importance of information gathering and full disclosure to generate credibility and investor interest.

(c) Rise or fall in share values of an enterprise soon after disinvestment does not by itself indicate that shares were under-priced or overpriced at the time of disinvestment.

(d) Difficulties of valuation in a multi-unit and multi-product scenario have to be reckoned.

5.3 In assessing the intrinsic worth of a share, the Committee recommends the following:

(a) Among the three criteria viz. Net asset value, profit earning capacity value and discounted cashflow value, discounted cash flow has the greatest relevance, though it is the most difficult.

(b) An explicit assessment of the scope and limits for selling non-income generating assets (land or buildings) and rationalising labour force (Voluntary Retirement Scheme etc.) should be made.

(c) Government policies affecting future profitability (such as disappearance of guaranteed offtake or guaranteed rate of return) may have to be spelt out. Such assurances wherever required may be extended only after careful assessment of the implications of such assurances on the economic efficiency rather than immediate attractiveness of the shares to investors.

(d) The influence of social constraints in the past working of the PEs and the extent of benefit accruing due to provision of certain under-priced facilities like land should be captured and presented. Likewise, costs of projects under construction should be evaluated on a realistic basis and presented while reckoning the intrinsic worth of the PEs.

5.4 As regards investor perception, the Committee recommends the following:

(a) Each company has to be studied carefully with the help of a merchant banking firm taking into account factors such as value of assets, its market share, potential profit earning capacity and the prevailing price in the market for shares of similar enterprises in the private sector.

(b) It is essential that the PE and merchant banker concerned present all positive aspects of the enterprise in the prospectus.

(c) While fielding PEs in the capital market, the main line of activity of the PE concerned and the extent of investors' fancy for the particular industry at the material time may have to be taken into account.

(d) In the offering memorandum and during investor presentations, the likely improvements in the efficiency of the PE concerned as a result of changed management attitudes and other relevant factors may need to be emphasised.

(e) Wherever disinvestment is made through public issues, the offering price would need to be fixed with a close assessment of the need to project the issues as a success to pave way for subsequent offering and at all the same time avoiding any criticism of under-pricing.

6. Target Clientele for Disinvestment

6.1 The Committee adopted the following approach in determining the relative roles of target clientele:

(a) The target clientele should include Mutual Funds, Financial Institutions, Merchant Bankers, Brokers, Employees of the respective public enterprises, Resident Investors, Non-resident Indian investors, as also Foreign Investors. In fact, there is no necessity to restrict the disinvestment among any particular groups or categories. Ideally, the purpose is best served by the shares being held by the widest cross section of the Indian public.

(b) Ceilings may be imposed in respect of preferential allotments of shares to the employees in all production / manufacturing oriented companies. However, such preferential allotments should not exceed 200 shares for each employee subject to an overall ceiling of 5%. In the case of "consultancy" companies, preferential allotment to the employees can extend upto 20 per cent again with a ceiling per employee. In case where employee-take-over is sought by employees, the ceilings and payment arrangements could be flexible.

(c) There can also be a ceiling for allotment if any to non-resident Indian investors or the extent of foreign holding that can be permitted. The same rules as are applicable to NRIs and foreign investors to buy the equity in private industry in India may be extended to the foreign investors to buy shares in PEs.

(d) The question of reserving a portion of the government shareholding proposed to be disinvested in favour of Foreign Institutional Investors may be considered when the role of FIIs expands in the Indian capital markets.

(e) It may be desirable to allow shareholding by technical collaborators in PEs on a preferential basis as part of modernisation and expansion. The new Industrial Policy allows foreign equity participation upto 51% in Indian enterprises. Rather than encouraging them to set up new units for the same purpose, it should be open to the existing foreign collaborators to buy into the equity of PEs operating in such areas. The public sector will derive two advantages through this method, viz. (I) continued technological and possibly fresh managerial involvement from foreign collaborators and (ii) scope for optimising the use of existing plant and other facilities to stage a global presence with the help of the foreign collaborators.

(f) There may be restrictions on the extent of equity sold to particulars group of clients. For example, foreign investors may not be allowed to buy more than 24% of equity except on those PEs concluding strategic alliances with overseas firms on terms approved by the government.

6.2 The Committee, therefore, recommends the following target clientele:

A. Where auction method or public offer is adopted, the target clientele should include:

(i) The general public;

(ii) Mutual funds;

(iii) NRIs and foreign investors on par with general principles governing their participation in the Indian equity market with no reservation for either of the categories;

(iv) Reservation restricted to employees who would get upto 200 shares per employee at a discount of 15% on the market price, enabling funding arrangements and a lock in period that is normally prescribed for reserved allocation of shares. While a ceiling is prescribed for each employee, where a trust or cooperative of employees is formed for the specific purpose, individual ceilings could be aggregated for the purpose;

(v) Under special circumstances, reservation for other stakeholders such as dealers in select activities like fertilisers depending on the extent of interest of such stake-holders, upto 500 shares per applicant at market price and subject to lock-in restriction as normally prescribed for reserved allocations.

B. In regard to technical collaborations;

- Technical collaborators may be existing or new;
- Emphasis on identification of enterprises that

would benefit from conversion into joint venture;

- Transparency through competitive offers (i.e. not restricting negotiations only to existing collaborator);
- Expanded equity base or disinvestment by negotiated price as well as stock options subject to any SEBI regulations;
- Where domestic industrial houses have synergy and offer collaboration arrangements to ensure efficiency, they should be treated at least on par with foreign technical collaborators.

C. Merchant bankers and stock brokers are essentially intermediaries and should not be treated as target-clientele. However, assistance of internationally renowned merchant bankers may be employed if the enterprise concerned expressly requests that this be done. Assistance of such foreign merchant bankers may be useful when foreign collaborations or investments have to be examined (including BIFR cases).

7. Other Issues

7.1 The Committee noted some important lessons of international experience in PSU disinvestment viz.

(i) In many countries, separate apex agencies have been created to design and implement disinvestment. In some cases, such an agency was established by law, so that the concerned law overcomes existing legal impediments to PE disinvestment.

(ii) The process of disinvestment was spread over two to three years, and where it was done in a hurry, it resulted in undesirable concentration, sometimes described as crony capitalism.

(iii) In the case of some countries, where a rigid time-table for disinvestment was caused by prescription of donors, there was an erosion of the negotiating strength of government agencies and possible loss of revenue.

(iv) Interested parties, including managers, bureaucracy and unions resisted such disinvestment but this was overcome with the chief executives and boards being packed with pro-chargers.

(v) Introduction of competition as part of the process of disinvestment was preferred. Consequently, to ensure competition and protection of consumers' interest, necessary policy/legal changes had to be brought about.

(vi) Concern with equity considerations has been an important issue in striking a balance between fiscal needs, consumers' interests and workers' welfare, but often special arrangements to protect income flows, if not jobs, were put in place for workers.

(vii) In some cases, quality of services and access of the poor to services suffered as a consequence of disinvestment but on the whole, results were positive.

(viii) There has been virtually universal criticism of under-pricing of shares wherever disinvestment has taken place. In some cases, flotation costs or gains by financial intermediaries such as underwriters and merchant bankers were considered excessive.

(ix) Pursuance of multiple objectives blurred proper evaluation of the impact of disinvestment.

7.2 Keeping in view the international experience and our own requirements, a Standing Committee on Public

Enterprise Disinvestment is recommended. The Committee may consist of both full and part time members and draw expertise from Government, Public Enterprises, Financial Sector, Professionals and academicians. The Commission's terms of reference may include;

(a) review of public enterprises with a view to recommending enterprise-specific actions for reforms, restructuring and disinvestment:

(b) suggesting, where appropriate, parameters for selection of Chief Executives Board of Directors to meet the requirements of reforms.

(c) Identifying the appropriate legal, institutional and procedural arrangements for protecting the interests of consumers, rural or backward areas while transforming organisational form into companies wherever needed and such arrangements may include breaking up of existing monopolies or encouraging new firms to promote competition;

(d) Proposing necessary incentives to enterprises to mobilise support for disinvestment;

(e) Applying the criteria suggested for establishing the percentage of disinvestment in regard to each enterprise;

(f) Providing guidance on modalities of disinvestment appropriate to each enterprise including share valuation;

(g) Monitoring the progress of disinvestment programme; and

(h) Arranging for independent evaluation of the progress of the disinvestment programme.

7.3 The proposed Committee would also be in a position to guide the public enterprises and the government in preparatory measures for disinvestment which include;

(a) financial restructuring especially debt / equity, accounting for and the settlement of dues between the government and public enterprises

(b) preparatory measures legally required for diversification of ownership including assistance in obtaining lenders' consent (external commercial or aid)

(c) assessing the medium term corporate plan with special reference to the proposed equity structure

(d) ensuring that data is gathered by each public enterprise and prospectus is prepared with due care

(e) the employment of merchant bankers, timing and management of issue, listing, share transfer etc.

7.4 The Committee commends for consideration of the government, establishing the Committee mentioned in para 7.2 on a statutory basis in view of the financial magnitudes involved, multiple ministries concerned impact on economic reform and the need to monitor use of proceeds of such disinvestment.

7.5 The Committee further commends for consideration, use of part of proceeds of disinvestment not only for National Renewal Fund (which may include financing of retraining of workers to enable redeployment), 10% incentive for PEs, and reduction in Government debt but also for channeling resources to social sectors like literacy, health and employment generation in rural area.

7.6 The Committee recommends that the following further measures in respect of PEs be initiated to ensure that the objectives of disinvestment are realised

(a) Government expectations from the PEs as majority / dominant shareholders should be documented in the form of MoUs but the focus of these MoUs will be different viz. Customers and capital markets.

(b) With diversified ownership coming into place after disinvestment, reconstituting PEs Boards with appropriate representation for non government directors as may be necessary.

(c) Each enterprise should be encouraged to commence work on corporate strategies and plans in alignment with ongoing reforms.

(d) Seminars and workshops could be held for the finance personnel and other senior executives of PEs on the subject of their new role in the liberalised economic environment, their relationship with the government, capital markets and their custormers etc. SCOPE could take the initiative in organising such workshops/seminars with guidance perhaps from SEBI.

(e) A deliberate policy of 'image building' through media and projecting performance is also necessary to ensure continues entry in to capital markets for raising resources.

Appendix-3

REPORT OF THE COMPTROLLER AND AUDITOR GENERAL OF INDIA

Overview

The Government of India sold the shares of selected Public Sector Enterprises (PSEs) during 1991-92. The sale was carried out in two phases in December 1991 and February 1992. The disinvestment exercise was not preceded by adequate preparatory study. No efforts were made to generate widespread investor enthusiasm among the financial institutions / mutual funds about PSE shares to encourage good response from them.

(Paragraph 5.1)

Some of the PSEs were included in the programme of disinvestment of shares though exclusion of these was advised by PSEs / Administrative Ministries on specific grounds. The result was that in the case of shares of some PSEs such as Steel Authority of India Ltd (SAIL) and Indian Petro Chemicals Ltd (IPCL), there was gross under-realization of sale receipts.

(Paragraphs 5.1, 5.15 and 5.16)

The method adopted by Government for sale of shares of PSEs in bundles depressed value realization of "Very Good" / "Good" PSEs as a result of their being clubbed together with "Average" PSEs. In four cases the average realization was even below the face value (Rs 10/-) of the share.

(Paragraph 5.3)

Offers received in the first phase of disinvestment were far below the reserve value of bundles based on reserve price fixed for share of each PSE. Reserve prices originally fixed on the basis of accepted criteria were reduced drastically without which the low offers received could not have been accepted. Such reduction ranged between 21.95 percent to 86.67 percent. In 24 out of 31 PSEs, reduction in valuation was above 50 percent. The reduction in original reserve price both at the time of first and second phase of disinvestment resulted in underrealization of value to the extent of Rs 3442 crores.

(Paragraphs 5.9, 5.10)

The Government had initially decided that in respect of PSE, whose shares were already listed on the stock exchanges, their shares would be off-loaded directly to mutual funds / financial institutions at the market price of their shares. The shares of Cochin Refineries and Andrew Yule listed on the Stock Exchange, were, however, clubbed in bundles along with the other shares and sold to financial institutions / mutual funds in the first phase of disinvestment in December 1991.

(Paragraph 5.3)

Composition of bundles of shares of PSEs for disinvestment were determined even before fixation of the reserve price of the shares of each PSE. As a result the value of each bundle instead of being around Rs 5 crores, as approved by the Government, ranged between Rs 8.61 crores and Rs 12.91 crores. The financial institutions / mutual funds being presumably under the impression that the bundle value was Rs 5.00 crores, quoted lower rats.

(Paragraph 5.5)

In the first phase of disinvestment, the Government offered shares valued at Rs 8000 crores on the basis of the original reserve prices fixed. This was far in excess of the perceived investible resources of around Rs 2000-2500 crores available with the financial institutions / mutual funds.

(Paragraph 5.6)

Tenders received in the first phase of disinvestment were non-competitive. 72.61 percent of the bids received had only one bidder. Out of the 406 bundles sold, in respect of 289 bundles representing 71 percent of the total bundles sold, only single bids had been received.

(Paragraph 5.7)

In the second phase of disinvestment of shares undertaken in February 1992, tenders received were again non-competitive. Four out of 19 bidders contributed 68 percent of total bids received.

(Paragraph 5.11)

A claw back provision was not incorporated in the terms and conditions of the sale to ensure realization by Government of a part of the profits likely to be made by the buyers in a subsequent sale of the shares.

(Paragraph 5.12)

The disinvestment served only to contain the fiscal deficit.

(Paragraph 5.14)

DISINVESTMENT OF GOVERNMENT SHAREHOLDING IN SELECTED PUBLIC SECTOR ENTERPRISES (PSES) DURING 1991-92

1. Introduction

The public sector has been central to India's economic development. In the pursuit of development objectives in a mixed economy, public sector enterprises in critical sectors of the economy have played an important role in preventing the concentration of economic power, reducing regional disparities and ensuring that planned development serves the common good.

The total investment including equity, loans and deferred credits in 246 PSEs amounted to Rs 1,13,233.68 crores as on 31st March, 1991. As against this the profit earned by these PSEs during 1990-91 was Rs 2367.74 crores and the dividend paid was a mere Rs 364.86 crores. Such minimal generation of surplus has been perceived by the Government as responsible for the inability of the PSEs to regenerate themselves in terms of new investments as well as in technology development. Proposal of raising resources for the PSEs through investment by the public sector financial institutions / banks in a basket of shares of both profit and loss making enterprises had been under consideration of the Government since July 1990 and it was decided in March 1991 to undertake partial disinvestment of shares of PSEs.

In the aforesaid background the Union Government announced in their statement on Industrial Policy on 24th July 1991 and in the Union Budget for 1991-92 presented on the same day that apart from revitalising the public sector, a part of the Government's share-holding in the public sector would be offered to mutual funds, financial institutions, general public and workers so as to raise resources and encourage wider public participation.

The Union Budget for 1991-92 provided for receipts of Rs 2500 crores on this account. In the two phases of disinvestment carried out in December 1991 and February 1992 the Government realized a sum of Rs 3038 crores from the sale proceeds of its shares held in 30 selected PSEs.

2. Organizational Setup

The PSEs are under the administrative control of the various Ministries and Departments of the Government of India. The Department of Public Enterprises (DPE) under the Ministry of Industry acts as the nodal agency for all PSEs and assists in policy formulation pertaining to the role of PSEs in the economy as also in laying down policy guidelines on performance improvement and evaluation, financial accounting, personnel management and in related areas. It also collects, evaluates and maintains information on several areas in respect of PSEs. The DPE also provides an inter-face between the administrative Ministries / Departments and the PSEs. In fulfilling its role it inter-acts with other Ministries and organizations as also premier management institutes in the country. The disinvestment of Government shares in selected PSEs during 1991-92 was carried out by the DPE in association with the concerned PSEs and their Administrative Ministries / Departments, Ministry of Finance and the Cabinet Secretariat.

3. Arrangement for Valuation and Sale of Shares of PSEs

After the announcement of the proposal for partial

disinvestment in the Union Budget 1991-92 and the Industrial Policy Statement 1991, the process of selection of PSEs whose shares were to be disinvested was undertaken by the Department of Public Enterprises (DPE). Out of the total 244 PSEs as on 1.4.1990, the DPE recommended disinvestment of shares of only 41 PSEs. PSEs which were (i) under construction stage, (ii) whose net asset value (NAV) per share was either negative or less than the face value, (iii) which were of insignificant size, (iv) where current level of profitability was low, (v) those falling under Section 25 of the companies act 1956, (vi) in which share-holding of the government was below 60 percent, (vii) those functioning in power generation / transmission sectors and (viii) those in the oil sector having special relationship with the Government and (ix) also those meeting defence needs of the country were excluded from the purview of disinvestment.

Out of these 41 PSEs, ten PSEs were later excluded at different stages for reasons such as some of them being consultancy firms, some having gone into losses during 1990-91 and the remaining engaged in production of strategic nature. Finally a list of 31 PSEs was drawn up in the first week of December 1991. Of the 31 PSEs, 8 were categorised as 'Very Good', 12 as 'Good' and 11 as 'Average'. The categorisation of these PSEs was apparently made on the basis of the Net Asset Value (NAV) / Share vis-à-vis face value Rs 10/- of the share of the PSEs as on 31st March 1991. The PSEs whose NAV was Rs 50/- per share and above were categorised as 'Very Good', between Rs 20/- per share to Rs 49/- per share as 'Good' and between Rs 10/- to Rs 19/- as 'Average'.

3.1 *Formulation of Guidelines for Valuation of Shares of PSEs*

In August 1991, the Ministry of Finance constituted a Committee under the Chairmanship of the Secretary (DPE) for formulating guidelines for valuation of shares of PSEs which were to be disinvested.

Based on the recommendations of the Committee submitted on 5th September 1991, the DPE issued detailed guidelines to the Chief Executives of the PSEs identified for disinvestment for valuing the shares by three different methods namely :

(a) Net Asset Value (NAV) Method.

(b) Profit Earning Capacity Value (PECV) method at capitalisation rate of 4 to 8 percent.

(c) Discounted Cash Flow (DCF) method – based on the future expected free cash flow streams for a period of about 5 years discounted at appropriate rates.

The PSEs were asked to submit the necessary data by 25th October, 1991 to enable the DPE to fix the 'reserve price' for sale of shares in respect of each PSE.

3.2 *Appointment of Consultant for Valuation of Shares*

The Government also appointed a private Consultancy firm in September 1991 to advise on the pricing of the shares of selected PSEs. The Government's intention was that if the value of shares computed by the consultants was higher than the values arrived at by the other methods it would be taken to increase the valuation of the shares. The Consultants submitted their report in three volumes on 10th, 12th and 18th December 1991. The Consultants based their recommended values taking into account prevalent stock market sentiment specific to the industry in which each PSE could be classified.

3.3 *Modus Operandi for Sale of Shares*

The following decisions were taken by the Government at the outset:

(a) Disinvestment would be done in phases, the first phase to be implemented in December 1991.

(b) Level of disinvestment would vary from 5 percent to 20 percent, keeping in view that Government shareholding would not fall below 51 percent.

(c) Shares of all selected PSEs would be offered in the

form of bundles consisting of nine PSEs (3 PSEs from each category viz., very good, good and average) through a process of bidding.

(d) Shares would be sold to only mutual funds and investment institutions in the Public Sector who would gradually off load these shares into the market so as to finally ensure a wider holding of the ownership of these shares.

(e) DPE would finalise the list of PSEs for disinvestment in consultation with the Administrative Ministries and Ministry of Finance, value them and prepare bundles.

While taking the above decisions in November 1991 the Government also decided that the Controller of Capital Issues (CCI) norms for share valuation would not be applicable for the envisaged disinvestment since they tended to generally under value shares. The CCI norms provide for share valuation by computing the average of NAV and PECV at 15 percent capitalisation rate for manufacturing companies subject to suitable adjustment with reference to the stock market prices in respect of listed companies. The Government decided that the valuation of shares of selected PSEs would be according to the three methods indicated in para 3.4 above. The average of the two highest values so obtained would be taken as the 'fair' value or the 'reserve price' for that PSEs share. It was also decided that the total value of the equity in each bundles would be about Rs 5 crores based on the fair value of the shares of each PSE. In the case of PSEs already listed on the stock exchanges, it was further decided that disinvestment of Government equity shares would be made directly to mutual funds and investment institutions at the market price.

3.4 Invitation of Bids, Fixation of Reserve Prices

The DPE issued notices, inviting bids for the sale of shares of 31 selected PSEs from 10 financial institutions / mutual funds on 10th December 1991. All the PSEs shares were grouped into 825 bundles each consisting of the shares of 9 PSEs in certain proportions determined by the DPE. On the basis of data furnished by the PSEs for the valuation of shares and the report submitted by the consultancy firm, the 'reserve price' of shares of each selected PSE was fixed by the DPE in consultation with the representatives of the PSEs concerned, Administrative Ministry of PSE and Ministry of Finance between the 14th and the 18th of December 1991.

3.5 *Revision of Reserve Prices*

After the bids were opened on 18th December 1991, it was found that the bid prices were far below the value of bundle computed with reference to reserve price and the number of shares in the bundles and, therefore, could not be accepted. Approval of the Government was, therefore, obtained on 24th December 1991 for empowering the DPE to sell the shares of selected PSEs by accepting the highest of the bids including single tender received, so long as these were above the average of the NAV and PECV computed using an average capitalisation rate of 10 percent. The price of the bundle so arrived at could further be reduced upto 10 percent, if necessary. The need for reducing the reserve price of each PSE share fixed earlier was justified on the ground that the reserve prices fixed earlier had been inflated due to optimistic projections of future cash flows by the PSEs.

Out of the 825 bundles offered for sale, bids were received from 9 mutual funds / institutions for 533 bundles. The bids were evaluated against the reserve price of each bundle worked out on the basis of the revised reserve price fixed for each PSE share as included in the bundle. 406 bundles for a total value of Rs 1427 crores were sold. Acceptances were sent by the DPE to the mutual funds / investment institutions on 1st January 1992. The bid amounts had been credited earlier to the Government account on 23rd and 24th December 1991.

3.6 *Second Tranche of Disinvestment*

For the second tranche of disinvestment, (February 1992), the Government decided on the following :

(a) The bundles of shares of PSEs remaining unsold in

the first tranche of disinvestment may be unbundled and fresh bundles of shares of 31 selected PSEs made with different proportion of shares of these PSEs.

(b) The fresh bundles of shares would be sold through the process of bidding to the mutual funds, financial institutions, investment institutions and banks in the public sector. The DPE would sell the bundles of shares for which the bids were equal to or above the price calculated according to the CCI guidelines.

(c) The DPE may sell shares in some selected PSEs beyond the 20 percent limit but in no case would this involve loss of Government control.

On 16th January 1992, the DPE orally requested the Delhi Regional Office of the Industrial Credit and Investment Corporation of India Ltd (ICICI) to evaluate and advise reasonable issue price for equity of selected PSEs. The ICICI submitted its recommendations on 29th January 1992 which inter-alia suggested non-inclusion of certain PSEs whose shares had been disinvested in the first phase. The prices suggested by the ICICI were higher than the earlier revised reserve prices in some cases. As a result of these recommendations a revised list of 16 PSEs for disinvestment was prepared by the DPE with the approval of Government. The valuation of the shares of these 16 enterprises was done with reference to the valuation done by the ICICI which was higher or equal to the revised reserve prices of the first phase of disinvestment.

The shares of the 16 PSEs were grouped in 120 bundles according to same categorisation as adopted earlier. Their reserve price were uniformly fixed at Rs 10.08 crores per bundle, which was also indicated in the notice inviting tenders and the bids were invited from 36 institutions, banks, on 11th February 1992. The terms and conditions stipulated in the notice inviting the bids for second phase were generally the same as those prescribed in the first phase of disinvestment. 273 bids were received from 19 institutions for all the 120 bundles. Bids for all the 120 bundles were accepted for a total value of Rs 1611 crores.

The shares of PSEs disinvested in the two phases taken together ranged from a minimum of 0.27 percent to maximum of 20 percent (Annexure I) and the total amount realised was Rs 3038 crores. The shares of one selected PSE namely Metal Scrap Trading Corporation remained unsold.

4. Scope of Audit

The arrangements made by the Government for the sale of shares of selected PSEs were examined in Audit to ascertain whether the preparation for sale had been adequate and satisfactory and whether the procedure for disinvestment was conducive to realizing the maximum receipts to the Exchequer. The records relating to disinvestment of Government shares in selected PSEs as supplied to Audit by the DPE and some of the concerned PSEs were examined in Audit and its findings based on these records are given in the succeeding paragraphs.

5. Audit Findings and Conclusions

5.1 Approach to Disinvestment Lacked Necessary Preparatory Work

Investors' enthusiasm for equity shares of a company is dependent to a large extent on the knowledge about its inherent financial strength, including inter alia profits earned and dividends paid in the past, growth in sales and assets, future plans of expansion, risks involved, the future of the industry including demand / supply imbalances, locational advantages and the competence of its management. Public issues of equity by private enterprises are invariably preceded by wide publicity about such aspects. The requirement of familiarising the investors both institutional and individual was more essential for PSEs due to their earlier lack of exposure to the stock markets.

While the Government had decided as early as in March, 1991 to disinvest a part of its shares in PSEs, it was noticed in Audit that no efforts were made to generate investor enthusiasm through wide publicity about the PSEs. In fact the identification of the 31 PSEs was completed in November 1991. The Government had asked the financial institutions like the Unit Trust of India (UTI) who were the prospective buyers to do their own valuation of shares of PSEs for which purpose they were advised to obtain information from the PSE concerned. No efforts were made to generate wide spread investor enthusiasm among the FIs / MFs about the PSEs shares to encourage a good response from these institutions.

The Department of Public Enterprises (DPE) stated in March 1993 that since the shares were sold to MFs / FIs only it was not considered advisable to incur expenditure on publicity and that MFs / FIs were given access to annual accounts, balance sheet, etc. of the PSEs.

The fact remains that though the decision to disinvest had been taken quite some time back, the MFs / FIs were left with very little time to make a realistic valuation of shares after the issue of DPE circular of October 1991 advising the PSEs to give necessary information as and when asked for by the MFs / FIs. This together with the lack of information on the seller's perception of the reserve price for the shares / bundles led to the low offers as well as number of bids received as explained subsequently in para 5.5.

Suggestion had been received from some of the Ministries and Departments of the Government of India as well as PSEs for exclusion of some PSEs from the proposed disinvestment. The justification given by the Departments / PSEs for their exclusion is indicated below:

Name of PSE	*Justification for Exclusion*
i) Indian Petrochemicals Ltd (IPCL)	These PSEs were intending to raise funds directly from the market by issue of fresh equity shares which taken together with the proposed disinvestment would result in Government's share-holding falling below 51 per cent.

ii) Cochin Refineries Ltd (CRL)	-do-
iii) Andrew Yule & Co (AY)	-do-
iv) National Aluminium Co (NALCO)	The volatility of international price of aluminium and fluctuations in profitability were quite low at that time.
v) Hindustan Zinc Ltd (HZL)	Full scale commercial production was expected in an year or two with the commissioning of a new project costing Rs 617 crores in October 1991 which would increase the share price of the enterprise in future.
vi) National Fertilizers Ltd (NFL)	Profit of these enterprises in 1990-91 was low which was going to increase substantiality in 1991-92 and as such disinvestment should be considered after the finalization of accounts for 1991-92.
vii) Fertilizers & Chemicals (Travancore) Ltd (FACT)	-do-
viii) Steel Authority of India Ltd (SAIL)	The valuation of shares under the three methods would not reflect the real values of the SAIL and Government would not get fair price till 1994-95. On control of steel distribution and pricing as well as modernisation of the plants was likely to improve profitability.

There was nothing on record to show that their suggestions were given due consideration. These PSEs were, however, included in the first round of disinvestment. Only in the second round were some of the companies excluded on the advice of

ICICI. The effect of this was that in the case of shares of IPCL and SAIL for example the realization turned out to be much lower than the original reserve price fixed as explained in paras 5.15 and 5.16.

The DPE stated that the Administrative Ministries / Departments and PSEs concerned were neither sellers nor buyers and the Government had to take a view for PSEs as a whole and as a seller based on macro considerations. The reply of the DPE is not convincing. It does not explain why the advice of the concerned Ministries / PSEs tendered, adducing specific grounds, was not accepted. As stated earlier, the Government subsequently, in the second phase, accepted the advice of ICICI for the exclusion of many PSEs from disinvestment.

5.2 Formulation of Guidelines for Valuation –Inadequacies

A scrutiny of the DPE's files relating to the setting up of the committee for formulating guidelines for valuation of shares of PSEs, revealed the following :

(a) The committee was to be assisted by Financial Advisers (FAs) of the Ministries as representative of the Department of Expenditure. The Chairman, however, decided not to associate the FAs on the ground that the committee had very little time and the selection of PSEs had not been finally completed.

The DPE stated that to complete the work in time, it was necessary to do away with the unwieldy size of the committee and to make maximum use of the available talents. It added that the absence of FAs of the Ministries in the committee was not of much consequence as representatives from available fields including PSEs were included in the committee. It was also stated that the disinvestment was not a normal activity for which rules were laid. The reply is not tenable as the committee constituted by the Ministry of Finance had, as its member, a representative of the Department of Expenditure. However, because of a subsequent decision by the

Chairman, the expertise of the Department of Expenditure could not be availed of.

(b) The final report was signed by only four out of 14 members of the committee, including 5 co-opted members. It may be inferred that the deliberations and recommendations of the committee did not reflect fully the expertise available even within the Government. Some of their suggestions which could have had important bearing on the outcome of disinvestment are reproduced below :

i. Shares should be offered not only to mutual funds and merchant banks but also to approved share brokers, public limited companies, approved pension funds, etc. for bringing more competition and better price and for preventing cartelisation. A limit should be fixed for purchase of shares by each financial institution for a wider dispersal of shares.

ii. The book value of shares of PSEs being very low, the assets of PSEs should be revalued at current price or replacement value for calculating the NAV. If this was not possible due to time constraints, the weightage of NAV in computing fair value may be reduced from 50 per cent as per CCI norms to 25 per cent.

iii. The rates of capitalisation for say the first ten among the best public sector units cannot be less than the average capitalisation rates obtaining in the first ten best private sector gilt edged shares.

iv. The disinvestment should be considered in stages with predetermined time schedule.

v. In view of the absence of market value it may be advisable to transfer the shares to selected mutual funds / public financial institutions at a reasonable value with a stipulation that as and when these shares are offered to the general public

90 per cent of the price gained would be transferred back to the Exchequer.

vi. If the Government have to raise the intended amount before 31.3.1992, the short term solution would be to raise a loan from the financial institutions against the collateral of shares which would in due course be offered to all parties including the financial institutions and the loan(s) be repaid.

Consideration of the above suggestions made by the various members representing different wings of the Government would have enabled an appraisal of the several options before embarking on disinvestment.

5.3 *Effect of Bundling of Shares on Prices of Very Good / Good PSEs*

The Government had decided to offer for sale the shares of the selected PSEs in bundles consisting of shares of 9 PSEs each, 3 'Very Good', 3 'Good' and 3 'Average'. It was stated that bundling was to facilitate disinvestment of shares of the average PSEs as the potential buyers would be compelled to buy them along with the Very Good and Good shares.

The method of offering shares in bundles made it difficult for the Government to assess how each share had been evaluated by the bidders. This was evident from the wide variation in the prices of shares of PSEs furnished later by the financial institutions / mutual funds, after acceptance of bids. But for bundling, it would have been possible to reject the offers for individual shares of PSEs which were below the reserve prices fixed by the Government. Thus, while it is not clear whether the bundling exercise would facilitate sale of the average PSEs shares, it would result in depressing the value realization of the shares of Very Good / Good PSEs. Details of eight cases noticed in Audit where the average realizations were less than even the revised reserve prices is given below. In four cases the average realization was even below the face value of the share of Rs 20/- :

S No	*Name of the PSE*	*Revised reserve price December 1991*	*Average price per share realized*	*Loss per share Rs.*	*No. of shares sold*	*Total Rs. lakhs*
1	IRCON	303	225	78	0.13	10.14
2	?	21	18.11	2.09	42.68	123.34
3	NCL	29	25.17	3.83	16.69	63.92
4	RCFL	13	9.87	3.13	311.36	974.56
5	NFL	10	8.46	1.54	111.63	171.91
6	NPF	10	8.00	2.00	191.90	383.80
7	CMC	10	8.00	2.00	25.28	50.56
8	DCI	36	10.00	26.00	4.02	104.52
					Total	1882.75

The invitation of bids for each PSE shares separately would have also resulted in higher value realisation for the Very Good and Good companies.

As mentioned in para 3.7 of the report, it was decided by the Government that in the case of PSEs already listed on the Stock Exchanges, their shares would be off loaded directly to mutual funds / financial institutions at the market price. Shares of Cochin Refineries and Andrew Yule which were already listed in the stock market were, therefore, not to be included for sale in the bundles. The inclusion of shares of these two PSEs in bundles was, therefore, contrary to the approval of the Government.

The DPE stated that sale of PSEs shares in bundles was considered as best method of realizing best prices in respect of all PSEs and it was not possible to say whether individual shares had been underpriced in this method of sale. The reply of the

DPE is not convincing. The sale of shares in bundles definitely had the effect of depressing the value realization of shares of Very Good / Good PSEs. In fact, during the disinvestment made in 1992-93, the Government took a decision of off-loading the shares of individual PSEs and not in bundles.

The DPE also contended that inclusion of shares of Cochin Refineries and Andrew Yule in different bundles was not contrary to any Government approval and was tactically sound. This cannot be accepted as the Government had taken a decision to off-load shares of these two PSEs which were listed in the stock exchange and whose market prices were known.

5.4 *Classification of PSEs – Basis Inadequate*

From a scrutiny of the files of DPE it emerged that the classification of PSEs as 'Very Good', 'Good' and 'Average' for the purpose of bundling of shares had apparently been done on the basis of NAV. This could not be considered as sufficient as the other financial criteria and macro economic parameters would substantially determine the market sentiment for each share. Reserve prices determined by the DPE and the valuation done by the consultants appointed by the Government were higher than the NAV of the PSEs used for the purpose of classification by the Government.

Taking into account the valuation done by the DPE and the consultants, classification made by the Government would have undergone a change. The table below indicates the classification as done by the Government, the consultant's valuation and the reserve price fixed by the DPE.

From the above table it is clear that classifications of PSEs for the purpose of bundling of shares had not been done taking all factors into account. PSEs listed at Sr Nos 2,4 and 5 could have been classified as 'Good' as the valuation done by the DPE and the consultants in these cases was higher than the valuation done in respect of HMT Ltd at Sr No 3.

S No	*Name of PSE*	*Classification the Govern-*	*Valuation as consul-*	*Reserve price fixed by DPE*

		ment as per NAV	*tants report (Average of High & Low Rs.*	*(Rs.)*
1	Madras Refineries Ltd	Good	65.25	65.00
2	MTN Ltd	Average	73.88	57.00
3	HMT Ltd	Good	56.62	46.00
4	Bongaigaon Refineries & Petrochemicals Ltd	Average	59.64	55.00
5	Hindustan Zinc Ltd	Average	88.76	85.00

Further, a substantial number of PSEs whose shares were disinvested operated in fields such as telecom, oil, communications, etc enjoying virtual monopoly and cash cow status. There was, therefore, adequate justification for believing that these PSEs would continue to maintain their position and become more profitable in the future. In fact the lowest reserve price fixed by the Government was Rs 35 for SAIL and there were only two other PSEs whose reserve prices were determined less than Rs 50/-. As against this 23 of the 30 PSEs had NAV less than Rs 50 and they were, therefore, not categorised as 'very good'. Classification of PSEs on the basis of reserve prices rather than NAV would have enabled bundling of shares in a more rational manner.

The DPE stated that shares floated in the primary markets were judged / gauged by NAV which was also followed by the Government for classification of PSEs. The Audit view was also stated to be not supported by an expert study or commercial practice. The fact remains that NAV alone is not the indicator of the classification of a PSE. There are other factors also which could have been kept in view for deciding the classification on rational basis.

5.5 Constitution of Bundles and Inviting of Bids Without Valuing the Shares

Government approved in November 1991 the offering of bundles of shares of 9 PSEs consisting of 3 very good, 3 good and 3 average, value of each bundle being kept around Rs 5 crores. The approval of Government also envisaged fixation of reserve price by taking the two highest values under the NAV, PECV and DCF methods.

The bids for all the 825 bundles were invited on 10th December 1991. Reserve prices of the shares of the selected PSEs were determined between 14th to 18th December 1991. Apparently, therefore, the bundles had not been valued before inviting bids and consequently the reserve price of bundle could not be indicated in the notice inviting the bids. As the approval of Government was for keeping the value of each bundle around Rs 5 crores, it was essential to fix the reserve price of shares to determine the value of each bundle before inviting bids.

Valuation done by Audit as a test check of bundle Nos 74, 90, 262, 277, 364, 385, 404, 460, 550, 580, 610, 674, 756, 788, 807 and 821 on the basis of reserve prices of shares of selected PSEs revealed that the value of these bundles ranged between Rs 8.61 crores to Rs 12.91 crores. Invitation of bids before fixation of reserve prices of shares, resulted in not keeping the value of each bundle around Rs 5 crores. There was also appreciable variation in the value of bundles, which was not in accordance with the approval of the Government.

The DPE had reported on 12th December 1991 that the financial institutions / mutual funds had been under the impression that each bundle of shares offered for sale would be around Rs 5 crores. It is not clear to Audit as to how the financial institutions / mutual funds gathered the impression that the value of each bundle was around RS 5 crores when the valuation of shares had not been made by the time the tenders were invited. The financial institutions / mutual funds quoted lower rates and the average realization per bundle worked out to Rs 3.51 crores.

The DPE stated that in the very first operation of its kind which had clear objective of raising resources, both underpricing and overpricing were obvious risks and it was for this reason that consultants' valuation and assessment of share prices by PSEs were not accepted. It was added that the value of internalized valuation of bundles without a buyer's perception, matching would not be material. The argument adduced are not convincing. The risks involved could have been minimised by a critical assessment of the best value of shares of individual PSEs by adequate preparatory company-wise / industry-wise study. The relevant factors indicated in consultants' report and the views of the PSEs could have been properly used to create favourable buyer's perception for realizing the best value.

5.6 Offer of Shares for Sale in Excess of the Perceived Investible Resources with the Institutions

On the basis of reserve price of shares determined by the Government between 14th – 18th December 1991, the average value of each bundle as worked out in Audit was about Rs 9.75 crores. The total value of 825 bundles was, therefore, around Rs 8,000 crores. From a note dated 18th December 1991 submitted by DPE before opening of the bids on that day, it was seen that the DPE had anticipated that all the institutions from whom bids were invited would be able to purchase shares of the value of around RS 2000-2500 crores against DPE's estimated value of over Rs 6000 crores.

When the financial limits of the financial institutions / mutual funds were generally known to the Government, offering shares in excess of the purchasing capacity of such institutions appears to be a financially imprudent decision. The apprehension regarding inadequate purchasing / bidding power was confirmed on opening of bids as only 710 bids for 533 bundles for a total value of Rs 2300.84 crores were received and the value of each bundle quoted was far below Rs 5 crores. This shows that planning in the disinvestment process was inadequate and incomplete.

The DPE stated that to sell a new commodity in the market for the first time it was considered prudent to make wider offer to sell lesser quantity. This argument is not convincing as with inadequate purchasing / bidding power of the buyers, offering of shares much in excess only led to uncompetitive bidding.

5.7 *Non-competitive Tenders in the First Phase of Disinvestment in December 1991*

The Government invited tenders for the sale of 825 bundles of shares of 31 PSEs from 10 institutions on 10th December 1991 which were opened on 18th December 1991. 710 bids were received from 9 institutions for 533 bundles as under :

	No of bundles	*No of bids*	*Percentage to total bundles*
i) No of bundles for which one bid was received	387	387	72.61
ii) No of bundles for which two bids were received	122	244	22.89
iii) No of bundles for which three bids were received	19	57	3.56
iv) No of bundles for which four bids were received	3	12	0.56
v) No of bundles for which five bids were received	2	10	0.38
	533	710	

72.61 per cent of the bundles had only one bidder. In 4.50 per cent cases only 3 or more bids were received. This clearly showed non competitiveness of the bids received.

Out of a total number of 710 bids for 533 bundles, one of the institutions submitted 389 bids valuing Rs 1267.42 crores which accounted for 55 per cent of the total bids received. Another financial institution offered 152 bids valuing Rs 449.34

crores which represented 21 per cent of the total bids received. The remaining 7 institutions / mutual funds together contributed only 24 per cent of the total bids valuing 584.08 crores. This indicated unequal bidding power of the institutions / mutual funds and the obvious corollary was that a couple of institutions had virtually dictated the prices.

After evaluating the above bundles with reference to the revised reserve prices fixed for PSE shares as outlined in Para 3.9, bids could be accepted only for 406 bundles of which 289 bundles were single bids representing 71 per cent of the total bundles sold. The position regarding allocation of these accepted bundles was as under :

Sl No	*Name of the institution / mutual fund*	*No of bundles allotted*	*Amount accepted (Rs Crores)*
1	Unit Trust of India	225	775.76
2	Canara Bank Mutual Fund	25	131.22
3	General Insurance Corporation	66	211.96
4	Life Insurance Corporation	59	184.31
5	Life Insurance Corporation · Mutual Fund	9	27.37
6	Punjab National Bank Mutual Fund	1	3.60
7	State Bank of India Capital Market	21	93.19

The DPE stated that when the bidders were uneven in terms of financial strength, bids naturally would not be even.

5.8 Extent of Variation in Prices of PSE Shares in Bundles Sold with reference to Original Reserve Prices

A scrutiny of the records of DPE revealed that there was no comparative statement on record indicating the amount of bids received with those worked out with reference to the original prices fixed for each PSE share. A test check conducted by Audit in this regard revealed the position as under :

Value in Rs Lakhs

Bundle No	*Value of shares in the bundle on the basis of Reserve Price originally fixed by the Government for shares of each PSE.*	*Bid price of the bundle accepted by the Government*	*Variation*
74	868.17	317.00	551.17
90	894.59	303.76	590.83
262	860.62	330.00	530.62
277	860.62	330.00	530.62
364	898.33	306.81	591.52
385	898.33	306.81	591.52
404	898.33	306.81	591.52
460	909.78	317.14	592.64
550	965.27	367.00	598.27
580	939.60	351.00	588.60
610	976.48	477.00	499.48
674	979.04	355.00	624.04
756	963.71	497.00	466.71
788	1286.14	338.05	948.09
807	1110.66	308.71	801.95
821	1291.23	327.77	963.46
Total	15600.90	5539.86	10061.04

The above study revealed that the Government accepted bids substantially lower (ie. 64 per cent) than the original reserve prices resulting in potential gains to the financial institutions / mutual funds at the cost of the Exchequer. The Department did not, however, bring out the above position in full details while seeking the approval of the Government for reducing reserve prices.

The DPE stated that different methodologies including

futuristic projection of DCF method resulting in higher reserve prices were specifically discussed and the pricing method finally accepted by Government was pragmatic. The reply does not clarify why the effect of lowering of the reserve prices to the extent of around 64 percent of the original reserve prices was not specifically brought to the notice of the Government at the time of seeking approval to the revision of the original reserve prices of the shares of the PSEs for acceptance of the tender bids of the MFs / FIs.

5.9 *Unjustified Reduction in the Reserve Prices of PSE Shares made after the Opening of Tenders*

The original 'reserve' prices for the sale of selected PSE shares were determined by the DPE in consultation with the PSE concerned, Ministry of Finance, Administrative Ministry of the PSE between 14th to 18th December 1991, on the basis of the data furnished by PSEs for the three methods of NAV, PECV, DCF as well as the valuation done by the consultants appointed by the Government.

On opening the tenders on the 18th December 1991, it was found by the DPE that no tender could be accepted if the bid for each bundle of shares was valued with reference to the reserve prices fixed. The Department attributed the shortfall in the bid prices vis-à-vis the reserve prices to the fact that the FIs and MFs did not share the PSEs optimistic expectations about future cash flows. The DCF method was, therefore, given up by the Government and the shares of PSEs were evaluated only with reference to the CCI formula, the PECV being calculated at a uniform capitalisation rate of 10 per cent which implied prices being determined at 10 times the Earning Per Share. Further, reduction of 10 per cent, if necessary, in the reserve price of the bundle arrived at with reference to reserve price of PSEs shares so fixed, was also stipulated. This revised criteria of valuation of shares resulted in reduction of the reserve prices ranging from 21.95 per cent to 86.67 per cent. In 24 of the 31 cases, the reduction in valuation was above 50 per cent. The details are given in Annexure II.

Such substantial reduction in reserve prices was not justified for the following reasons :-

i. The valuation committee and the government had earlier rejected the CCI formula as being too conservative and inapplicable for valuation of PSE shares. The CCI formula provides for suitable adjustment in the capitalisation rate on the basis of the stock market price of share. Under the CCI regime premium was allowed only to existing listed companies. Since the PSEs were not listed on the stock exchanges, the adoption of the CCI formula would have required their share value worked out with appropriate adjustment / of the capitalisation rate having regard to the reserves, profitability and market presence. In the earlier valuation exercise the PECV had been arrived at by adopting the appropriate Industry Capitalisation Rate for each PSE. Whereas these ranged from 4.65 to 7.78 per cent in a majority of the cases the Government finally adopted a uniform rate of 10 per cent for all PSEs which is not rational.

ii. The reduction in the reserve prices to bring them in consonance with the market response was also not reasonable. The bids received were in fact highly non-competitive in nature. For 72.61 per cent bundles only single bids had been received. Only in 4.50 per cent bundles 3 or more bids were received. 55 per cent of the bids were tendered by only one institution namely the UTI. Such non-competitive response could not be taken to reflect the market perception of the fair value of the PSEs shares. These aspects had not been adequately considered by the Government while deciding to reduce the reserve prices.

iii. While the earlier reserve prices had been determined by the DPE in consultation with the Administrative Ministries and the Chief Executives of the PSEs concerned, the subsequent proposal to the Government for revising the criteria in refixing reserve prices was done without consulting them.

Considering the factors detailed in the preceding para it would have been appropriate for

the Government to attempt negotiations with the bidders who were Public Sector financial institutions / mutual funds by explaining / justifying the basis on which the original reserve prices had been fixed.

The DPE stated that it was not required to negotiate with the bidders as it would tantamount to retendering and that all factors were taken into account and the price was fixed as per principles finally approved by Government. The reply is not convincing. The original reference price was fixed by the Government based on the valuation of shares by consultant and also keeping in view the methods mentioned above. These methods of valuations could not, therefore, be discarded only on the ground that the MFs / FIs had quoted lower rates for bundle of shares within their available means of resources. Negotiation or retendering could have facilitated obtaining of reasonable prices for the shares.

5.10 Fixation of Reserve Price for the Second Tranche of Disinvestment of PSEs Shares Bundles in February 1992

The second tranche of disinvestment of PSEs shares in bundles was undertaken in February 1992. Some PSEs were withdrawn from the second tranche on the advice of the ICICI. Out of shares of 31 PSEs offered in the first phase, unsold shares of only 16 PSEs were offered in fresh 120 bundles to all the Public Sector financial investment institutions, mutual funds and merchant banks. The reserve price of Rs 10.08 crores of each bundle for the second phase was based on the valuation of shares of each of the 16 PSEs done by Industrial Credit and Investment Corporation of India (ICICI). The reserve price of Rs 10.08 crores of each bundle was made known to all the bidding parties in the notice inviting bids.

A scrutiny of the 'advice' of ICICI revealed that their recommendations had not taken into account the following parameters.

i. Profitability projections made by the PSEs.

ii. Major changes contemplated by the PSEs in the future plans.

iii. Any future major restructuring of the PSEs.

iv. Impact of decontrol of steel on the profitability of SAIL.

The reserve price thus recommended were not based on relevant factors and were much lower than the reserve prices of shares of PSEs originally fixed.

The unjustified reduction in the reserve prices in response to lower bids received in two tranches of sale resulted in under-realisation of receipts aggregating Rs 3441.71 crores to Government as detailed in Annexure IV.

The DPE stated that ICICI, who were one of the expert agencies in the field in the country, recommended reserve price after taking into consideration all those factors provided by the PSEs and the DPE. It was further stated that subsequent to disinvestment of PSE shares, these did not show any remarkable recovery except some sporadic higher quoting in very limited off loading. In fact most of the scrips were not being traded regularly and based on hypothetical calculations, even notional losses to Government could not be taken as logical.

As already stated in the para above, the ICICI had not taken a number of relevant factors for the valuation of shares of PSEs. Their valuation was much lower than the reserve prices originally fixed. It may also be stated that as per Annexure III of this Report, the market price of some of the PSEs as on 30th October 1992 were much higher than the prices recommended by ICICI. The extent of benefit availed of by the FIs/MFs of the high prices prevailing at this time by selling the shares of 10 PSEs, held by them is not ascertainable. In a test check of 19 PSEs listed on the stock exchanges it was seen that in March (2nd, 6th) and April (7th) 1993, the prices quoted for their shares were much higher than the average prices realised in the two tranche of disinvestment.

5.11 Uncompetitive Biddings of PSEs Shares in the Second Tranche of Disinvestment in February 1992.

In the second tranche of disinvestment, bids for 120 bundles of PSEs shares were invited on 11th February 1992 which were opened on 24th February 1992. 273 bids were received from 19 institutions / mutual funds / merchant banks for all the 120 bundles.

Analysis of the bids received from different parties indicated the position as under :

Bundles	*No of Bundels*	*No of bids*	*Percentage total bundles*
i) No of bundles for which only one bid was received	30	30	25
ii) No of bundles for which only two bids were received	48	96	40
iii) No of bundles for which only three bids were received	27	81	22.5
iv) No of bundles for which only four bids were received	9	36	7.5
v) No of bundles for which only five bids were received	6	30	5

It would be seen from the above that only in 35 per cent cases three bids or more had been received which showed lack of competition even in the second tranche of disinvestment despite the fact that the number of bidders had been increased by including merchant banks.

Out of the 273 bids received, 120 bids were received from a single financial institution amounting to Rs 1580.75 crores. The other three bidders contributed 66 bids valued at Rs 768.65 crores. Thus these four bidders contributed 68 per cent of the total bids and this represented 69 per cent of the total value of the bids amounting to Rs 3416.50 crores. The contribution of the remaining 15 bidders taken together was, therefore, insignificant. This clearly showed that in the second phase also there was lack of competition.

The DPE stated that when the bidders were uneven in terms of financial strength, the bids made by them were bound to have high variations. It may, however, be stated that in the second phase of disinvestment though the scope of inviting tenders from parties was enlarged but the number of shares included in each bundle was so large that the reserve price of each bundle was fixed at Rs 10.08 crores which was very high. Further, though the number of PSEs was reduced in the second phase from 31 to 16, the shares offered for sale was high and could not be expected to generate better competition keeping in view the limited investible resources of the bidders.

5.12 Market Price of Disinvested Shares

A scrutiny of the market prices as prevalent at the end of October 1992 of 10 PSEs shares since listed as given in Annexure III, revealed that the potential gain to the financial institutions / mutual funds / banks ranged between 126.62 per cent to 615.53 per cent over the average price at which these shares were sold in the two phases of disinvestment during 1991-92. The response of the stock market to the PSEs shares also revealed that the reserve prices for PSEs shares fixed by taking an average of NAV + PECV at 10 per cent capitalisation or at ICICI valuation rate, was grossly under estimated. In fact in 6 out of the 10 PSEs listed in the stock exchanges so far, the reserve prices originally fixed under NAV, PECV, DCF and Consultant's method were also lower than the ruling market price.

To save the Government from substantial under-realisation from such sales, it was necessary that a 'claw-back' provision should have been incorporated in the terms and conditions for the sale of shares to the effect that as and when these shares were subsequently sold by the financial institutions / mutual funds to the general public, a reasonable fixed percentage of the gain on these sales would be transferred back to the Exchequer. Since the government had no past experience and was disinvesting its shares in PSEs for the first time and most of them were not listed, it was all the more necessary to include such a special clause.

The Chief Advisor (cost), Ministry of Finance as well as the Chief Executive of BPCL had in fact suggested, in August 1991, stipulation of a clause that as and when these shares are offered to the general public, 90 per cent of the difference of the price gained by the financial institutions / mutual funds should be transferred back to the Central Government.

The DPE sated that stipulation of claw-back provision was not practicable and FIs/MFs might have desired inclusion of a similar provision for Government meeting their losses or reduced profits in the subsequent sales of shares by them. The incorporation of a claw-back provision has to be viewed in the context that the disinvestment exercise was undertaken for the first time. A claw-back provision was an assurance that in the event of windfall profits obtained by the FIs/MFs on off-loading these shares in the market within a short given period, a part of profits would flow back to the Government. Inclusion of a suitable claw-back provision was also suggested by the Chief Adviser (Cost). Non inclusion of a claw-back provision cannot be considered to be in the best interest of the tax payer.

5.13 Irregular Forward Trading of Shares of PSEs after Disinvestment.

While approving the first round of disinvestment the Government had also decided that the shares of the selected PSEs would be listed on the stock exchanges to enable the financial institutions / mutual funds to off-load them to the general public at the appropriate time. The terms and conditions on which bids were invited from the financial institutions, mutual funds and merchant banks for sale of shares of selected PSEs also specified that the purchasers would be free to off-load their share-holding in these PSs through the normal stock exchanges transactions. Securities and Exchange Board of India (SEBI) had intimated to all the stock exchanges in the country that the shares of PSEs should be listed by the stock exchanges and traded only after disclosure documents were submitted and approved by the SEBI and stock exchanges.

It was brought to the notice of the Government that some banks and financial institutions which had purchased shares of PSEs had subsequently sold them in transactions outside the stock exchanges violating the terms and conditions of the sale. The Ministry of Finance sought comments on such forward trading of PSEs shares from the DPE. The DPE, however, held the view that the purchasers were not debarred from effecting any forward sale of shares of PSEs before their actual listing on the stock exchanges as the sale of shares from the Government to the institutional buyers in the public sector was a purely commercial deal.

As already stated above the purchasers were free to off-load their share holding in these PSEs only through the normal stock exchange transactions. The view held by the DPE that the purchasers were not debarred to sell shares before actual listing on the stock was thus contrary to the decisions taken at the outset by the Government and terms and conditions prescribed for sale of shares as well as the instructions issued by the SEBI to all stock exchanges in April 1992.

The DPE stated that for any violation of stock exchange regulations the empowered organs like SEBI etc. were to take necessary action and not the DPE.

5.14 Non achievement of objectives of disinvestment

The objectives behind partial disinvestment of its shares in the selected public sector enterprises, as stated in the statement of Industrial Policy and the Budget speech for 1991-92 of July 1991, were to raise non inflationary resources, encourage wider public participation and promote greater accountability of these enterprises.

The Budget Estimates for 1991-92 provided capital receipt of Rs 38174 crores including Rs 2500 crores to be realised from disinvestment of PSE shares and capital expenditure at Rs 32039 crores. The estimated surplus on the capital account was,

increase the authorised capital of the company to RS 400 crores. The company also pointed out that they had the experience of raising funds from public through bonds and debentures and they had been advised by experts that their shares market value would be significantly higher than its book value. Despite these observations the DPE went ahead and disinvested 20 per cent of equity representing 372 lakh shares of face value Rs 10 amounting to Rs 37.20 crores in the two disinvestments carried out in December 1991 and February 1992 at an average price of Rs 65.24 per share.

For the sale of its shares in IPCL in the first phase of disinvestment in December 1991 the Government originally fixed a reserve price of Rs 175/- per share which was reduced to RS 37/- after the tenders were opened. For the second phase of disinvestment the reserve price was, however, refixed at Rs 60/- on the basis of the valuation done by ICICI.

A study of the consideration paid by various institutions indicated that the price per share ranged from RS 35 to Rs 140.60. In the second phase of disinvestment the price per share paid by three parties was less than the reserve price of Rs 60/- which resulted in the under-realisation of Rs 232.77 lakhs to the Government.

Sl No	*Name of the institution*	*No of shares sold*	*Revised Reserve Price per share 2nd phase Rs.*	*Price at which shares were sold Rs.*	*Loss share*	*Total loss (Rs. lakhs)*
1	Indian Bank Mutual Fund	336700	60	48.96	11.04	37.17
2	Allahabad Bank	335000	60	52.00	8.00	26.80
3	Corporation Bank	675200	60	35.00	25.00	168.80
	Total					232.77

Subsequently IPCL raised Rs 320 crores from the public by

sale of fresh equity shares of Rs 10/- each for cash at a premium of RS 150/- per share.

The public issue of IPCL opened on 16th November 1992 and despite the stock market being bearish it was fully subscribed closing on the earliest closing date viz., 19th November 1992. The public issue was preceded by prolonged publicity in News Papers, Magazines, Television etc. about the strength of the company as well as its future plans. The offer was made directly to the public without fixing any minimum limits. Not only has the IPCL succeeded in raising resources for financing its future plans but also widened its equity holding. The public issue of IPCL of November 1992 at a price almost 3 times realized in the earlier disinvestment has highlighted the following major shortcomings of the latter.

a) Disinvestment was not preceded by adequate public exposure of the PSEs.

b) The offer for sale was restricted to MFs/FIs, the minimum size of bundles being Rs 3 to Rs 3.5 crores in the first tranche and Rs 10.08 crores in the second.

c) The concerned PSEs were not associated with the disinvestment exercise thereby foregoing the benefit of their expertise and the confidence in their respective organisations in determining realistic reserve price.

6. Summing Up

- The disinvestment exercises was not preceded by adequate preparatory study. No efforts were made to generate enthusiasm among financial institutions / mutual funds about PSE shares to encourage good response (Paragraph 5.1)
- Some PSEs like SAIL, IPCL were included against the advice of these PSEs/Administrative Ministries resulting in under realisation of share value in respect of shares disinvested in the PSEs (Paragraphs 5.1, 5.15 and 5.16).

- The method of sale of shares of PSEs in bundles had the effect of depressing the value realisation of 'very good / good' PSEs shares as a result of clubbing together with 'average' PSEs. The disinvestment of shares of Cochin Refineries and Andrew Yule which were listed on the stock exchange to financial institutions / mutual funds in the first tranche was contrary to Government decision (Paragraph 5.3).
- Making bundles before fixation of reserve prices of shares of PSEs resulted in failure to contain the value of each bundle to around Rs 5 crores as approved by the Government. There was also appreciable variation in the value of bundles ranging between Rs 8.61 crores to Rs 12.91 crores. By quoting rates of bundles below Rs 5 crores the financial institutions / mutual funds made adventitious gains at the cost of the Exchequer (Paragraph 5.5).
- Despite being aware that the financial institutions / mutual funds would be able to purchase shares only around Rs 2000-2500 crores in the first phase of disinvestment in December 1991, the Government offered shares whose value on the basis of reserve prices was around Rs 8000 crores, ie., far in excess of the perceived investible resources with the institutions / mutual funds (Paragraph 5.6).
- Tenders received in the first phase of disinvestment were non-competitive. 72.61 per cent of the bids received had only one bidder. Out of 406 bundles sold, 289 bundles were single bids representing 71 per cent of the total bundles sold (Paragraph 5.7).
- In 16 bundles test checked at random in Audit the extent of variation in prices of PSEs shares in bundles accepted with reference to the original prices fixed in the first phase of disinvestment in December 1991 amounted to Rs 10061.04 lakhs (Paragraph 5.8).
- Reserve prices were reduced ranging between 21.95

per cent to 86.67 per cent. In 24 out of 31 cases reduction in valuation was above 50 per cent. The reduction in original reserve price resulted in under-realisation of share value to the extent of Rs 3442 crores (Paragraphs 5.9 and 5.10).

- In the second phase of disinvestment also the tenders received were uncompetitive. There was also unequal bidding power. Four out of 19 bidders contributed 68 per cent of total bids received (Paragraph 5.11).
- Non incorporation of claw back provision in the terms and conditions of the sale resulted in Government not being able to realise a part of the huge profits made / likely to be made by the buyers in after sale of shares of the PSEs (Paragraph 5.12).
- The off-loading of shares after purchase by some institutions otherwise than through the normal stock exchanges was violative of Government policy and the terms and conditions of the sale (Paragraph 5.13).
- The disinvestment served only to contain the fiscal deficit (Paragraph 5.14).

Annexure – I

REFERRED TO IN PARAGRAPH 3.6

List of Disinvested Public Sector Enterprises

S No	*Name of PSEs*	*Percentage of Disinvestment*
1	Hindustan Petroleum Corporation Ltd (HPCL)	20.00
2	Indian Railway Construction Co. Ltd (IRCON)	00.27
3	Minerals & Metals Trading Corporation (MMTC)	00.67
4	Bharat Petroleum Corporation Ltd (BPCL)	20.00
5	Bharat Earth Movers Ltd (BEML)	20.00
6	Videsh Sanchar Nigam Ltd (VSNL)	20.00
7	State Trading Corporation (STC)	07.98
8	Bharat Heavy Electricals Ltd (BHEL)	20.00
9	Shipping Corporation of India (SCI)	20.00
10	Indian Petrochemicals Corporation Ltd (IPCL)	20.00
11	HMT Ltd (HMT)	05.43
12	Dredging Corporation of India Ltd (DCI)	01.44
13	Bharat Electronics Ltd (BEL)	20.00
14	Cochin Refineries Ltd (CRL)	10.01
15	Indian Telephone Industries (ITI)	20.00
16	Andrew Yule (AY)	13.57
17	Hindustan Organic Chemicals Ltd (HOCL)	20.00
18	Hindustan Cables Ltd (HCL)	03.64
19	Madras Refineries Ltd (MRL)	20.00
20	Mahanagar Telephone Nigam Ltd (MTNL)	20.00
21	Rashtriya Chemicals & Fertilisers Ltd (RCFL)	05.64
22	Steel Authority of India Ltd (SAIL)	05.00
23	Neyveli Lignite Corporation (NLC)	05.00
24	National Aluminium Co Ltd (NALCO)	02.72
25	Hindustan Zinc Ltd (HZL)	20.00
26	Bongaigaon Refineries & Petrochemicals Ltd (BRPL)	20.00
27	National Fertilizers Ltd (NFL)	02.28
28	Fertilizers & Chemicals (Travancore) Ltd (FACT)	01.54
29	Hindustan Photo Films Manufacturing Co Ltd (HPF)	16.05
30	CMC Ltd (CMC)	16.69

(Source : Annexure IV of Annual Report of Department of Public Enterprises for the year 1991-92)

ANNEXURE – II

Referred to in Paragraph 5.9

Statement of fixation of reserve prices for PSE shares in the first phase of disinvestment in December 1991.

(Face Value – Rs 10/-)

S No	Name of Public sector Enterprises	Price recommended by the consultant appointed by Government			Reserve price fixed by Government during 14th - 18th December 1991	Reserve price refixed by Government as an average of NAV plus PCEV at 10 per cent	Reduction in percentage in value of share in Colum 5 with reference to Col. 4
		High	*Low*	*Average*			
1	AY	92.14	82.72	87.43	82.00	39.00	52.44
2	BEML	242.72	228.17	235.45	225.00	133.00	40.89
3	BEL	104.22	58.66	81.44	80.00	29.00	63.75
4	BHEL	56.10	47.82	51.96	66.00	37.00	43.94
5	BPCL	351.50	333.32	342.41	350.00	181.00	48.29
6	BRPL	68.18	51.09	59.64	55.00	18.00	67.27
7	CMC	82.03	67.51	74.77	75.00	10.00	86.67
8	DCI	148.70	115.65	132.18	132.00	36.00	72.73

(Contd.)

S No	Name of Public sector Enterprises	Price recommended by the consultant appointed by Government			Reserve price fixed by Government during 14th - 18th December 1991	Reserve price refixed by Government as an average of NAV plus PCEV at 10 per cent	Reduction in percentage in value of share in Colum 5 with reference to Col. 4
		High	Low	Average			
9	FACT	80.85	53.77	67.31	70.00	10.00	85.71
10	HCL	39.29	30.24	34.77	70.00	29.00	58.57
11	HOCL	147.08	115.22	131.15	132.00	46.00	65.15
12	HPCL	238.88	222.10	230.49	305.00	191.00	37.38
13	HPF	96.12	77.16	86.64	70.00	10.00	85.71
14	HZL	93.77	83.74	88.76	85.00	16.00	81.18
15	HMT	60.94	52.30	56.62	46.00	21.00	54.35
16	IPCL	107.14	101.30	104.22	175.00	37.00	78.86
17	IRCON	250.00	208.00	229.00	440.00	303.00	31.14
18	ITI	80.80	69.38	75.09	100.00	35.00	65.00
19	MRL	73.95	56.55	65.25	65.00	32.00	50.77
20	MTNL	79.57	68.18	73.88	57.00	22.00	61.40

(Contd.)

S No	Name of Public sector Enterprises	Price recommended by the consultant appointed by Government			Reserve price fixed by Government during 14th - 18th December 1991	Reserve price refixed by Government as an average of NAV plus PCEV at 10 per cent	Reduction in percentage in value of share in Colum 5 with reference to Col. 4
		High	*Low*	*Average*			
21	MMTC	225.17	210.33	217.75	204.00	93.00	54.41
22	NALCO	35.18	21.17	28.18	38.00	10.00	73.68
23	NLC	84.47	72.38	78.43	57.00	11.00	80.70
24	RCF	94.37	66.30	80.34	64.00	13.00	79.69
25	SCI	63.58	36.44	50.01	75.00	22.00	70.67
26	NFL	63.88	38.27	51.08	65.00	10.00	84.62
27	STC	74.96	63.17	69.07	123.00	96.00	21.95
28	SAIL	35.00	35.00	35.00	35.00	10.00	71.43
29	VSNL	264.24	249.62	256.93	220.00	77.00	65.00
30	CRL	NOT RECOMMENDED			145.00	58.00	60.00

ANNEXURE III

Referred to in Paragraph 5.12

Statement showing the market price vis-à-vis the average price at which the shares of selected PSEs were disinvested

Sl No	Name of the PSE share	Reserve price of Price originally fixed during 14th-18th December 1991	Revised Reserve fixed fixed for 1st stage of dis-investment in December 1991 NAV + PECV at 10% cap. rate	Reserve Price which second phase of disinvestment 1992 (ICICI)	Average Price at share value of Rs 10/- was sold	Market price as Economic Times 31.10.92				Gain to financial institutions/mutual funds/banks lowest of closing prince 30.10.92 average of 52nd week	
						Closing price 31.10.92	52nd High	52nd Low	Average	Gain per share	Percentage of gain
		Rs	Rs	Rs	Rs	Rs	Rs	Rs	Rs	Rs	Rs
1	2	3	4	5	6	7	8	9	10	11	12
1	BPCL	350	181	300	243.89	750	1275	650	962.50	506.11	207.52
2	BHEL	66	37	37	38.05	140	200	130	165.00	101.95	267.94

(Contd.)

3	HCL	70	29	-	25.17	65	65	60	62.50	37.33	148.31
4	HOCL	132	46	46	56.92	143.75	220	135	177.50	86.83	152.55
5	HPCL	305	191	225	242.70	550	1200	550	875	307.30	126.62
6	HZL	85	16	17	21.65	58.75	65	47.50	56.25	34.60	159.82
7	HMT	46	21	-	18.11	80	85	67.50	76.25	58.14	321.04
8	SAIL	35	10	12	13.24	42	80	41.25	60.62	28.76	217.22
9	RCPL	64	13	-	9.87	43.75	55	41	48	33.88	343.26
10	NLC	57	11	11	11.46	82	NA	NA		70.54	615.53

ANNEXURE - IV

Referred to in Paragraph 5.10

Statement showing under-realisation of value of PSEs shares in the first and second phase of disinvestment during 1991-92

Sl. No	Name of PSE	No. of shares disinvested (Face Value Rs. 10) (In Lakhs)	Percentage of disinvestment to equity	Original reserve price per share fiex Rs.	Average realisation per share Rs.	Under realisation per share Rs.	Total amount under-realised (Rs. in Lakhs)
1	AY	10.15	13.57	82	NA	-	-
2	BPCL	100.00	20.00	350	243.89	106.11	10611.00
3	BHEL	489.52	20.00	66	38.05	27.95	13682.08
4	BEL	160.00	20.00	80	30.00	50.00	8000.00
5	BRPL	399.61	20.00	55	30.75	24.25	9690.54
6	BEML	60.00	20.00	225	148.31	76.69	4601.40
7	CRL	42.19	10.01	145	98.40	46.60	1966.05
8	CMC	25.28	16.69	75	8.00	67.00	1693.76
9	DCI	4.02	1.44	132	10.00	122.00	490.44
10	FACT	52.32	1.54	70	10.00	60.00	3139.20
11	HPCL	127.68	20.00	305	242.70	62.30	7954.46

(Contd.)

Sl. No	Name of PSE	No. of shares disinvested (Face Value Rs. 10) (In Lakhs)	Percentage of disinvestment to equity	Original reserve price per share flex	Average realisation per share	Under realisation per share	Total amount under-realised
				Rs.	Rs.	Rs.	(Rs. in Lakhs)
12	HCL	16.69	3.64	70	25.17	44.83	748.21
13	HMT	42.68	5.43	46	18.11	27.89	1190.35
14	HPF	191.90	16.05	70	8.00	62.00	11897.80
15	HZL	807.46	20.00	85	21.65	63.35	51152.59
16	HOCL	98.70	20.00	132	56.92	75.08	7410.40
17	IPCL	372.00	20.00	175	65.24	109.76	40830.72
18	IRCON	0.13	0.27	440	225.00	215.00	27.95
19	ITI	175.38	20.00	100	49.45	50.55	8865.46
20	MTNL	1200.00	20.00	57	46.26	10.74	12888.00
21	MRL	193.16	20.00	65	39.63	25.37	4900.47
22	MMTC	3.34	0.67	204	93.00	111.00	370.74
23	NALCO	351.00	2.72	38	13.13	24.87	8729.37
24	NFL	111.63	2.28	65	8.46	56.54	6311.56

(Contd.)

Sl. No	Name of PSE	No. of shares disinvested (Face Value Rs. 10) (In Lakhs)	Percentage of disinvestment to equity	Original reserve price per share fiex Rs.	Average realisation per share Rs.	Under realisation per share Rs.	Total umount under-realised (Rs. in Lakhs)
25	NLC	717.91	5.00	57	11.46	45.54	32693.62
26	RCFL	311.36	5.64	64	9.87	54.13	16853.92
27	STC	23.93	7.98	123	67.00	56.00	1340.08
28	SCI	522.46	20.00	75	34.41	40.59	21206.65
29	SAIL	1990.75	5.00	35	13.24	21.76	43318.72
30	VSNL	120.00	20.00	220	123.29	96.71	11605.20
TOTAL :		8721.25					344170.74

INDEX

❑❑❑